Comparative Law *in* Warsaw 1800–1835

JCL Studies in Comparative Law:
Second Series

Series Editors

Professor William E. Butler
Professor Michael Palmer

1. W. E. Butler and O. V. Kresin (eds.), *Discovering the Unexpected: Comparative Legal Studies in Eastern and Central Europe* (Clark, New Jersey, Talbot Publishing, 2021). ISBN 9781616196554

2. Simon Palmer and Zhai Xiaobo (eds.), *Bentham Around the World* (Clark, New Jersey, Talbot Publishing, 2021). ISBN 9781616196561

3. O. V. Kresin, *Comparative Law in Warsaw: 1800-1835*, transl. W. E. Butler (Clark, New Jersey, Talbot Publishing, 2021) ISBN 9781616196585.

KORETSKY INSTITUTE OF STATE AND LAW,
NATIONAL ACADEMY OF SCIENCES OF UKRAINE
KRZYSZTOF SKUBISZEWSKI FOUNDATION (WARSAW)
UKRAINIAN ASSOCIATION OF COMPARATIVE JURISPRUDENCE
THE VINOGRADOFF INSTITUTE, DICKINSON LAW
PENNSYLVANIA STATE UNIVERSITY

Comparative Law *in* Warsaw 1800–1835

O. V. Kresin
ДОКТОР ЮРИДИЧНИХ НАУК
HEAD, CENTER OF COMPARATIVE JURISPRUDENCE
KORETSKY INSTITUTE OF STATE AND LAW,
NATIONAL ACADEMY OF SCIENCES OF UKRAINE
ASSOCIATE, INTERNATIONAL ACADEMY OF COMPARATIVE LAW
SECRETARY-GENERAL, UKRAINIAN ASSOCIATION OF COMPARATIVE JURISPRUDENCE

EDITED AND TRANSLATED BY
William E. Butler
ACADEMICIAN, NATIONAL ACADEMY OF SCIENCES OF UKRAINE;
NATIONAL ACADEMY OF LEGAL SCIENCES OF UKRAINE

TALBOT PUBLISHING
Clark, New Jersey

ISBN 9781616196561

TALBOT PUBLISHING

AN IMPRINT OF
The Lawbook Exchange, Ltd.
33 Terminal Avenue
Clark, New Jersey 07066-1323

Please see our website for a selection of our other publications and fine facsimile reprints of classic works of legal history
www.lawbookexchange.com

Library of Congress Cataloging-in-Publication Data

Names: Kresin, Oleksiĭ, 1976- author. | Butler, William Elliott, 1939- editor, translator.
Title: Comparative law in Warsaw, 1800-1835 / O. V. Kresin, doktor iuridichnikh nauk, Head, Center of Comparative Jurisprudence, Koretsky Institute of State and Law, National Academy of Sciences of Ukraine, Associate, International Academy of Comparative Law, Secretary-General, Ukrainian Association of Comparative Jurisprudence; edited and translated by William Elliott Butler, Academician, National Academy of Sciences of Ukraine, National Academy of Legal Sciences of Ukraine.
Description: Clark, New Jersey : Talbot Publishing, [2021] | Series: JCL studies in comparative law: second series ; no. 3 | Includes bibliographical references and index. | Summary: "A study of the history of comparative jurisprudence in early nineteenth-century Poland"-- Provided by publisher.
Identifiers: LCCN 2021037952 | ISBN 9781616196585 (hardcover)
Subjects: LCSH: Law--Poland--Foreign influences--History--19th century. | Law--Europe, Eastern--Foreign influences--History--19th century. | Comparative law--Poland--History--19th century.
Classification: LCC KKP470 .K74 2021 | DDC 349.43809/034--dc23
LC record available at https://lccn.loc.gov/2021037952

Printed in the United States of America on acid-free paper

Contents

Preface

W. E. BUTLER

The present volume continues a series of studies by Dr. Oleksiy Kresin devoted to the history of comparative jurisprudence with special reference to developments in Eastern and Central Europe. For the western reader these collectively represent an introduction to comparative legal developments in a part of the globe little understood and appreciated. But more than new names and new debates are illuminated. There is a re-examination of primary sources which casts new light on classical versions of the formative years of comparative jurisprudence; what is widely and traditionally understood as a western European dialogue is, in fact, trans-European. We outside the region have painted for ourselves a partial and limited account of developments, whereas the reality is rather more complex, interesting, and interactive.

Poland is a rich source of comparative legal experience in the period here considered – principally the first third of the nineteenth century, with occasional forays back into the sixteenth to eighteenth centuries. The successive Partitions of Poland by her neighbors (Austria-Hungary, Prussia, and Russia) and, in the period here considered, the initial triumphs of Napoleonic France led to constant receptions of foreign law, challenging issues of whether and how to introduce respective foreign law on Polish territories, and to what extent Polish substantive legal regulation and Polish legislative style should be allowed or encouraged to survive or be adapted. The ensuing discussions engaged the full repertoire of comparative legal dialogue at the time, with ultimately considerable weight being given to German legal thought.

Kresin has been at the forefront of comparative legal science in Ukraine and the other post-Soviet republics for the past two decades. He began by persuading colleagues to join him in producing a ten-volume Encyclopedia of Comparative Jurisprudence containing an impressive bibliography, an anthology of translations of works by leading comparatists from around the world, biographical resources, a manual of Ukrainian and foreign centers of comparative law research and teaching, and a monograph on comparative legal methodology. For nearly a decade he initiated a series of annual conferences on comparative jurisprudence attended by comparatists from around the world. Conferences were used as occasions for a separate series of "master classes" by distinguished comparatists, each of which was separately published, as were the collections of reports delivered at conferences. From 2005 to 2014 Kresin was the editor of the first specialist journal in Ukraine devoted to comparative law; for two years he edited an international journal, *Comparative Jurisprudence*, published in Ukrainian, Russian, and English editions.

He has introduced the international world of comparative law to the post-Soviet republics by producing extensive accounts of the history of the International Academy of Comparative Law (of which he is an Associate Member), International Association of Legal Sciences, and the Inter-American Association of International and Comparative Law.

The present writer has collaborated with Kresin for some two decades in various ways, including the publication of collected articles on comparative legal topics and the translation in two volumes of Kresin's habilitation dissertation – all listed in the Sources of the present study. In this volume Kresin continues his assault upon the traditional perception of Eastern and Central Europe as primarily the recipients and transmitters of western European ideas; a closer look, he suggests, gives evidence of the historically creative contributions made by scholars in Poland.

Translation Note

The present study has been translated from a Russian-language version of a work originally prepared in the Ukrainian language and published in Ukraine. The source materials are mostly in the Polish language, as will be reflected in the footnotes. Some are drawn from archival sources, including the Annex. Biographical and bibliographical details have been added to this version, and citation style conforms to a modified version of the University of Chicago manual of style.

Where Ukrainian and Russian names or words are transliterated, the Library of Congress system of transliteration is used or adapted in simplified form. Polish language materials require no transliteration and are given as in the original.

The first mention of a deceased natural person is accompanied whenever possible by the full name of the individual, followed by the years of birth and death. Further mentions of the individual are not accompanied by this information, usually just by the surname. On two occasions individuals are related and distinguishable only by forenames. In that event initials may be supplied unless it is otherwise clear from the context or footnotes precisely which individual is being discussed. The Index of Names will give access to the first mention, if required.

W. E. Butler

Newville, Pennsylvania

July 2021

Acknowledgements

The history of comparative jurisprudence and comparative legal thought during recent decades has attracted the attention of dozens of legal scholars. It is not a matter of the genealogy of one science or one project, but a material clarification of understanding the genesis of all contemporary legal sciences in the context of changes in the thinking of jurists. The present writer has devoted several studies to this problem in which the topicality, problem, theory, and methodology of such inquiries have been substantiated and a synthesis undertaken of the respective European doctrines of the second half of the eighteenth and first third of the nineteenth centuries. The Polish element in these works had been touched upon only in passing and required broader and more complex treatment. I want to express my gratitude to the Krzysztof Skubiszewski Foundation for supporting a lengthy research period in Warsaw during which I was able to collect the necessary materials and consult with colleagues.

O. V. Kresin
Kyiv, July 2021

Introduction

The temporal framework chosen for this study is no accident. It was repeatedly singled out by Polish specialists on the development of legal thought. Nonetheless, as Pomianowski noted, there are no general works on legal thought of these years for the central Polish territories.[1] The year 1807 acts as the political determinant, marking the restoration of Polish statehood (the Duchy of Warsaw and to a significant degree the successor Kingdom of Poland) and the defeat of the November Uprising (1830-1831) with the subsequent direct measures of the Russian authorities in 1831 and 1832 to limit the autonomy of the Kingdom of Poland in principle. The founding in 1807 of the School of Law (later the Faculty of Law and Administration of Warsaw University), which became the first specialized institution of higher legal education in the central Polish territories, the closure of Warsaw University in 1831, the significant emigration in that year of scholars, and the elimination of the Society of Friends of Sciences in 1832 were intellectual benchmarks.

The vast legacy of Polish comparative jurisprudence during this period requires lengthy and fundamental studies. This book is confined to the legal thought of Warsaw jurists. In a few instances we step outside this framework. For example, in analyzing the works of Tadeusz Czacki, not written in Warsaw and dating in part from before the period of concentration here. The contributions of Ignacy Daniłowicz are analyzed, although written in Vilnius. Attention is given to W. A. Maciejowski and his history of Slavic legislation, the first volume of which appeared in 1832. Individual works are considered by authors who were not jurists. But these exceptions are appropriate, for they are closely related to the development of comparative legal knowledge and the comparative legal thought of Warsaw jurists during the years 1807 to 1831.

1 P. Z. Pomianowski, "Główne nurty ideologiczno-metodologiczne w środowisku warszawskich prawników przed wybuchem powstania listopadowego", Zeszyty Prawnicze UKSW, XI (2011), p. 405.

Part One
Theoretical Foundations of Comparative-Legal Knowledge in Doctrines of Warsaw Jurists

Chapter 1
Contextual Development of Legal Thought

§1.1. Political Context

Aspirational changes in the territorial affiliation and political status of the central Polish territories, accompanied by fundamental changes in the system of the sources and application of law, were a major element in the political and legal context of forming a special scientific picture of the world on the part of Warsaw jurists in the early decades of the nineteenth century. The 1794 Prussian Land Statute was extended to the former *Rzecz Pospolita* which, after the Partition, were in the Kingdom of Prussia; the old civil law there became subsidiary *de facto*. Civil procedure was regulated by the 1793 General Judicial Ordinacija for the Prussian *lände*, and criminal law by the 1805 Prussian Criminal Ordinacija.[2]

After these lands were occupied by French troops in 1806, a provisional system of State administration was created. By instruction of the Secretary of State of the French Empire, Count Hugues-Bernard Maret (1763-1839), 1st duc de Bassano, of 14 January 1807, a Governmental Commission of seven persons was formed to administer these lands and agreed with the Directorate – five ministers-directors (justice, armed forces, police, finances, and internal affairs).[3] The Governmental Commission decided to reinstate the private law of the *Rzecz Pospolita* while retaining Prussian norms as *renvoi* norms. An "Abridged System of Civil

[2] P. Z. Pomianowski, *Początki polskiego czasopiśmiennictwa prawniczego. Seria pierwsza „Themis Polskiej"* (Warsaw, 2015), pp. 15-16.

[3] S. I. Shchegolev, «Польша в системе наполеоновской Европы. Создание Герцогства Варшавского» [Poland within the System of Napoleonic Europe. Creation of the Duchy of Warsaw], Вестник СПбГУ [Herald of St. Petersburg State University], Series 2 (History), no. 1-2 (2004), p. 76.

Procedure" based on Prussian legislation was introduced, and the 1805 Prussian Criminal Ordinacija was left in force.[4]

According to the Treaty of Tilsit between France and the Russian Empire of 25 June (7 July) and 27 June (9 July) 1807, the lands of the Kingdom of Prussia were partly partitioned, and the majority of territories seized by it as a result of the Partitions of the *Rzecz Pospolita* (except the Gdansk Pomerania, Warmia, and the Białystok regions) were transformed into a formally independent Duchy of Warsaw (or often called in Polish literature – the Principality of Warsaw).[5] Napoleon transferred authority over it as a separate State under the Treaty to the King of Saxony, Friedrich August I (1750-1827), a descendant of the kings of the Rzecz Pospolita (grandson of August III (1696-1763), great-grandson of August II (1670-1733), great-greatgrandson of Jan III Sobieski (1629-1696)), once elected to be the successor of Stanisław-August Poniatowski (1732-1798). He was given the title of Duke of Warsaw.[6] The formally independent State was controlled politically by the French Empire. Napoleon's plans to restore the Kingdom of Poland or the entire *Rzecz Pospolita* were equivocal and, in any event, at the insistence of Emperor Alexander I (1777-1825), this was officially denied in France. Only during the War of Napoleon (1769-1821) in 1812 against Russia was the slogan of reviving the old statehood proclaimed.[7]

According to the Constitution of the Duchy of Warsaw (Article 69) signed by Napoleon on 22 July 1807 and by the Governmental Commission of the Duchy on 23 July 1807, the Code Civil of France should have been introduced into force, even though the majority of influential political and Roman Catholic forces hoped for the restoration of the political system and law of the *Rzecz Pospolita* and a continuation of reform efforts.[8] The Directorate of Justice headed by Count Feliks Walejzuscz Władysław Łubieński (1758-1848), anticipating the intentions of Napoleon, prepared a Report for him in advance: "View on the Organization of Court Proceedings" and

[4] Pomianowski, note 2 above, p. 16.

[5] Ibid., p. 16.

[6] Shchegolev, note 3 above, p. 76-77.

[7] Ibid., pp. 77-78.

[8] M. Gałędek, "The Problem of Non-Adaptability of National Legal Heritage: Discussion on the Reform of Civil Law in Poland in the Course of Work of the Reform Committee in 1818", *Romanian Journal of Comparative Law*, VIII, no. 1 (2017), pp. 10-11, 14.

"Certain Ideas Given Ex Promptu with Reflections: Is the Code of Napoleon the Great Appropriate for Our Nation?", setting out a substantiation of the inadvisability and even harmfulness of extending French legislation to the territories of the former *Rzecz Pospolita*. The Emperor, however, at a reception in Dresden on 19 June 1807 did not listen to them and dictated the Constitution for the Duchy on the basis of the French with a command relating to the implementation of the Code.[9] It entered into force in the Duchy on 1 May 1808.[10] As Prince Adam Jerzy Czartoryski (1770-1861) later noted, the sole reason for the adoption of the Code became the "submissiveness to the vassalage of Napoleon"; the Polish factors acted here merely as an "instrument of the dominant force".[11]

According to the Treaty of Schönbrunn of 14 October 1809 between France and the Austrian Empire, Western Galicia and part of the Eastern, or so-called Old Galicia (Zamoiski District and Podgor'e), which after the Partitions of the *Rzecz Pospolita* were part of the Holy Roman Empire of the Germanic Nation (then the Austrian Empire) and were incorporated in the Duchy of Warsaw.[12] The operation of the French Code Civil was extended to these lands on 15 August 1810; the Criminal Code (Franciscana), which had operated in Western Galicia from 1796 and in all other Habsburg possessions from 1803, remained in force there.[13]

Any criticism or effort to change the legislation introduced were complicated by Napoleon's aspiration to extend the law of France to all the countries under its control. Nonetheless, the Code Civil was criticized, albeit without success. The Minister of Justice, Łubieński, spoke out against individual provisions relating to mortgage, land surveying, and others. Severe criticisms were heard at the Sejm in 1811 with respect to deviations of the marriage

[9] J. J. Litauer, "Przeciwnicy Kodeksu", *Gazeta Sądowa Warszawska*, no. 22 (1908), p. 365; H. Grynwaser, "Kodeks Napoleona w Polsce", in Grynwaser, *Pisma* (Wroclaw, 1951), I, pp. 16-18; M. V. Syrko, Цивільний кодекс Франції 1804 року та його вплив на цивільне законодавство країн Європи (на прикладі Польщі та Румунії) [Civil Code of France of 1804 and Its Influence on the Civil Legislation of European Countries (Examples of Poland and Romania)] (Lviv, 2015), p. 88 (diss. kand. iurid. nauk).

[10] Gałędek and A. Klimaszewska, "A Controversial Transplant? Debate over the Adaptation of the Napoleonic Code on the Polish Territories in the Early 19th Century", *Journal of Civil Law Studies*, XI, no. 2 (2018), p. 270.

[11] Litauer, note 9 above, p. 365.

[12] Shchegolev, note 3 above, p. 77.

[13] Pomianowski, note 2 above, p. 16.

and family provisions of the Code and the secular understanding of marriage differing from the canon law.[14] On 21 December 1811 the King received a petition from deputies of the Sejm to repeal provisions of the Code, and in 1812 the Council of General Confederation was created to these demands, especially from landowners and the Catholic clergy.[15]

King Friedrich August I indicated on several occasions to the authorities of the Duchy that the Code Civil was not subject to change; only drafts on issues not encompassed therein might be prepared. A Decree of the King of 5 July 1810 noted: "Taking into account the close link between the Code Napoleon and other parts of French legislation ..., we decree that the French system shall be taken into account as a model in drafts supplementing the insufficient laws and provisions".[16] Moreover, the King pointed out the failure of decisions of the State Council already adopted to conform to Code provisions, pointing especially to limitations adopted on the rights of Jews.[17]

The 1806 French Code of Civil Procedure entered into force in the Duchy in 1808, and the 1807 French Code de commerce, in 1809. The new civil procedure norms and court organization were unacceptable to parts of society, and the State Council of the Duchy dragged out their adoption.[18] The Code de commerce was enacted without discussion and protests.[19] But the resistance to the criminal and criminal procedure codes proved to be effective, and these Napoleonic acts were not borrowed.[20]

After the conquest of the Duchy of Warsaw by the Russian Empire in 1813-1814, Emperor Alexander I decided to preserve

[14] S. Godek, "Już Napoleon w swoim Kodeksie rozwody upoważnia". Kilka uwag w związku z książką Piotra Zbigniewa Pomianowskiego, Rozwód w XIX wieku na centralnych ziemiach polskich. Praktyka stosowania Kodeksu Napoleona w latach 1808-1852", *Czasopismo prawno-historyczne*, LXXI, no. 1 (2019), pp. 377-378; Klimaszewska and Gałędek, "The Implementation of French Codes on the Polish Territories as Instruments of Modernization – Identifying Problems with Selected Examples", in A. Albarian and O. Moréteau (eds.), *Le droit comparé et ...: Actes de la conference annuelle de Juris Diversitas* (Aix-Marseille, 2015), pp. 79-80.

[15] Grynwaser, note 9 above, pp. 64-68.

[16] Ibid., pp. 37-40.

[17] Ibid., p. 51.

[18] Ibid., pp.40-41.

[19] Klimaszewska and Gałędek, note 14 above, pp. 80-82.

[20] Gałędek and Klimaszewska, note 10 above, p. 275.

Polish statehood. One may assume that Adam Czartoryski, the Minister of Foreign Affairs of the Russian Empire from 1804 to 1806 and author of schemes to restore the Kingdom of Poland as a State in an ancestral personal *unie* with the Russian Empire, had a significant role in this.[21] At the initiative of Czartoryski, Emperor Alexander I instructed the process of transformation of the legal order of the Duchy to begin by Edict of 19 May 1814, for which a special committee was formed (known as the Civil Reform Committee).

A Memorandum from Czartoryski to the Emperor dated 7(19) February 1814, which inspired the Edict of 19 May 1814, said: "The Code Civil of Napoleon and judicial procedure should be repealed and may be provisionally replaced by Polish laws and the Statute [1588 (third) Statute of the Grand Duchy of Lithuania, Rus, and Samogitia – ок], and also by forms which were applied before the introduction of French procedure". An Imperial instruction "Items with Which the Committee Should be Engaged" added to the Edict was strengthened by the words "as soon as possible" and made provision for forming the Reform Committee; it was provided that the Committee shall "discuss whether the codes should be entirely or partly repealed and when this repeal may occur. It also should propose a plan and the composition of a separate commission which would be responsible for drafting new civil, criminal, and procedure codes and for the final organization of court proceedings".[22] And in the "Items" referred to above it was noted: "The will of His Majesty the Emperor that all general changes and all possible reforms in the contemporary system of administration of the Principality should be introduced without haste in order to avoid the catastrophic consequences of all possible unanticipated

[21] A. M. Ziuzin, «Адам Чарторыйский и формирование государственной политики по польскому вопросу (конец XVIII – начало XIX веков» [Adam Czartoryski and the Formation of State Policy on the Polish Question (End of XVIII and Early XIX Centuries)], Всероссийский журнал научных публикаций [All-Russian Journal of Scientific Publications], no. 5 (2011), p. 22.

[22] S. Askenazy, "Zagrożenie Kodeksu Napoleona przy utworzeniu Królestwa Polskiego", *Gazeta Sądowa Warszawska*, no. 22 (1908), p. 333; Gałędek, note 9 above, pp. 14-15; Gałędek and Klimaszewska, "The Work of the Civil Reform Committee on the New Regulation of Catholic Marriages in 1814", *Krakowskie Studia z Historii Państwa i Prawa* (Special Issue; 2018), p. 180; Gałędek, Klimaszewska, and Pomianowski, "Prace Komitetu Cywilnego Reformy nad przygotowaniem narodowej kodyfikacji prawa cywilnego i procedury cywilnej w przededniu utworzenia Królestwa Polskiego (1814-1815) – edycja ***źródłowa***. Część I", *Krakowskie Studia z Historii Państwa i Prawa*, XII, no. 2 (2019), pp. 244, 261-262.

changes".[23] This Edict commenced many years of discussions, organizational forms, drafts, and, finally, material changes in legislation.

Czartoryski had suggested this reform to Emperor Alexander I in February/March 1814 and hoped that other territories of the former *Rzecz Pospolita* would become part of the Duchy of Warsaw from the Russian Empire, and the 1588 Lithuanian Statute would become the basis of a single legal order in this State.[24] Nikolai Nikolaevich Novosil'tsev (1761-1838), the Commissar empowered by the Emperor and attached to the Governmental Council of the Kingdom of Poland, actively resisted this plan.[25] The views of Czartoryski were well-founded, for the possibility of expanding the Duchy of Warsaw by incorporating other former territories of the *Rzecz Pospolita* which were part of the Russian Empire had been reserved by the last in the Final Act of the Congress of Vienna of 28 May (9 June) 1815.[26] That such apprehensions relating to the strengthening of the Duchy were seriously considered in Russian political thought is demonstrated by the later caution of a leading Russian historian. Nikolai Mikhailovich Karamzin (1766-1826): "The restoration of Poland will be the fall of Russia".[27]

[23] Gałędek, Klimaszewska, and Pomianowski, note 22 above, p. 263.

[24] Askenazy, note 22 above, p. 333; Grynwaser, note 9 above, p. 68-71; Gałędek, note 8 above, p. 16; Gałędek, Klimaszewska, and Pomianowski, note 22 above, p. 245; A. Zarzycka, "Próby zmian prawa rzeczowego z Kodeksu Napoleona w Królestwie Polskim w latach 1815-1818", *Krakowskie Studia z Historii Państwa i Prawa*, II (2008), p. 192. Also see Ziuzin, note 21 above, p. 21. Regarding t1he unfoundedness of these expectations and the reaction to them of Alexander I, see A. R. Sokolov, «Русские в Варшаве в 1813-1815 годах: от Герцогства Варшавского к Царству Польскому» [Russians in Warsaw in 1813-1815: From the Duchy of Warsaw to the Kingdom of Poland], Новый исторический вестник [New Historical Herald], № 2 (2018), pp. 125-126.

[25] Grynwaser, note 8 above, p. 78; Godek, note 13 above, p. 373; W. Sobociński, "Jan Wincenty Bandtkie obrońca Kodeksu Napoleona", *Rocznik Lubelski*, III (1960), p. 167. For clarification of the position of Novosil'tsev, see O. A. Liubeznikov, «Попытки проведения Н. Н. Новосильцовым общеимперской национальной политики в Западных губерниях России и Царстве Польском в 1810-1820-е годы» [Attempts of N. N. Novosil'tsev to Carry Out the Imperial National Policy in the Western Governates of Russia and the Polish Kingdom in 1810-1820s], Труды исторического факультета Санкт-Петербургского университета [Proceedings of the Faculty of History of St. Petersburg University], no. 11 (2012), p. 163.

[26] S. M. Fal'kovich, «Польский вопрос в решениях Венского конгресса 1815 г. и причины краха венских договоренностей» [Polish Question in Decisions of the 1815 Congress of Vienna and Reasons for the Collapse of the Vienna Arrangements], Славянский альманах [Slavic Almanac], no. 3-4 (2015), p. 25.

[27] N. M. Karamzin, Мнение русского гражданина [Opinion of a Russian Citizen]

The political context of legal developments in the region changed materially after the Kingdom of Poland was created under Emperor Alexander I. Under a Treaty between Russia and Austria-Hungary "On Ensuring the Well-Being of Poles" of 21 April (3 May) 1815, part of Eastern Galicia went to Austria which had previously been integrated with the Duchy of Warsaw, and Krakow became a Free City. A large portion of the Duchy passed forever to the Russian Empire. Both empires were at liberty to determine the political status of the Polish lands. These provisions were confirmed by a Treaty between Russia and Prussia of 27 April (8 May) 1815, the Final Act of the Congress of Vienna of 28 (9 June) 1815, and by a Russian-Austrian-Prussian Treaty of 14 (26) September 1815.[28] These treaties "finally withdrew the 'Polish problem' from the domain of international relations into a municipal stratum".[29] The Manifesto of Alexander I of 9 (21) May 1815 proclaimed the accession of part of the Duchy of Warsaw to the Russian Empire and granted to it a special system of administration as the Kingdom of Poland.[30]

Czartoryski submitted on 25 May 1815 the Fundamental Principles of the Constitution of the Kingdom of Poland to the Emperor for consideration. These were confirmed on 25 January 1816 with the status of a provisional law (but Alexander I regarded them as higher than a constitution and as a permanent act). The Fundamental Principles provided in §8: "The civil and criminal laws presently in force shall not lose their force before the moment when new books of laws which we ordered to be compiled will receive sanction and will be promulgated".[31] It should be noted that

(available online).

28 N. Iu. Gromakova, «"Польське питання" на Віденському конгресі 1815 р. й утворення Королівства Польського» ["Polish Question" at the 1815 Congress of Vienna and the Creation of the Kingdom of Poland], Збірник наукових праць Харківського національного педагогічного університету ім. Г. С. Сковороди: Серія «Історія та географія» [Collection of Scientific Works of G. S. Skovoroda Kharkiv National Pedagogical University: Series "History and Geography"], no. 53 (2016), p. 155.

29 Ibid., p. 156.

30 Ibid.

31 Grynwaser, note 9 above, p. 73; Zarzycka, note 24 above, p. 175; Zarzycka, "Rola organów władzy Królestwa Polskiego w pracach legislacyjnych nad narodowym prawem rzeczowym w latach 1815-1830", *Studia z Dziejów Państwa i Prawa Polskiego*, VIII (2003), p. 125; Sobociński, "Prawo francuskie w Niemczech a w Polsce: nowe opracowania niemieckie recepcji i refleksje porównawcze", *Annales Universitatis Mariae Curie-Skłodowska*, XXXVII (1982), p. 181 (Sectio F:

all drafts of the Constitution of the Kingdom contained provisions concerning the rapid preparation of a Code, but these provisions were not mentioned in the confirmed "Fundamental Principles".[32] Later Czartoryski noted in his diary "It is not necessary to destroy everything French in a code".[33]

The new orientators should doubtless be sought in the military, political, and international legal context: the final removal of Napoleon from the political arena and consolidation of the territory of the Kingdom of Poland for the Russian Empire additionally guaranteed by the Russo-Austrian-Prussian alliance enabled the reception of French law no longer to be regarded as a threat of French revanche. In a sense, this law had lost its sovereign-owner and its international political character – it had been depoliticized. Czartoryski, moreover, had changed his views, and they satisfied the Russian Emperor. The orientation in favor of a new national codification remained; although there was no declared urgency, and a temporary substitution of legislation in force with older Polish or Lithuanian legislation had not been provided for. This transformed the framework for discussions and the grounds for organizational forms. This same approach was used by the "trustee-States" when the Krakow Republic was established in 1815: national codes were to be drafted, but the French Code Civil was temporarily to remain in force.[34]

All the same, the Russian imperial power was interested in accelerating a new codification of law in the Kingdom of Poland. The Viceroy of the Kingdom, Józef Zajączek (1752 - 1826), said this in an address to the Council of State.[35] But as the first Sejm of the Kingdom of Poland approached in 1818, the position of the authorities changed. On 19 July and 22 August 1817, the Viceroy suggested there was no rush to draft the new codes; one should concentrate on the adoption of urgent changes to the legislation in force: "It would be improper that a book of national laws might be prepared within such a brief time, and therefore one should embark upon a modification of the codes which prove to be

Humaniora).

32 Grynwaser, note 9 above, p. 78.

33 Ibid., p. 73.

34 K. Sójka-Zielińska, *Wielkie kodyfikacje cywilne. Historia i współczesność* (Warsaw, 2009), p. 261.

35 Zarzycka, note 24 above, p. 181.

immediately necessary". Let the "Commission consider whether there are in the existing codes some items which are unsuitable or harmful for our country, with the change of elimination of which need not await the era of creating a national code".[36]

Soon this view was confirmed by the position of the Emperor expressed in an appeal of the State secretary of the Empire of 24 August (5 September) 1817: work on drafting a new original civil code should be deferred indefinitely, and instead changes in legislation in force should be drafted before the 1818 Sejm with respect to concrete urgent issues (registration of civil status, surveying disputes, marriage and divorce, mortgage), as well as a criminal code.[37]

According to a draft of the Emperor of 19 (31) July 1818, a new civil code was to have been prepared by the Governmental Commission of Justice – retaining the system of the Code Napoleon.[38] On 14 August 1818 the Viceroy confirmed a plan agreed with the Commission to prepare national codes.[39] At this time a prepared draft of the first and second books of a national civil code, approved in 1820 by the Council of State, the Emperor rejected. Several instructions of Alexander I in 1820, 1823, and 1825 and of Emperor Nicholas I (1796-1855) in 1829 were directed towards accelerating the preparation of a new civil code, and in the absence of a finished result – to prepare necessary changes in the existing Code. On 14 August 1821 the Emperor in an appeal to the State Secretary ordered that when preparing the Code the "dogmas and discipline of the Catholic Church" be adhered to. After consideration of the draft book two of the Civil Code submitted by the Minister of Justice, the Council of State on 15 June and 30 November 1829 decreed to cease work on this book.[40]

In 1818 the Prussian and Austrian criminal law in force in various parts of the Kingdom of Poland was replaced by a new Criminal Code. Changes relating to mortgage were made in 1818 and in 1823 in the Civil Code.[41] The Sejm in 1825 adopted the

36 Grynwaser, note 9 above, p. 88; Zarzycka, note 24 above, p. 184.

37 Grynwaser, note 9 above, p. 89; Zarzycka, note 24 above, p. 185.

38 Zarzycka, note 31 above, p. 127.

39 Grynwaser, note 9 above, pp. 117-118.

40 Zarzycka, note 31 above, pp. 127-128, 131-132; Grynwaser, note 9 above, p. 139; Sójka-Zielińska, note 34 above, p. 263.

41 Pomianowski, "The National Codification of Civil Law in Poland at the

first book of the Civil Code of the Kingdom of Poland (on natural persons) on the basis of the Code Napoleon, but with material changes. Among others, the institution of secular marriage was abolished, and the regime of spousal ownership was changed.[42]

Consideration of the draft book two of the Civil Code was lengthy and postponed, although Nicholas I opposed everything Napoleonic and considered the French Code Civil to be the dregs, born from a combination of Satan and revolution.[43] Consideration was renewed pursuant to a letter of the Minister State Secretary to the Chairman of the Administrative Council of 11 November 1829, but thereafter was sabotaged by the Council of State. As a result, the Sejm in spring 1830 only made amendments to the Civil Code in force.[44]

Summing up this concise account of the political and legal context of the development of legal ideas of Warsaw jurists during the first third of the nineteenth century, we make reference to a modern Russian specialist: "The cause of the confrontation was that the Poles saw in the granting of autonomy the first step towards restoration of the *Rzecz Pospolita*, and the Russians – the first step towards the smooth integration of Polish lands into the Empire of the Romanovs".[45]

The policy of the Russian Government relating to Polish intellectual life was a separate context. After the Sejm of 1820, a course was taken to "calm down by the most effective means any activity directed towards the disturbance of quiet or which may give occasion for dissatisfaction" and "suppress the revolutionary spirit" in the Kingdom.[46] The opposition press was closed, election results vacated to a number of local agencies, the convocation of the next session of the Sejm postponed for an indefinite period, protective political activity of the ordinary and secret police and of spy networks activated, various circles, societies, and Masonic

Beginning of the 19th Century. Sources and Inspirations", in V. Amorosi and V. M. Minale (eds.), *History of Law and Other Humanities: Views of the Legal World Across Time* (Madrid, 2019), p. 238.

[42] Ibid., pp. 238-239; Gałędek, note 8 above, p. 35.

[43] S. Posner, "Dziś a przed stu laty. Nasz stosunek historyczny do kodeksu", *Gazeta Sądowa Warszawka*, no. 22 (1908), p. 358; Grynwaser, note 9 above, p. 157.

[44] Pomianowski, note 2 above, p. 208.

[45] Sokolov, note 24 above, p. 134.

[46] Fal'kovich, note 26 above, p. 30.

lodges were dispersed, military servicemen were prohibited from participating in any associations, travel abroad to study was prohibited, and the possible closure of Warsaw University was considered.[47] Russian authorities strengthened censorship and simultaneously supported *sub rosa* the publication of scholarly works, including legal, advantageous for their views and conclusions, such as, for example, of a Slavophile nature.[48]

This all intensified the anti-Russian, anti-monarchical, and anti-governmental mood in society, the aspiration to create a unified Polish State, and led to the forming of secret organizations, acts of insubordination, and, in turn, to greater repression, especially extra-judicial, and to open violations of the Fundamental Principles of the Constitution of the Kingdom of Poland by the Russian authorities.[49] Ultimately, on 29 November 1830 a uprising began in the Polish Kingdom against the Russian authorities, the suppression of which brought an end to formally autonomous statehood under the authority of the Russian Emperor. As one specialist observed: "the constitutional construction erected at the Congress of Vienna was destroyed; it did not withstand the test of time and forces which pressured it".[50] One outcome of the suppression of the uprising of 1830-1831, in addition to the elimination or transformation of virtually all institutions connected with the development of legal thought, was mass emigration, temporary or permanent, of a significant portion of the Polish intelligentsia, including jurists, which led to prolonged intellectual stagnation in the Kingdom of Poland.[51]

Thus, as a result of the Partitions of the *Rzecz Pospolita* and during the period here investigated, the central Polish lands underwent several times a change of State subordination, loss, and new acquisition of statehood. As a result of the changes between 1807 and 1831, for the first time a purely Polish (and not Polish-Lithuanian-Prussian-Ukrainian-Belarus-Baltic) national State

[47] Ibid., pp. 30-31.

[48] I. S. Troiak, «Польская историческая россика первой половины XIX в.» [Polish Historical Rossica of the First Half of the XIX Century], Гуманитарные науки в Сибири [Humanities in Siberia], no. 3 (2011), pp. 83-84.

[49] Fal'kovich, note 26 above, pp. 31-34.

[50] Ibid., p. 34.

[51] See, for example, M. Iłowiecki, *Okręty na oceanie czasu. Historia nauki Polskiej do 1945 roku* (Warsaw, 2011), p. 165.

was created on part of the Polish lands. The Polish population participated extensively in the struggle for the restoration of Poland. The formal independence of the Polish State (a monarch in common with other States, Saxon or Russian, incorporation not legally provided for or dependence on another State) should have been and was perceived as indefinite, under threat, not fully-fledged, having regard to the limitations, and then repressions on the part of the governments of the ruling monarchs.

Together with the political developments, material changes occurred in the sources and principles of law and the application of law. Foreign (Prussian, Austrian, French) law was compulsorily introduced on the central Polish lands, and the sphere of application of law from the times of the *Rzecz Pospolita* was narrowed in principle. The aspirations and the protests of the Poles were not taken into account. All this acted as the context of thinking about and conceptualizing a new Polish legal order.

§1.2. Institutional Context

The formation of a number of legislative-drafting agencies, educational and scientific institutions, and publication projects which in various forms served as channels for the expression of ideas were linked with the political and legal challenges which arose during the period of Polish legal thought here considered.

Legislative-Drafting Agencies. In 1808 under the aegis of the Governmental Commission of Justice, Łubieński formed a commission of jurists to analyze the law in force and the application thereof and prepare draft normative legal acts for the Council of State. The possibility of deviating from the Code Civil or of making changes in it was allowed, and this generated the aforementioned categorical reaction from Friedrich August I.[52]

Pursuant to an Edict of 19 May 1814, Czartoryski was appointed chairman of the Committee of Reform and materially influenced its membership, but was not present at the majority of sessions because he was taking part in the Congress of Vienna. By Edict of the Emperor, Nikolai Novosil'tsev was appointed, among others, to the Committee in his capacity as Deputy Chairman of the Provisional High Council of the Duchy of Warsaw (and replaced Czartoryski in his absence); the woewod and President of the

[52] Grynwaser, note 9 above, pp. 37-40.

Senate, Tomasz Adam Ostrowski (1735-1817); the State Chancellor and advisor in Lublin, Franciszek Grabowski (1750-1836), among others.[53]

The discussions in the Committee were lengthy and lively. The discussion encompassed the Code Civil, Code of Civil Procedure, Code de Commerce, and various issues of court organization. Because it was impossible to argue for the preservation of French legislation without changes or the uselessness of a new Polish codification, having regard to the Edict of Alexander I, the views of Committee members were divided: (1) relative to the future period before the adoption of Polish codes: between complete repeal of French legislation with a return to the law of the *Rzecz Pospolita* and necessary changes thereof – and retention of French legislation and modifications thereof; (2) relative to the sources of future Polish legislation: primarily sources of the *Rzecz Pospolita,* retention of the structure and basic provisions of the French codes, rational synthesis of legislation of contemporary States; (3) relative to the duration of the transition period.[54] A Memorandum by Novosil'tsev read out at a session of the Committee on 8 July 1814 showed, at first glance, the impartiality of the representative of the Emperor, a readiness to adopt any decision which the Committee would approve, but at the same time confirmed: the final aim was to replace Napoleonic codes with Polish.[55]

The Committee was in session twice a week between 4 July 1814 and 18 June 1815, meeting for 92 sessions in all. Within the Committee, legal issues were considered in priority at the section on courts and cities (which later was named the judicial and legislative section), headed by Grabowski. In addition to the Committee members, auxiliary individuals were appointed to the section, among them the legal scholar Jan Wincenty Bandtkie (1783-1846).[56]

In the summer and autumn of 1814, the Committee determined that a new codification of material and procedural law should be undertaken, and until the completion thereof the law in force

[53] Gałędek and Klimaszewska, note 22 above, p. 181; Gałędek, Klimaszewska, and Pomianowski, note 22 above, p. 261.

[54] See, for example, Gałędek, note 8 above, p. 17-19.

[55] Gałędek, Klimaszewska, and Pomianowski, note 22 above, pp. 270-271.

[56] Gałędek, note 8 above, p. 20; Gałędek and Klimaszewska, note 2 above, pp. 182-183; Gałędek, Klimaszewska, and Pomianowski, note 22 above, p. 252.

should be retained with changes deemed to be necessary.[57] The Committee approved on 27 November 1814 an instruction for the future codification commission.[58] The Committee considered the draft Civil Code approved by the sections, the structure of the Civil Code, draft laws or conceptual foundations thereof on urgent partial changes in the law in force (especially with respect to family law and the system for the registration of acts of civil status). But not a single one of the drafts adopted by the Committee ever entered into force.[59] The Civil Reform Committee ceased activity in June 1815.

The work of the Committee was described by a member, Andrzej Gorodiski:

> The entire ... work was rather a result of joy in connection with the announced changes of domestic affairs for the better than a cold calculation, and it emanated from ... the unrestrained wish to make improvements as soon as possible, and it ... did not determine the state of domestic relations beforehand, and instead the aspiration to work on a full reform according to own inspiration and facts, which were found in unsure memory.[60]

On 25 September 1815 a Preparatory (Codification) Commission was formed by Decree of the Provisional Government.[61] The draft had been prepared by Czartoryski. Antoni Bieńkowski (1760-1834) headed the Commission, a former judge on the Court of Appeal in Warsaw. Professional practitioners and legal scholars were members of the Commission: Jan Wincenty Bandtkie; M. Lewicki; an advokat of the Court of Appeal in Warsaw, Alojzi Orchowski (1767-1847); a former referendarii, Józef Kalasanti Szaniawski (1765-1843); and a former refendarii of the Council of State, Antoni Wyczechowski (1780-1844). They were to draft an instruction and

[57] Gałędek, Klimaszewska, and Pomianowski, note 22 above, pp. 270-271.

[58] Gałędek, note 8 above, pp. 24, 26.

[59] Ibid., pp. 26-34; Gałędek and Klimaszewska, note 22 above, p. 199; Gałędek, Klimaszewska, and Pomianowski, "Prace Komitetu Cywilnego Reformy nad przygotowaniem narodowej kodyfikacji prawa cywilnego i procedury cywilnej w przededniu utworzenia Królestwa Polskiego (1814–1815) – edycja ***źródłowa***. Część ***II***", *Krakowskie Studia z Historii Państwa i Prawa*. XII (2019), pp. 388-389.

[60] Gałędek and Klimaszewska, note 10 above, p. 281.

[61] Gałędek, note 8 above, p. 35; Gałędek, Klimaszewska, and Pomianowski, note 22 above, p. 251; Zarzycka, note 24 above, p. 175.

work plan for the future codification deputation.[62] Moreover, Czartoryski in 1815 requested jurists to provide their opinion on the need to replace the French codes with another law and in response received memorials from Bandtkie and Wyczechowski.[63]

That the Preparatory Commission was not autonomous in its work is demonstrated by the decision of the Viceroy of the Kingdom of Poland, Zajączek, of 2 January 1816: all work on the development of the constitutional foundations of the Kingdom was to be undertaken under the guidance of Czartoryski, and he would submit drafts for the Administrative Council to consider.[64] As for the orientation of the work of the Commission (organization, determination of the sources of the future codes), Czartoryski and the Governmental Commission of Justice had differing positions. Ultimately, in 1817 the Viceroy approved the plan submitted by the last; it provided for maximum retention of Napoleonic legislation in the new codes.[65]

The will of the Emperor, expressed in a communication of the State Secretary on 24 August (5 September) 1817, was to postpone the drafting of a new original national civil code, but a new organ should be formed by the Viceroy of the Kingdom of Poland – a Drafting Commission, which was to prepare before the Sejm assembled in 1818 a number of draft changes in existing legislation. The membership was proposed by the Governmental Commission of Justice and confirmed by the Viceroy on 4 October 1817.[66] Branch deputations were formed within the Commission, and their work began to be supervised by the Governmental Commission of Justice pursuant to the Order of the Viceroy of 18 September 1817.[67] The drafting Commission was dissolved by Order of the Viceroy of 11 August 1818.[68]

Under an Edict of Alexander I of 19 (31) July 1818, the individual books of the Civil Code should have been drafted by designated

[62] Zarzycka, note 24 above, pp. 175-176.

[63] Ibid., p. 177.

[64] Ibid., p. 181.

[65] Ibid., pp. 182-184.

[66] Grynwaser, note 9 above, p. 164; Zarzycka, note 24 above, pp. 185, 187; Zarzycka, note 31 above, p. 127.

[67] Zarzycka, note 24 above, pp. 186-187.

[68] Ibid., p. 193.

editors.[69] The Council of State of the Kingdom of Poland on 27 May 1819 rejected the plan for the Civil Code prepared by Bieńkowski. Thereafter the first and second books of the Civil Code were prepared, which Emperor Alexander I did not approve. On 1(13) October 1820 at the behest of the State secretary, the Emperor commanded to create a general legislative deputation. In the same way, on 27 November (9 December) 1823 and in the instruction of 24 December 1823 the Emperor ordered the deputation to limit the work on these books to urgent changes and to cease work on the codification of civil procedure and criminal law in order to have more time to prepare a national civil code.[70]

After the adoption of book one of the Civil Code in 1825, work on books two and three and on the code of civil procedure and the criminal code was assigned to a new (second) Sejm deputation created at the behest of the State Secretary of 1(13) January 1825. This deputation prepared the draft book two of the Civil Code. But the initiatives of the deputation were slowed down because of the conservative position of the Governmental Commission of Justice, and ultimately of the Council of State. In a behest of the Minister State Secretary of 12 (24) March 1829, Nicholas I terminated the work of the deputation on the third book of the Civil Code and ordered book two to be completed first and necessary changes therein to be drafted. On 16 June 1829 the Council of State decreed to change the work format of the deputation, to prepare only individual changes in the Code in separate drafts, but Emperor Nicholas I insisted that the preparation of the Code be continued through a letter of the Minister State Secretary to the chairman of the Administrative Council of 11 November 1829. At the end of 1829 and in the first half of 1830, the deputation drafted seven laws making changes of the Civil Code.[71] On 10 December 1830 the deputation was eliminated by one of the first decrees of the Provisional Government of the Kingdom of Poland during the uprising and its functions were transferred to the Commission of Justice.[72]

[69] Zarzycka, note 31 above, p. 127.

[70] Ibid., pp. 127-128, 131-132.

[71] Ibid., pp. 128, 133; Pomianowski, note 2 above, p. 207; Grynwaser, note 9 above, p. 155.

[72] Grynwaser, note 9 above, p. 163.

Work on the national codification continued until 1831.[73] Between 1815 and 1831 no attempts were made to introduce any norms or principles of Russian law into the Kingdom of Poland.[74] In general, albeit with significant reservations, one may agree with a contemporary specialist who commented on life in the Duchy of Warsaw and the Kingdom of Poland between 1813 and 1831: "Of the three States which partitioned the *Rzecz Pospolita*, Russia, especially after Alexander I took the throne, gave the largest space of freedom to the Poles".[75]

Legal Education and Science. The organizational forms of the development of legal education and science in the Duchy of Warsaw and the Kingdom of Poland comprised yet another element of the institutional structure transforming legal thought.

At the time it was formed, there were no institutions of higher education on the territory of the Duchy of Warsaw.[76] A School of Law was opened in Warsaw in 1807 at the initiative and with the material support of the Minister of Justice, Count Łubieński, and, thanks to the enthusiasm of a group of jurists: Antoni Łabęcki (1773-1854), Prince Franciszek Ksawery Szaniawski (1768-1830), and Antoni Wyczechowski.[77] During the first year, these were unofficial courses for the raising of qualifications. As Łubieński noted, "in order to satisfy an acute need for cognition of the Code of Napoleon the Great ... intelligent men were called upon ... to set out: the French Code Civil, the theory of criminal law, the theory of civil and criminal procedure, and the French code of civil procedure".[78]

[73] Gałędek, note 8 above, p. 35.

[74] Pomianowski, note 2 above, p. 16.

[75] T. Matlęgiewicz, "Idee słowianofilskie w Warszawskim Towarzystwie Przyjaciół Nauk (1800-1830)", *Athenaeum*, XXXIII (2012), p. 98.

[76] A. Rosner, "Dzieje Wydziału Prawa i Administracji Uniwersytetu Warszawskiego w latach 1808-1831", in G. Bałtruszajtys (ed.), *Zarys dziejów Wydziału prawa i administracji Uniwersytetu Warszawskiego* (2d ed.; Warsaw, 2016), p. 12.

[77] Ibid.

[78] Cited in ibid., p. 12. Also see Rosner, "Nauka prawa ... stała się nieuchronnie potrzebną nie tylko przez swą użyteczność, lecz obowiązki, jakie nas łączą w obywatelskim stanie". O tradycji i nowoczesności w nauczaniu prawa w Księstwie Warszawskim i Królestwie Polskim (1807-1830)", *Krakowskie Studia z Historii Państwa i Prawa*, VIII (2015), p. 233.

Pursuant to a Decree of Friedrich August of 18 March 1808, the School of Law was re-founded, or officially founded, the personnel establishment confirmed, and the syllabus expanded: natural law, Roman law, civil law, French Code Civil, criminal law, "all possible relations with the administration, police, and public law", and additional lectures. In addition, public lectures occurred at the beginning of each academic year.[79] Later the following courses were added: State system of contemporary States; history of law; canon law, selected questions of philosophy, and others.[80] The model for the School of Law was the École special de droit.[81]

Despite the presence of natural law in the syllabus, studies in the School of Law were primarily positivist in spirit, historically-oriented, and comparative legal to a significant degree; legal science was understood as fundamental and social, and not merely practical in the French exegetic understanding at the time.[82] The School was not subordinate to the Chamber of Education of the Duchy; it remained within the jurisdiction of the Minister of Justice. The high status of the School was underpinned by a royal decree in July 1809, pursuant to which occupying a number of judicial offices required a graduation certificate from the School.[83] A School of Administrative Sciences was founded in May 1811 by royal decree; in actuality a dual School of Law and Administration had been formed.[84] Between 1808 and 1815, 572 persons studied in the School of Law, but only 74 completed the entire course of study.[85]

By edict of Emperor Alexander I of 19 November 1816, an institution of higher education of the university type was founded – the Chief School, with the rights to grant educational and scientific degrees and to censure the works of lecturers.[86] In 1818 under a

[79] A. Oniszczuk, "Doświadczenia Księstwa Warszawskiego w zakresie edukacji prawniczej", *Krytyka Prawa*, VIII, no. 3 (2016), p. 76.

[80] Rosner, "Tradycja i nowoczesnośc w nauczaniu prawa. Doświadczenie Rzeczpospolitej szlacheckiej i Szkola Prawa w Księstwie Warszawskim", in H. Izdebski (ed.), *Nauka i nauczanie prawa. Tradycja i przyszłość* (Warsaw, 2009), p. 55.

[81] Grynwaser, note 9 above, p. 28.

[82] See, for example, Rosner, note 76 above, p. 22.

[83] M. Mycielski, "Uniwersytet Królewski, 1816-1831", *Dzieje Uniwersytetu Warszawskiego. 1816-1915* (Warsaw, 2016), p. 54.

[84] Oniszczuk, note 79 above, p. 78.

[85] Cited in Rosner, note 76 above, p. 23.

[86] Mycielski, note 83 above, p. 61.

new statute the School became the Royal Warsaw University.[87] The Faculty of Law was the largest in the University. In 1821 of 491 students in five faculties of the University, 256 studied in the Faculty of Law; that is, more than half.[88]

Education both in the School of Law and in the Faculty of Law was regarded primarily as practical and applied education. As was observed in 1821 by the Rector, Wojciech Szweykowski (1773-1838), "Any theory, insofar as possible, should be adapted to practice, namely, to application in the requirements of the country". As one specialist noted, the University "was not a contemporary arena of an experimental-scientific character, although gradually such trends could be clearly traced".[89] Another specialist noted, "during the existence of the Principality, French legislation began to knit together with Polish legal culture thanks to contemporary approaches in the domain of education".[90]

But the teaching syllabus, personality of the lecturers and their works, and the brilliant Pleiad of legal scholars among the graduates of the School of Law and Warsaw University leave no doubt that the legal education there was of a significantly more profound character there than was assumed. One indicator is that the Law Faculty of Warsaw University took from the School of Law and strengthened the historical, comparative, and philosophical elements of education that transcended the dogmatic study of legislation and judicial practice.[91] One of the leading legal scholars of that time ascribed to Warsaw education the role of custodian of the people.[92]

It should be noted that Krakow University when the city of Krakow was part of the Duchy of Warsaw had chairs of: natural law, political law, law of nations, and general political economy; Roman law and history of all laws; Code Napoleon, Code de Commerce, mining law, and "laws established at the last Sejm"; the practice of all judicial and political instances of the Principality

[87] Rosner, note 76 above, p. 27.

[88] K. Wójcicki, *Warszawa, jej Życie Umysłowe i Ruch Literacki w Ciągu Lat Trzydziestu (od 1800-1830 r.)* (Warsaw, 1880), p. 141.

[89] Rosner, note 78 above, pp. 233, 235.

[90] Oniszczuk, note 79 above, p. 89.

[91] Rosner, note 76 above, p. 36; Mycielski, note 83 above, p. 160.

[92] A. Heylman, "Myśli o nauce prawa i prawodawstwie w kraiu naszym", *Themis Polska*, VII (1830), p. 135.

of Warsaw; political economy and country statistics; and canon law (although the last two chairs were not held for a long time).[93] The nomenclature of the chairs makes clear that legal education in that institution went far beyond the applied practitioner model.

The privileges received by Warsaw University, especially the autonomy of censorship, enabled legal ideas to develop and to be disseminated to a certain extent. Both elements of dialogue and compromise and the instability of the last with respect to freedom of lecturers to express their views may be seen in the persecution of a young University lecturer on legal history, Romuald Hube (1803-1890) in 1826 to 1827. Because he was an open adherent of the ideas of Georg Friedrich Wilhelm Hegel (1770-1831) but not a consistent Hegelian, the Commission of Education decided that the Chair of the History of Law……. was unnecessary. Ultimately, protests by the Dean of the Faculty of Law, Jan Wincenty Bandtkie and the students helped save both the Chair and the lecturing career of Hube.[94]

Following the suppression of the November uprising, Warsaw University was closed by decision of Emperor Nicholas I on 19 November 1831 – exactly fifteen years after it was founded. Vilnius University was closed that same year, and Krakow University entered into a period of long decline.[95] One specialist observed:

> When after the collapse of the November Uprising and closure of the University, legal instruction was undertaken in courses at gymnasiums, the Tsarist authorities watched to ensure that it was purely of a practical, professional character, and any delving into theory or comparison with the legislation of other States was strictly prohibited.[96]

Among Warsaw scientific institutions, the most important and authoritative was the Society of the Friends of Science, founded

[93] Oniszczuk, note 80 above, p. 83.

[94] M. Paszkowska, "Romuald Hube 1803-1890", *Portrety uczonych. Profesorowie Uniwersytetu Warszawskiego 1816-1915* (Warsaw, 2016), p. 251.

[95] Rosner, "Jan Wincenty Bandtkie 1783-1846", ibid., p. 66; Szymaniec, "Nauka prawa jako działalność pro bono. Uwagi na temat polskiej nauki prawa w latach 1807-1831", M. Marszal and J. Przygodzki (eds.), *Pro publico bono – idee i dzialalność* (Wroclaw, 2016), p. 102; Iłowiecki, note 51 above, p. 165.

[96] Sójka-Zielińska, "Nauczanie historii prawa w czasach przemian ustrojowych", in A. Turskiej (ed.), *Humanizacja zawodow prawniczych a nauczanie akademickie* (Warsaw, 2002), p. 44.

in 1800. Modern specialists note that it "set the tone of Warsaw intellectual life".[97]

Five divisions operated within the Society, one of which was devoted to the science of law. In 1808 the Society received semi-official status in the Duchy and was renamed the Royal Warsaw Society of Friends of Science.[98] The Society was liquidated in July 1832.[99]

Publishing activity. The publication of scholarly works was another form of institutionalizing the science of law, especially the publication of scholarly journals. Between 1801 and 1832, 695 legal works were published in Warsaw (whereas in Wilna – 100; Krakow – 82; Lviv – 62; Poznan – 32). One specialist noted: "The leading role of Warsaw in the Polish science of law was undoubted".[100]

There was a certain evolution to be seen in scientific, scientific-popular, and literary and scientific periodical publications. In general the periodicals of the Duchy of Warsaw and then the Kingdom of Poland exceeded in number all the newspapers and journals which appeared on Polish territories under the authority of Austria and Prussia taken together.[101] From 1802 the Society of Friends of Science published yearbooks irregularly. There were few legal articles in these publications.[102] Legal articles did appear in the *Nowy Pamiętnik Warszawski. Dziennik historyczny, polityczny, tudzież nauk i umiejętności* (1801-1805). Sections devoted to the "Science of Law" and to "Legislation" did appear in the *Pamiętnik Warszawski* (1809-1810). There was a rubric "Science of Law" in the *Pamiętnik Warszawski czyli Dziennik Nauk i Umiejętności* (1815-1823).[103]

97 Rosner, note 76 above, p. 20.

98 B. Szyndler, "Towarzystwo Warszawskie Przjyaciól Nauk w dobie Ksiestwa Warszawskiego (szkic do monografii)", *Teka Komisji Historycznej Oddziału Lubelskiego PAN*, I (2007), p. 15.

99 Rosner, note 95 above, p. 66.

100 W. Witkowski, "Warszawa jako ośrodek polskiej nauki prawa w dobie zaborów", *Krakowskie Studia z Historii Panstwa i Prawa*, VIII, no. 1 (2015), p. 49.

101 Польша и Россия в первой трети XIX века. Из истории автономного Королевства Польского. 1815-1830 [Poland and Russia in the First Third of the Nineteenth Century. From the History of the Autonomous Kingdom of Poland. 1815-1830] (Moscow, 2010), p. 449.

102 Szyndler, note 98 above, I, p. 15; Pomianowsi, note 4 above, p. 37.

103 Pomianowski, note 2 above, pp. 37, 43-45.

But the first Polish legal journal with scientific aspirations became *Themis Polska* (1828-1830).[104] Although the view of one specialist that the Polish science of law was born on the pages of this journal[105] is an exaggeration and undervalues the preceding two decades in the evolution of Polish legal science, but there is little doubt that the *Themis Polska* significantly influenced the development of the science of law in Poland. And the authors themselves were aware of this; they regarded the journal (in the context of the publication of specialized scientific legal journals as a whole) as a factor contributing to the formation of a national jurisprudence.[106]

Thus, within the period here considered the institutional infrastructure was created for the development of legal doctrine, education, science, and relevant publishing activity in the central Polish region. The reception of French law in the Duchy of Warsaw provided the direct and indirect impetus, initially as an idea and then as a reality. The introduction of a foreign element into Polish legal life served as an irritant for public and scholarly discussion and a profound transformation of Polish jurisprudence. The discussions in the changing lawmaking bodies should have concentrated on the preservation, transformation, or rejection of French law, and likewise of Austrian and Prussian. Preservation would have entailed a consideration and either a synthesis or a choice to be made between them. The idea of rejecting French law or the transformation thereof would have engaged the conceptualization and rethinking of the law of the former *Rzecz Pospolita*, the identification and designing of a Polish national law on the basis of autochthonic sources and/or by way of a synthesis of foreign experience. The contradictory policy of the Russian Imperial government, changes in the positions of influential national political groups, the existence of institutionalized channels for the expression of ideas all facilitated the crystallization and re-evaluation of discussions that were in essence comparative legal discussions that went beyond practical issues in the search for arguments and generalizations.

[104] Ibid., p. 254.

[105] Ch. E. Mecke, "Dyskurs o zasadniczej myśli prawniczej w 'Themis Polskiej' (1828-1830) na tle programu historycznej szkoły prawa w Niemczech", *Forum prawnicze* (2018), p. 18.

[106] A. Heylman, note 92 above, p. 136.

The founding in the central Polish region of institutions of higher education – School of Law, School of Law and Administration, Faculty of Law of Warsaw University – was dictated primarily by practical considerations. One primary requirement was the implementation of the received French legislation. But legal education from the outset went beyond these practical aims. Influenced by European trends and the broad interests of Polish jurists, legal education became fundamental, with historical and comparative legal dimensions. The scientific, and not only applied, nature of the legal profession developed thanks to the Society of the Friends of Science as an academic institution, and by the publication of books and a number of periodical publications.

§1.3 Intellectual Context: Outside Influences

Intellectual factors, namely, outside influences, were another important context for the development of legal thought among Warsaw jurists. The education of Polish jurists abroad, familiarization with and translations of the works of foreign authors, and the self-identification of Polish authors with certain foreign scientific schools and orientations were the instruments of these influences.

A significant number of the leading Warsaw jurists studied in universities of the German *lände*: Berlin (Hube, Maciejowski, Zaborowski); Göttingen (Heylman, Maciejowski); Halle (Bandtkie).[107] No doubt this list is incomplete. But information about Polish jurists studying in other countries is rarely encountered. Some Polish jurists retained links with their German professors for a long time. Witkowski is probably correct when he says that scientific legal life in Warsaw was dominated by graduates of German universities.[108]

Significant foreign works on law were translated at Warsaw. During the last quarter of the eighteenth century a number of works of importance for the formation of the modern legal sciences had been translated into Polish, among them Montesquieu's *Spirit*

[107] Szymaniec, note 95 above, pp. 121-122; J. Bardach, "Waclaw Aleksander Maciejowski 1792-1883", in note 94 above, pp. 337-338; Paszkowska, note 94 above, pp. 248, 250; Rosner, note 95 above, p. 56; Witkowski, "Nowe pokolenie prawników Królestwa Polskiego I połowy XIX wieku", *Rejent*, no. 4 (2000), p. 190.

[108] Witkowski, note 100 above, p. 48.

of the Laws.[109] Also translated were Immanuel Kant (1724-1804) on perpetual peace[110] and on the idea of universal history,[111] and Gaetano Filangieri (1752-1788) on the science of legislation.[112] Among other relevant foreign jurists who appeared in the Polish language during the first third of the nineteenth century were Paul Johann Anselm Ritter von Feuerbach (1775-1833) on German jurisprudence,[113] together with excerpts from his piece on court organization and procedure in France;[114] extracts from Jean Louis Eugène Lerminier (1803-1857) on the state of French legislation;[115] and contributions to the world of law by Jean Baptiste Blonde (1784-1854), Sosthene de la Rochefoucauld (1785-1864), Antoine Marie Demante (1789-1856), Carl Joseph Anton Mittermaier (1787-1867), Alphonse Honore Taillandier (1797-1867), and two articles by Eduard Gans (1798-1839) and Johann Michael M. Birnbaum (1792-1877).[116]

Polish jurists read and cited (or sometimes did not cite, but drew upon) these translations during the first third of the nineteenth century: Gans (W. A. Maciejowski, C. Zaborowski, K. A. Heylman, R. Hube);[117] Friedrich Carl von Savigny (Zaborowski, Heylman,

[109] Ch. de Montesquieu (1689-1755), *Duch czyli treść praw albo o stosowności którą powinny mieć prawa z ustawą rządu każdego, obyczaimi, położeniem kraiu, religią etc. Z przydatkiem dociekania praw Rzymskich względem sukcessyi, praw francuzkich i praw lennych* (Lipsk, 1777). 2 vols.

[110] I. Kant, Projekt wieczystego pokoju, transl. S. Bielski (Königsberg, 1796), cited from M. Żelazny (comp.), "Bibliografia polskich przekładów prac Immanuela Kanta (do roku 2004)", *Filo-Sofija*, no. 1 (2004), p. 89.

[111] Kant, *Wyobrażenie do historii powszechnej we względzie kosmopolitycznym*, transl. J. Bychowiec (Königsberg, 1799), cited in Żelazny, note 110se above, p. 89.

[112] G. Filangieri, *Nauka prawodawstwa przez Kawalera Kaietana Filangieri*, transl. W. R. Karczewski (Warsaw, 1791-1793). 8 vols.

[113] P. Feuerbach, "O prawodawstwie", *Pamiętnik Warszawski*, II (1822), pp. 199-209, 301-315.

[114] Feuerbach, "Wyciąg z dzieła Feuerbacha, pod tytułem: Über die Gerichtsverfassung und das gerichtliche Verfahren Frankreichs, in besonderer Beziehung auf die Öffentlichkeit und Mündlichkeit der Gerechtigkeitspflege (Giessen 1825)", *Themis Polska*, IV (1828), pp. 83-129; VIII (1830), pp. 221-260.

[115] J. Lerminier, "Uwagi nad stanem prawodawstwa francuzkiego", *Themis Polska*, VII (1830)

[116] Pomianowski, note 2 above, pp. 96-100.

[117] W. Maciejowski, "Ogłoszenie prenumeraty", *Themis Polska*, V (1829), pp. 419-420; [C. Zaborowski], "Rozbiór krytyczny dzieła pod tytułem: Upominek pogrobowy ś.p. Kazimierza Pliszki Podlesianina; rzecz o sukcessii ...", *Themis Polska*, VI (1829), p. 213; A. Heylman, "Wywod zasad ogolnych nauki prawa i prawodawstwa", *Themis Polska*, VII (1830), p. 21; R. Hube, "Niektore uwagi nad historya nauki prawa (1830)", in Hube, *Opera*, ed. K. Dunin (Warsaw, 1905), I,

Hube);[118] Ch. de Montesquieu (Maciejowski, Zaborowski);[119] Feuerbach (Maciejowski, Hube);[120] Hegel (Heylman, Hube);[121] Gustav von Hugo (1764-1844) (Heylman, Hube);[122] Jeremy Bentham (1748-1832) (Zaborowski);[123] Giovanni Battista Vico (1668-1744) (Maciejowski);[124] and Kant (Hube).[125]

Among Polish works of a comparatist character, Maciejowski cited the largest number of foreign authors in his history of Slavic legislation. He noted that he was inspired to undertake his studies by the works of Johann Gottfried Herder (1744-1803), Pavel Jozef Šafárik (1795-1861), Edouard Gans (1798-1839), Friedrich Majer (Maier) (1772-1818) – the author of works on the comparative legal history of the Germanic peoples; Friedrich Bluhme (1797-1874), and the Polish translation of Feuerbach.[126]

The self-identification of Warsaw legal scholars with certain European scientific schools becomes clear by 1827. The views of Warsaw legal scholars on the distinctive national features of the development of the science of law are interesting. Although German legal science was not the ideal to imitate unconditionally, it was at least the principal point of departure for a significant number of Polish jurists. Hube noted in 1827 and later that German legal science was universal, not tied down to the "requirements of some concrete legislation", and as theory developed, the "Germans became the cradle for the history of law" (at the end of the eighteenth century) and the science of the philosophy of law. This

p. 53; Hube, "Uwagi nad systematem Kodexu cywilnego francuskiego", *Themis Polska*, V (1829), p. 298.

118 C. Z[aborowski], "Jurysprudencya sądu kassacyinego Xięstwa Warszawskiego i związek instytucyi kassacyinéy z ogólném życiem prawném w kraju", *Themis Polska*, VI (1829), p. 366; Zaborowski, note 117 above, p. 213; Heylman, note 92 above, p. 111; Heylman, note 117 above, pp. 11, 15; Hube, note 117 above (1830), p. 50.

119 Maciejowski, note 117 above, pp. 414-415; Zaborowski, note 117 above, pp. 213, 240.

120 Maciejowski, note 117 above, p. 415; Hube, note 117 above (1829), pp. 298, 306.

121 Heylman, note 117 above, p. 7; Hube, note 117 above (1830), p. 54.

122 Heylman, note 117 above, pp. 10, 40; Hube, note 117 above (1830), p. 53.

123 Zaborowski, note 118 above, p. 362.

124 Maciejowski, note 117 above, p. 414.

125 Hube, note 117 above (1830), p. 54.

126 Maciejowski, *Historya prawodawstw słowiańskich* (Warsaw, 1832-1835), I, pp. vi, 1, 4, 7, 34, 57.

imparted to the "German School of law incontestable supremacy in comparison with all preceding schools".[127] Instead, Hube considered French jurisprudence to be oriented towards practice, one-sided, based on dogmatics and causistics – the interpretation of national codes and generalization of their application, born after the appearance of the codes and not adequately developed scientifically, but having prospects in the course of the critical analysis of legislative development.[128]

On the whole, Maciejowski shared the views of Hube; he also described the state of French legal science as primitive, having changed little from the eighteenth century, but approved with some restraint the achievements of German jurisprudence.[129] Hube and Heylman linked these distinctions with the differing political and legal development of the Germanic States and France.[130]

Moreover, beginning at least from 1827 Warsaw legal scholars identified themselves with certain foreign scientific schools more clearly. Hube in 1827 identified himself primarily with the historical school of law, but pointed out the advisability of combining its principles with the philosophical school of law.[131] The approach of the philosophical school was evident by 1829 in the Gans variant, together with criticism of the historical school.[132] By 1830 these positions become sharper, up to the proclamation of the conceptions of the historical school to be not sufficiently scientific and obsolete, but the emphasis was retained on the need to combine the principles of the two schools.[133] Hube ultimately noted in 1830 that both schools are necessary and are historical in their principles, but have a differing understanding of the philosophy of the historical-legal process: the superiority of the philosophical school is discovered namely in this sphere.[134]

[127] Hube, "Krotki rys historyi literatury prawa (1827)", in Hube, *Opera*, note 117 above, I, p. 54.

[128] Hube, "O stanie nauki prawa w naszych czasach (1827)", note 117 above, pp. 5, 9; Hube, note 117 above (1829), pp. 304-306.

[129] Maciejowski, note 117 above, p. 414-415.

[130] Heylman, note 117 above, p. 30.

[131] Hube, note 127 above, p. 68; Hube, note 128 above, p. 11.

[132] Hube, note 117 above (1829), pp. 298, 304, 311.

[133] Hube, note 117 above (1830), pp. 38-39, 42-43, 50-56.

[134] Ibid., p. 57.

As an unequivocal proponent of the historical school and opponent of the philosophical school, Heylman identified himself, but he perceived and speculatively interpreted the positions of the school too broadly, by proceeding from the logical generalization of its ideas and partially accepted the ideas of the philosophical school.[135] In 1829 Zaborowski clearly identified himself with the historical school of law, although he acknowledged the importance of the ideas of the philosophical school.[136] Maciejowski more or less considered himself to be associated with the historical school and endeavored to follow its principles consistently.[137]

The emphasis by some modern authors on what they consider to be the major influence of the exegesis school[138] requires, in our view, separate consideration because the originality of the theoretical postulates of that school was not significant (at most from the perspective of later legal positivism); they were based on early positivism in law as set out in the German works of the second half of the eighteenth and early nineteenth centuries. Possibly that explains why Warsaw jurists of the first third of the nineteenth century did not identify themselves with that School.

The foregoing enables us to conclude that Warsaw legal scholars of that period unambiguously identified themselves with the German model of the science of law as they understood it, but irrespective of whether they inclined to the historical or the philosophical school of jurisprudence which originated during the first third of the nineteenth century in Germany and spread to other countries, to a greater or lesser degree Polish jurists accepted the foundations of both schools. Our earlier studies demonstrate that this gradual combining in various correlations and forms was not distinctive to Poland; this happened everywhere, including in Germany itself even among the founders of the respective schools.[139] Therefore, we consider inadvisable the reflections of contemporary proponents of the understanding of these schools as some pure models with a supposedly not fully adequate understanding of

135 Heylman, note 92 above, p. 111; Heylman, note 117 above, pp. 2, 7-8, 10-11, 15-19, 21, 29, and 40.

136 Zaborowski, note 118 above, pp. 366, 368; Zaborowski, note 117 above, p. 213.

137 Maciejowski, note 126 above, I.

138 Pomianowski, note 1 above, pp. 405-407; Szymaniec, note 95 above, p. 120.

139 See Kresin, *Comparative Legal Studies: 1750 to 1835. Approaches to Conceptualization*, ed. & transl. W. E. Butler (London, 2019), 2 vols.

their grounds and an insufficiently sharp juxtaposition by Warsaw legal scholars of the first third of the nineteenth century.[140]

The emphasis accorded by Warsaw legal scholars to the foundations of these schools[141] should not be regarded as a declaration of loyalty to or blind reproduction of their views, but as a point of departure for developing their ideas and adaptation of these to national Polish realities. Moreover, just as in the German science of law during the 1820s, the sharp tone among Warsaw jurists in disputes about the virtues and shortcomings of these two schools[142] reflected exercises in rhetoric more than a substantive dispute between the two programs which had a single foundation and increasing drew closer to one another.

To some extent recourse to the conceptions of European scientific schools performed the role of a starting point for the development by Warsaw scholars of their own ideas, some of whom had studied in German universities, and to some degree determined the agenda for discussions or frameworks within which they attempted to embody their discussions, and also might partially shape the conceptual language, but not the outcome, of these discussions. For example, as one observer noted: "The discourse concerning the future national codification of civil law was purely a Polish scientific and politico-legal discussion. But it remained, just as a similar discussion in Germany, in a European context" without being a simple reflection of western European discussions.[143] Another specialist noted the same with regard to the proposition of the historical school concerning the time being appropriate or inappropriate for creating national legislation: "It should be noted that the same conclusion had completely different practical consequences in the Kingdom (where French civil law was in force) and Germany (where local laws were principally in force)".[144]

[140] Mecke, note 105 above, p. 32; Szymaniec, note 95 above, pp. 121, 123; Pomianowski, note 2 above, p. 131.

[141] Mecke, note 105 above, p. 23, 37; Paszkowska, note 94 above, p. 252.

[142] Pomianowski, note 1 above, p. 412; also see Pomianowski, note 2 above, p. 118.

[143] Mecke, note 105 above, p. 37.

[144] Pomianowski, note 1 above, p. 412. Also see Pomianowski, note 2 above, p. 118.

The situation of Bandtkie is especially illustrative. In October 1814 Bandtkie expressed ideas similar to those of Savigny as set out in his work on the vocation of our age,[145] but before von Savigny's volume was published in Germany the same year. A modern scholar wrote in this connection: "The Warsaw scholar have, however, ... have had information about the debates in Germany when preparing his text for press", but concludes that "two clear parallels between the positions of Bandtkie and Savigny were linked with the intellectual climate of Europe of that time".[146] Therefore, the conclusion of another specialist with respect to Bandtkie being the founder of the Warsaw historical school of law[147] also is tentative, for the historical school of law itself was regarded by contemporaries in at least two senses, was not an isolated pure model which in unchanged form traveled about Europe, but a complex of ideas gradually formed by various scholars and on some issues in parallel with one another.

One cannot concur with the view that it is "difficult to seek serious, original theoretical ideas in the works of Warsaw legal scholars". The works which appeared in Warsaw were primarily a reflection of ideas which arose in the West, or an attempt to compile and adapt them to local conditions"; as a result of the superficiality of the philosophical erudition of Warsaw jurists "it also is difficult to speak about some, albeit eclectic, legal doctrine arising".[148] Perhaps the grounds of doctrine may lie deeper, and not eclectically, than observers have searched, and instead of a presumed reflection, the national distinctive features may be discovered as being to a certain extent European and, partially, Central and Eastern European ideas.

[145] F. C. von Savigny, *Of the Vocation of Our Age for Legislation and Jurisprudence*, transl. Abraham Hayward (London, 1831; reprint ed.; 1996).

[146] Szymaniec, note 95 above, p. 103.

[147] Rosner, note 95 above, p. 67.

[148] Pomianowski, note 2 above, pp. 131-132; Pomianowski, note 1 above, pp. 415-416.

Chapter 2
Institutionalization of Comparative Legal Knowledge

§2.1. Foundations of Positivist Legal Science

Dualism was characteristic of European legal thought in the mid-eighteenth century – the parallel development of the knowledge of positive law and a speculative doctrine of natural law. These were not synthesized, although they might be arbitrarily combined, and did not constitute a single jurisprudential discipline.

During the second half of the eighteenth century more or less in parallel the doctrine of the separation of knowledge about positive law from philosophy (including the doctrine on natural law) and the formation on the basis thereof of positive, social, and empirical legal science was elaborated by the Göttingen School of Johann Stephan Pütter (1725-1807), the Königsberg professor, Immanuel Kant, and the Italian scholar, Gaetano Filangieri. They pointed to: the exclusiveness of positive law as law proper; the normativity or legality as the nature of positive law distinct from morals and morality, although linked with them; the lawfulness and rationality of positive law as an expression of social experience and will, its non-incidentalness and self-value as the subject-matter of research; its empirical nature as the foundation of the cognition of law; and the systematization of knowledge concerning positive law and the formalization thereof in the science of law.

At the outset of the nineteenth century, the grounds for a new (or, in principle, transformed) science of law were clarified by the leading scholars of the period. For the historical-philosophical doctrine on law there were Hegel, Feuerbach, Anton Friedrich Justus Thibault (1772-1840), and others; they subordinated positivist legal science to empirical and positive philosophy, including the philosophy of law, but with recognition of the separateness of both spheres, the impossibility of levelling their limits, and condemnation of the formalism of metaphysics, including the theory of natural law. Savigny's historical doctrine on law proclaimed the separation of jurisprudence from philosophy. Common to both doctrines was the proclamation of the autonomy of the science of positive law, including the formation of an own system of concepts on the basis of empirical studies, and also denial of the possibility of natural law as a proper law – as a consequence of which these orientations of legal thought could be deemed to be different aspects of the early development of positivism.

The so-called "codification debates" – a public discussion from 1810 to 1817 that became key in the forming and precise delimitation of the positions of the historical-philosophical and historical schools, and also the clarification and enrichment thereof on general grounds – played a major role in the development of the science of law. Among these general grounds were: (1) forming of the doctrine concerning law on the basis of empirical studies of positive law, the unity of empirical knowledge and legal doctrine; (2) recognition of the profession and vocation of the legal scholar – independent of legal practice and lecturing; (3) recognition of pluralism of the forms of organization of legal knowledge – the fundamental legal science of the German model, and the practice-oriented doctrines of the English and French models. Therefore, this discussion, especially in 1814 at the peak thereof, may be considered the last benchmark en route to overcoming the dualism of legal knowledge and the forming of a positive and social science of law (or its corresponding transformation in principle).

The further development of the ideas of the historical-philosophical and historical schools concerning the science of law until 1833 was linked with the divulgence and mutual-influence of their programs. Georg Friedrich Puchta (1798-1846), for example, declared that in and of itself the concept of law is elaborated outside empirical positivist jurisprudence – by the philosophy of law. Gans insisted that empirical research data acts as the basis thereof, and philosophy provides only its method for this, but not speculative abstractions. Feuerbach said that the philosophy of law had to be founded on the basis of comparative (general) jurisprudence. The construction of a positivist jurisprudence separate from philosophy was reflected in legal education, and the encyclopedia of positive law became the basic discipline.

Disputes among scholars in this period concerned whether the philosophy of positive law should be included in the science of law or in philosophy, and also the practicality of jurisprudence, on which the historical school insisted, or the liberation thereof from practical purposes, which the historical-philosophical school manifested. An issue of principle was linked with the last dispute in the context of this study – the respectively national or universal character of the subject-matter of the science of law. But the said disputes did not deny the convention of the two most influential German and, to a significant degree, European schools with respect to the autonomous character of the science of law and its positivist and social theoretical grounds.

Together with the idea of the integral nature of the science of law, especially in the context of its separation from theology, philosophy, ethics, and complex disciplines (cameralistics), the doctrine of its differentiation developed. The idea of its division into branches according to the division of law, and also purely instructional constructions in the sphere of education during the mid-eighteenth century, began to grow into a substantiation of the system of legal sciences. Scholars proposed a differentiation of the doctrine on law by branches, dogmatics, general positivist jurisprudence (jurisprudence, history of law) and the same positivist philosophy of law (science on the forms and concepts in law). Some scholars emphasized the comparative nature of knowledge within general jurisprudence or expressly identified the last with comparative jurisprudence. Also proposed was relegating disciplines to general jurisprudence which were interdisciplinary or had a specialized character – such as legal hermeneutics, legal linguistics, comparative jurisprudence.[1]

In considering the question of what legal science should be or what legal sciences were in the thinking of Warsaw jurists, we begin with Józef Kalasanty Szaniawski. In his work "What is Philosophy? (1802), using the concepts and terminology of Kant, Szaniawski proclaimed the supremacy and primacy of pure reason with respect to practical reason, *a priori* cognition with respect to sensation and experience. Therefore, for Szaniawski all sciences are parts of philosophy, and this creates uniform grounds which are only applied to cognized subject-matter, including law.[2] The science of law in this understanding could not be regarded as an autonomous phenomenon. On the contrary, Tadeusz Czacki

[1] O. V. Kresin, *Comparative Legal Studies: 1750 to 1835. Approaches to Conceptualization*, ed. & transl. W. E. Butler (2019), II, pp. 133-135.

[2] *Wiek XIX. Sto lat mysli Polskiej. Zyciorysy, streszczienia, wyjatki* (Warsaw, 1907), II, p. 313.

(1765-1813), who relied on Cesare Beccaria (1738-1794), Filangieri, and other legal scholars, confirmed the existence of a science of legislation; that is, positive jurisprudence.[3]

Commencing at least by 1808, Prince F. K. Szaniawski proposed a new vision of the science of law without which the legal sphere could not exist in full measure.[4] The need arises in legal science because of the complexity of law, an understanding of which requires special skills, and this assumes the existence of a special legal profession, the special vocation of judge, researcher, and legislator.[5] In a rather confused definition, Szaniawski identified the subject-matter of the science of law ("lawyerness" as the "development and application of prescriptions to human actions") and object as the "eliciting of useful truth in lawyerness" – which simultaneously might designate the practical and deeply scientific aspects of jurisprudence.[6] In his view, the science of law had been formed during the era of the ancient Roman State.[7]

According to Szaniawski, the path to cognition in the science of law should proceed from individual impressions of sensations, experienced cognition of elements of the past and present law (partial notions) to their interpretation, comparison, and generalization, systematization, "intellectual imitation", and the forming of general, complex, and abstracted ideas or concepts, and not *vice versa*.[8] Szaniawski called this empirical science of law a "real philosophy, a science of the human intellect"; namely, sciences in his vision acquire general truths.[9] Szaniawski noted that empiricity

[3] T. Czacki, *O litewskich i polskich prawach o ich duchu, żródłach, związku, i o rzeczach zawartych w pierwczym statucie dla Litwy, 1529 roku wydanym* (Krakow, 1861), II, pp. 293-294.

[4] F. K. Szianiawski, *O usposobieniach potrzebnych do uczenia się prawa. Rzech czytana przy otwarciu Szkoły prawa w Warszawie dnia 14 Pożdziernika 1808 roku* (Warsaw, 1808), pp. 3-4.

[5] Ibid., p. 5. Also see X. S. [Xaw. Szaniawski], "O przyczynach wielu uprzedzeń i sarkań przeciwko prawnictwu", *Pamiętnik Warszawski*, I, no. 1 (1815), p. 3. Niemcewicz in 1808 also emphasized the combining of theory and practice within the legal profession. See [J. U. Niemceswicz], *Przestroga dla społziomków na rok 1809* (Wrocław, 1808), p. 19.

[6] X. S. [Szaniawski], note 5 above, pp. 2-3, 9, 11.

[7] Szaniawski, note 4 above, p. 10.

[8] Ibid., pp. 6-7; F. K. Szaniawski, *Wiadomości początkowe w nauce prawa* (Warsaw, 1817), pp. v-vii, 2.

[9] Szaniawski, note 4 above, p. 7; Szaniawski, note 8 above, p. viii.

in the science of law, being a moral science, is not experimental, but of experience, and concepts thus cannot be precise.[10]

Within the framework of the science of law, Szaniawski distinguished the historical and philosophical approaches to cognition, the first being the empirical foundation of the second.[11] By 1817 Szaniawski had proclaimed the history of law to be a separate science.[12] He constantly emphasized the comparative method in both approaches,[13] and in 1819 substantiated the existence of a separate "statics of law or science of comparison in law".[14]

Even more consistent was the vision of a positivist historically-oriented science of law set out by Bandtkie commencing at least by 1812. Just as Szianawski, Bandtkie traced the science of law back to ancient Rome, but in his later works linked the formation of legal science with the professionalization of courts and the achievements of the Glossators in the twelfth century, an era in which the law of each people matures and becomes more complex while in the transition to State-social life.[15] The thoughts of Bandtkie on the independence of jurists from being elected by the municipal community and impartiality of their decisions not being agreed or linked with the understanding of feasibility by the general population are related to the matter of professionalization of legal activity without being confined to a particular period.[16] A transformation occurred in the sixteenth century, Bandtkie noted, when the science of law was turned from dogmatics and philosophizing to historical-legal analysis (probably he referred to the *mos gallicus* school).[17]

[10] F. K. Szaniawski, *Statyka prawa, czyli nauka porównywań w prawie* (Warsaw, 1819), p. 3.

[11] Szaniawski, note 4 above, pp. 7-8.

[12] Szaniawski, note 8 above, p. 284.

[13] Szaniawski, note 4 above, p. 9; Szaniawski, note 8 above, pp. v-xii.

[14] Szaniawski, note 10 above.

[15] Bandtkie, "Wywod historyczny praw mieyskich w Polsce dawney obowiązuiących", in J. W. Bandtkie, *Zbiór rospraw o przedmiotach prawa polskiego* (Warsaw, 1812), pp. 175-176; Bandtkie, *Uwagi o potrzebie nauki prawa w naszym kraju w szczegolności, a o użytku onejże w ogolnością* (Warsaw, 1814), pp. 5-6, 29-30, 32, 38; Bandtkie, "Co stanowi prawnika", *Pamiętnik Warszawski*, VI (1816), pp. 311-312.

[16] Bandtkie, note 15 above (1814), p. 10.

[17] Ibid., p. 31.

The historical analysis of law, in his view, combined with impartial critique is the basis of cognition in the science of law – which, of course, did not diminish the need for a purely dogmatic mastery of law in force for a practical purpose.[18] Bandtkie affirmed that the purely dogmatic interpretation of the letter of the law without a historical comprehension of its true significance and the reasons for the appearance thereof would lead to mistakes in principle.[19] He noted that among other sciences "law and the history thereof are the most valuable science which to the highest degree promote the happiness of the people, discover not only virtues or the futility of all political society and the composition thereof, but even the prosperity or suffering of individuals".[20]

Bandtkie condemned the *a priori* theorizing and philosophizing as anti-historical and deceptive and ridiculed the Kantian doctrine on pure reason and practical reason as disadvantageous in any profession without combining the last with science.[21] Instead he considered it possible to form an own philosophical discourse on the basis of the generalization of knowledge about positive law of the past and the modern day, namely in "the proclamation of truths verified by experience" embodied in the "high vocation of" the science of law.[22]

But Bandtkie devoted more attention in his writings to legal education than to the science of law. He also called legal education a science, which made his ideas more difficult to understand. He supported the professionalization of all legal occupations and legislative work, emphasizing the insufficiency of a practical education, the important role of the legal historical component of education, especially the history of national and foreign (particularly German and French) law, Roman law, canon law,

[18] Bandtkie, "O uprawnieniu dzieci przez zaszly zwiazek malzenski czynionem", in Bandtkie, note 15 above (1812), p. 258; Bandtkie, note 15 above (1812), pp. ix, 127-128; Bandtkie, note 15 above (1814), p. 18; Bandtkie, note 15 above (1816), pp. 311-313.

[19] Bandtkie, note 18 above (1812), p. 248; W. Sobociński, "Jan Wincenty Bandtkie obrońcą Kodeksu Napoleona", *Rocznik Lubelski*, III (1960), p. 160.

[20] Sobociński, note 19 above, p. 160.

[21] Bandtkie, "O karze śmierci na kradzież stanowionéy rzecz podług praw kraiowych uwazana", in Bandtkie, note 15 above (1812), p. 276, 284; Bandtkie, note 15 above (1812), p. 87; Bandtkie, note 15 above (1814), pp. 30,33-34; Bandtkie, "Co stanowi prawnika", *Pamiętnik Warszawski*, VI (1816), pp. 309, 322-325.

[22] Bandtkie, note 15 above (1814), pp. 33-35.

general history, and philosophy.[23] On the practical and educational importance of the history of Polish law he said: it

> shows, on one hand, that new provisions [received French law – OK] to a great extent are similar to older prescriptions, and the more they are researched, the more we will like them; on the other hand, what the Government does best is to give instruction on adaptations which fully replace them with laws which might completely become part of the customs of the people and thus achieve the final purpose of each legislation ... to show the wise laws of our ancestors, which often because of misunderstanding unjustly are criticized, and thus create in the hearts of youth a connection with fatherland laws and customs and a real devotion to the country.[24]

As Bandtkie noted, "lawyerliness ... makes its followers the trustees of the prosperity of peoples".[25]

Hube presented a distinctive vision of the science of law. He considered the emergence of the science of law to be recent, a "product of our time".[26] Moreover, Hube noted that the scientific organization of historically, theoretically, and philosophically-oriented knowledge about law was not universal; it was one thing among certain peoples (Germans), and otherwise among others, which could be affected by the distinctive features of their development: "any science should be considered a manifestation of the intellectual life of the people".[27] Legal knowledge in France, for example, was practice-oriented, based on casuistics and the interpretation of codified legislation, but begins to be transformed

[23] Bandtkie, note 18 above (1812), p. 215; Bandtkie, note 15 above (1814), pp. 18-22, 25, 28-37; Bandtkie, note 21 above (1816), pp. 311-316, 319-321, 333; Bandtkie, *O poważaniiu dawnieyszém w Polszcze prawników uczonych", in Posiedzenie publiczne Królewskiego-Warszawskiego Uniwersytetu, na uczczenie pamiątki uczonych mężow, a mianowicie polakow, odbyte dnia 15 lipca 1825 roku* (Warsaw, 1825), pp. 36, 39.

[24] Bandtkie, note 18 above (1812), pp. 216-217.

[25] Bandtkie, note 21 above (1816), p. 333.

[26] R. Hube, "Krotki rys historyi literatury prawa (1827)", in Hube, *Opera*, ed. K. Dunin (Warsaw, 1905), I, p. 67; Hube, "Uwagi nad systematem Kodexu cywilnego francuskiego", *Themis Polska*, V (1829), pp. 303-304.

[27] Hube, note 26 above (1827), p. 68; Hube, "O stanie nauki prawa w naszych czasach (1827)", in note 26 above (1905), I, pp. 5, 10; Hube, note 26 above (1829), V, pp. 306-307; Hube, "Niektore uwagi nad historya nauki prawa (1830)", in note 26 above (1905), I, p. 34.

into a science thanks to the emergence of a critical vision of the last.[28] The Polish science of law should, he said, be distinctive because it should combine theoretical knowledge about law and empirical knowledge about the Polish law in action and the received legislation.[29]

He named as being among the legal sciences and instructional disciplines the following: general history of law; history of the institutions of new nations; systems of legislation of individual States; history of national legislation (and the history of national law); history of legislation of the Slavic peoples; philosophy of law; the "science of the comparison of law" (in 1830); and he wrote about the "system of the science of law".[30]

Hube wrote in 1827 that historical legal cognition was the foundation of the legal sciences, being capable of discovering the cause and effect link in the past and in contemporary legal development. Such cognition, moreover, was capable of creating criteria for an evaluation of the "subject-matter value of legislation".[31] The forming of a contemporary science of the history of law, in Hube's view, was completely new, highest stage of the development of the legal sciences.[32]

Whereas the history of law in Hube's vision investigates the "kind and nature of changes", the philosophy of law addressed that which is "absolutely stable, immutable, solely true in legal relations". But these immutable grounds, unlike earlier times, are sought in society, in the contemporary order of things; this quest leads not to abstractions and illusions, but to a cognition of existing relations, pointing out what in these relations is basic, and what is subject to changes and historical development, combines with the history of law, and augments the last.[33] The concepts of the philosophy of law must be based on the generalization of

[28] Hube, note 27 above (1827), pp. 9-10; Hube, note 26 above (1829), pp. 304-306, 309, 329; Hube, note 27 above (1830), p. 34.

[29] Hube, note 26 above (1829), p. 312.

[30] Hube, note 26 above (1827), pp. 69, 71, 74-75; Hube, note 27 above (1827), p. 10; Hube, note 27 above (1830), pp. 34, 48-49; Hube, "O starożytnych zbiorach praw Czeskich", *Themis Polska*, V (1829), p. 3.

[31] Hube, note 26 above (1827), pp. 10-11.

[32] Ibid., p. 10.

[33] Ibid., pp. 10-11; Hube, note 26 above (1829), p. 308.

empirical materials.[34] Hube also mentioned theory (of law), but its role and status were not revealed.[35]

Hube stated in 1829 that the science of law had acquired in his time a universal character and liberated itself from "views limited by locality"; this meant that the science of law should encompass the law, legal concepts, and conceptions of all ancient and contemporary peoples.[36] The elements of the science of law are the history and philosophy of law, and its principal tasks – to develop a universal history of legislation and create a philosophy of law on its own. History looks at the past, and the philosophy of law, on the basis of reflecting on history, "ensures an improved vision of the spirit of the future".[37]

If a universal science of law discovers scientific truths, then a science of legislation (following Gans, we call it legal knowledge) has a national (individual) and more practical character; it is directed towards the improvement of own national law, also performing a cognitive function – the "cognition of the individual character of its nation".[38] The science of law provides the foundations of the science of legislation, and the materials are the law of the nation, especially judicial practice.[39] But when reading Hube, the impression is given that he is referring not to two sciences, to two systems of knowledge, but to different levels, facets, and functions of a single science. For example,

> But not only the reward and merit of the science of law, but even exclusively its true honor, is that the foundations obtained by it on the path of reflections, well-foundedly contrasted with the needs of society, are subsequently included in the laws governing the destinies of the same society. What the theory, sanctified by the authority of time, deemed to be advisable the legislators cannot deny.[40]

[34] Hube, note 26 above (1829), p. 339; Hube, note 27 above (1830), pp. 35-36.

[35] Hube, note 26 above (1829), p. 307.

[36] Ibid., pp. 299-300, 304, 306-207.

[37] Ibid., p. 300.

[38] Ibid., p. 301.

[39] Ibid., p. 301.

[40] Ibid., p. 335.

Hube offered a new generalization of the history of the science of law in 1830. In his view, historically legal knowledge when notions of divine judgment dominated could not become a science; it reposed within other systems of knowledge (theology and others).[41] The science of law was born when and where people feel themselves the power to autonomously create law or at least "appropriate to themselves the prescriptions of laws".[42]

The most ancient science of law which originated in Ancient Rome Hube called exegetics (dogmatic), the "permanently live exposition of a particular once given law" connected with an "interpretation of the expressions of law and the adaptation thereof to the development of human relations" and the first attempts to find the link of the letter of the law with the development of social life and to change law in connection with social changes.[43] After the fall of the Roman Empire, Europe gradually liberated the individual and gave to him/her the possibility of political participation in the creation of law. Reflection occurred on customary law in the process of its being combined with Roman dogmatic, thanks to which the concepts of the science of law were formed.[44]

The science of natural law developed in the late Middle Ages on the basis of the dogmas of the generalization of Roman law, and this generated an acute and problematic dualism between theoretical and practical legal knowledge and simultaneously the "liberation of the individual spirit which began to cognize itself".[45] The merit of the theory of natural law and the philosophy of law based on it became the universalization of the doctrine of law (notwithstanding the universalization being contradictory and often artificial in substance, and therefore merely provisional) and the extensive use of the comparative method, in spite of its express rejection.[46] There followed the enlightened and revolutionary idea relating to the dominance of reason, this led to the rejection of customary and Roman law, and the dominance of the last ceased in the science of law. And this in turn led to legislative reforms everywhere, which stimulated the rebirth of the science of law

[41] Hube, note 27 above (1830), pp. 38-39.

[42] Ibid., pp. 39-40.

[43] Ibid., pp. 40-41.

[44] Ibid., pp. 42-44.

[45] Ibid., pp. 45-48.

[46] Ibid., p. 48.

in a philosophically abstract variant because "reason must be the highest legislator".[47]

The new period of "rest" and the reaction connected with the forming and dominance of the history of law had reverse, individualized grounds, rejected abstractions, and discovered the inadequacy thereof. Instead, the science of law turned to the development of the *socium*, became social. A new philosophy of law emerged that relied on the problematic of the theory of natural law but rejected *a priori* speculations and began to analyze and generalize positive law. Reality and abstract thought were combined in these two disciplines.[48]

In Hube's view, the contemporary period in the development of the science of law was linked with the dialogue of the historical and philosophical schools. The foundations of the historical school were formed during the second half of the eighteenth century, particularly in the works of Hugo and, later, Savigny. They consisted of a pragmatic consideration of the historical development of law in the context of the evolution of society and a collective consciousness.[49]

The philosophical (more correctly, the historical-philosophical) school was no longer elevated above the world; it was directed towards the cognition of the contemporary state of law, just as the historical school. Hube regarded Gans as the founder thereof. It shared a number of grounds with the historical school, but understood the historical process differently. It considered the reasons for changes in social and legal institutions to be changes in human thought. Therefore, unlike the historical school, it encompassed within its studies and generalizations phenomena not only of the national, but also of universal, dimensions. Moreover, according to Hube, the philosophical school elaborated more precise criteria for evaluating historical materials and suggested, on the basis of the complete rejection of the principle of *a priori* ("the ideal philosophy of law is not at all a science of law") and generalization of positive law, the definition of its immutable foundations.[50] Relying on these and other arguments, Hube

47 Ibid., p. 49.

48 Ibid., pp. 48-51, 53.

49 Ibid., p. 52.

50 Ibid., pp. 53-57.

actually asserted not dialogue, but a dialectical succession of the two schools: the improved historical school becomes philosophical, which is more consistently historical.[51]

According to Zaborowski, who expressed his view in 1829, the science of law was an integral part of the legal life of a nation, and therefore a legal knowledge inseparable from practice, acting purely as a technical element of law. It arises as a requirement of a nation to "impart a scientific form to their main thoughts", provides for the ordering of law, transfer of experience of the past, provision of an expanded interpretation of legislation and ensuring the application thereof, and also the substantive development of law in spheres not linked with social tradition and convictions; that is, as legal skills.[52] Legal scholars must, if not exclusively, then primarily, investigate the law of their own nation, confining themselves basically to the history and dogmatic of law, and Zaborowski had a critical attitude towards the philosophy of law (as *a priori*).[53]

According to Maciejowski, the science of law was formed in the early nineteenth century; prior to then, it existed in a primitive state, despite the efforts of individual illuminators. The basic approach was historical – the cognition of legal phenomena in the historical context of their origin and development.[54] He drew attention to the differences in the development of the science of law in various countries, pointing to the low level in France and the high level in Germany; the reasons for the differences in the level of science being the level of the development of the nation. Among the historical disciplines, Maciejowski singled out the history of national law, the history of Slavic legislation, and the "universal history of legislation".[55]

Heylman believed that the science of law should above all investigate the law of one's own nation: "There are as many

[51] Ibid., p. 57.

[52] C. Z[aborowski], "Jurysprudencya sądu kassacyinego Xięswa Warszawskiego i związek instytucyi kassacyinéy z ogólném życiem prawném w kraju", *Themis Polska*, VI (1829), pp. 362-364, 366, 368-371.

[53] Ibid., pp. 370-371; [Zaborowski], "Rozbiór krytyczny dzieła pod tytułem: Upominek pogrobowy ś.p. Kazimierza Pliszki Podlesianina; rzecz o sukcessii ...", *Themis Polska*, VI (1829), p. 240.

[54] W. Maciejowski, "Ogłoszenie prenumeraty", *Themis Polska*, V (1829), pp. 414, 416.

[55] Ibid., p. 414-415, 419.

different jurisprudences as there is individual legislation".[56] The task of the science of law is to generalize the dogmatic of positive law, find its national principles on the basis of popular convictions, and create from law a "single scientific whole", and on the basis of this draft legislation create norms by means of judicial decisions.[57]

According to Heylman, historical and dogmatic studies should dominate within the system of a science of positive law (for him, the same as a science of legislation); the philosophy of law is also present.[58] The science of law also acts as a system of legal sciences because all three elements mentioned in Heylman's works are also called sciences.[59] The science of law had not existed in this form in the past: philosophy and dogmatics have ancient origins, but the historical approach arose recently in Germany.[60] Heylman pointed to the differences in the development of the science of law in Germany and France; these derive from different paths of development of their law, as a result of which historical-legal studies were dominant in Germany and dogmatic studies in France.[61] In the works of Heylman, the science of law and legal practice become concepts virtually inseparable from the outset of the academic era in the development of law (according to Hugo and Savigny).[62]

The subject-matter of the history of law is the genesis of law in force, because laws are formed historically, and not simply by the will of the legislator or the highest authorities of a country. Cognition of the essence of legislative norms is impossible without their historical explanation. Therefore, "history now occupies first place in the science of positive law".[63] The subject-matter of the dogmatics of law is only the law of a nation in force, and its development emanates from theory to practice and from practice

[56] A. Heylman, "Myśli o nauce prawa i prawodawstwie w kraiu naszym", *Themis Polska*, VII (1830), p. 123.

[57] Ibid., pp. 124-125, 128-130, 134; Heylman, "Wywod zasad ogolnych nauki prawa i prawodawstwa", *Themis Polska*, VII (1830), pp. 26-27, 29.

[58] Heylman, note 56 above, pp. 124-125, 131; Heylman, note 57 above, pp. 1, 5-11, 19.

[59] Heylman, note 57 above, p. 31.

[60] Ibid., pp. 1, 6-7.

[61] Ibid., p. 30.

[62] Ibid., pp. 14-15, 26-27.

[63] Ibid., p. 5.

to theory. It must elicit the link of norms and extract from that link the real bases of contemporary law: "it also elicits contradictions, lacunae, lack of purpose, harmful directions, and what impedes the flourishing of a nation and each person".[64] Heylman saw the philosophy of law as divided into three parts (and simultaneously, three sciences) distinguished by the "gradation of the subject-matter", but having common grounds: the philosophy of law in force; the "philosophy of all positive laws"; and the philosophy of ideal law. The philosophy of law in force, which he considered to be an innovation, explains and critically analyzes the positive law of one's own country, "draws out the model of external and internal life which a nation leads at the contemporary moment", has the "purpose to maintain a harmony between law and the degree and regime of morality and the enlightenment of a nation".[65]

The "philosophy of all positive laws" (or the "philosophy of diverse laws"), noted Heylman, despite their designation, in fact is not universal, being "always confined by the consideration of positive laws of a small number of nations". This is justified and should apply to "those nations which are equal to us in civilization or exceed us in enlightenment and in practical morality or in social institutions and legislation". It is impossible to cognize everything, and the study of the law of nations, being at a lower level of development, has no practical use. This science must be based on a combination of the historical and comparative approaches, and the purpose is cognition of the correlation of uniformity and diversity in the legal regulation of social relations, an evaluation of the existing models and principles, a critical evaluation of national law for the purpose of its improvement.[66]

The philosophy of ideal law, in Heylman's view, is the highest philosophy of law, the "theoretical construction of thoughts and feelings which an entire human species deemed to be positive law", but has no relation to theories of natural law. This philosophy evaluates the universal development of positive law and "seeks harmony between the spirit of that law and the wisdom of the spirit which has Providence above all humanity". Therein the difference disappears between law and morality, and positive

[64] Ibid., p. 31; Heylman, note 56 above, p. 129.

[65] Heylman, note 57 above, pp. 39-40, 44-47.

[66] Ibid., pp. 48-52.

law acts as reason and justice; that is, as the highest philosophical human law.[67]

On the basis of the foregoing, we disagree with a contemporary specialist that Polish jurists of the first third of the nineteenth century conventionally ascribed to the science of law and the history of law solely a service function, and also confined the problematic of the history of law as being solely or primarily national.[68] Warsaw jurists in the period here considered formulated the grounds of a positivist science of law. These grounds included: recognition of the autonomy of legal knowledge; the construction thereof on the basis of the generalization of empirical data, the combining of practical and theoretical knowledge, and a renunciation of any metaphysical and speculative philosophizing and forming of an own philosophical discourse.

It was declared that the sciences – and the science of law in particular – are capable of autonomously cognizing the "truths". Therefore, the science of law is independent of *a priori* thought, is not a part of philosophy, and creates itself a real philosophy – the philosophy of positive law ("truths, verified by experience"). The difference was recognized between technical and natural ("exact") and socio-humanities ("moral") sciences: knowledge within the last is not experimental knowledge, but of experience (*a posteriori*), and therefore the concepts are imprecise.

The discussion of the essence of the science of law was reflected in the vision of its history. The authors of the works analyzed herein devoted attention to the development of legal knowledge and the legal specialty beginning at least in Antiquity. Attention was drawn to the transformation, professionalization, and socialization of knowledge. The direct dialectical predecessor of the contemporary science of law was considered to be the separate systems of the dogmatic of law in force and natural law. The formal achievements were acknowledged of natural law doctrine in the universalization (albeit artificial) of legal knowledge and the creation of its problematic. But virtually all scholars emphasized the substantive meaningful break in principle with natural law – the replenishment of its forms with new philosophical positivist

[67] Ibid., pp. 52-55.

[68] P. Szymaniec, "Nauka prawa jako działalność pro bono. Uwagi na temat polskiej nauki prawa w latach 1807-1831", M. Marszał and J. Przygodzki (eds.), *Pro publico bono – idee i działalność* (Wroclaw, 2016), p. 124.

knowledge on the basis of empirical studies and generalization of the results thereof.

Changes of principle were linked with the end of the eighteenth and early nineteenth centuries, which enabled the science of law to be regarded as a new or a qualitatively renewed phenomenon. In the view of Warsaw scholars, the science of law became social and historical, and also a comprehensive system, and not merely the aggregate of knowledge and doctrines. The new conceptual character of this science, separated from preceding eras, provided that it has its own precisely determined "motherland" – the German states, and a sphere of dissemination, to which Warsaw scholars unanimously relegated the Polish lands. Following German colleagues in recognizing the aforesaid criteria of the scientific nature of legal knowledge, these writers admitted the temporary or permanent possibility of the existence of other forms for organizing such knowledge.

Warsaw legal scholars saw the contemporary period of the development of the science of law as an arena of dialogue and competition between the historical and philosophical (or historico-philosophical) schools of legal thought and primarily manifested their affiliation to one of those schools, but expressing their own distinctive thoughts or undertaking an original synthesis of the ideas of the two schools. Both schools were understood by them to be historical and, consequently, in the understanding of that time, as positivist in their fundamentals. In the vision of proponents of the historico-philosophical school, it might be regarded as a dialectical continuation of the historical school.

The historical, dogmatic, and philosophical approaches to the science of law were generally recognized at the time. They were seen as three spheres of the "system of the science of law" or individual sciences within the system of the sciences of law. The history of law must generalize the types and nature of changes in law. The philosophy of law finds the immutable foundations or principles of law on the basis of the generalization and abstracting of empirical knowledge. However, the history of law was regarded as absolutely dominant.

The major divergence in the positions of Warsaw jurists was the subject-matter and object of the new science of law. One group believed that the science of law was primarily of an applied character, in actuality a science of legislation. This assumed that one's national law was the principal subject-matter, and one might explain the differences in the organization of scientific knowledge in different countries by the character of their law – solely codified (as in France) or partially codified or primarily customary (as in the German states and in the Duchy of Warsaw or Kingdom of Poland). The improvement of the national legal order was the object of the science of law for these legal scholars. Knowledge of foreign law in this vision also was primarily applied knowledge, affected by the concrete requirements of understanding or improving own national law.

For the other legal scholars, the science of law had a fundamental character. The subject-matter was universal, and the object was the extraction or derivation of legal "truths". The incorporation in the subject-matter of studies on equal grounds of foreign law together with national law was normal for this group, and a comparative approach was formulated as one of the basic, if not the leading, approaches together with the historical, dogmatic, and philosophical.

§2.2. Role of Comparative Knowledge in Jurisprudence

The separate status of the science of law substantiated by European scholars objectively raised the question of the ways and principles for building a general doctrine on law – separate from philosophy. Moreover, beginning at least from the Pütter School, comprehension of the diversity and interaction of legal orders was relegated to the subject-matter of the science of law. Legal scholars regarded constant and large-scale comparison and generalization of the positive law of various nations as the means of resolving these problems.

Both the historical and the historico-philosophical schools acknowledged that the dogmatics of branches of national law were not sufficient to build a new science of law. Isolated national legal knowledge was declared to be unscientific; one's law should be cognized in the context of other legal orders; and the general doctrine on positive law should encompass ideally all legal orders. Both schools by their character were positivist and social, and therefore in attempts to build a universal science of law distanced themselves from *a priori* rationalist or idealist philosophies of law. Therefore, a comparative approach became the principal instrument for building a legal picture of the world and a new science of law. The new science of law, in the unity of its object, subject-matter, and methodology, was born as expressly comparativistic, which to a significant extent was a concentrated and substantive expression of its social and positive character.[69]

In 1806, when examining the history of jurisprudence in the *Rzecz Pospolita* and its territories prior to the Partitions, Bandtkie cited only two works of a comparative legal character. One was by a Lviv scholar and professor at the Zamość (Zamojska) Academy, T. Drezner (1550-1616), published at Paris in 1602;[70] the second was by P. B. Orzechowski (1626-1694), published at Breda, now in The Netherlands, in 1647.[71] Both compared Roman law with the law of the *Rzecz Pospolita* (called Polish law in the title).[72] Joachim Lelewel (1786-1861) named as among the works where Roman law was compared with the law of the *Rzecz Pospolita* the textbooks of Bieńkowski and T. Ostrowski (1750-1802) published in the eighteenth century.[73]

The legacy of legal thought in the *Rzecz Pospolita*, just as other States before the end of the eighteenth century, is not replete with the conscious and targeted application of a comparative approach. The work by Drezner was truly of a comparative-legal character in which the law of the *Rzecz Pospolita* was compared not only with Roman law, but with Byzantine, French, Spanish, and canon law.[74] As Bondaruk noted, Drezner designated one hundred legal problems where he found similarities and differences in the legal orders being compared.[75] Other works associated with the Zamość (Zamojska) Academy were by Polish and Ukrainian legal scholars: Bazyli Rudomicz (c. 1620-1672) on a comparison of the monarchies

[69] Kresin, note 1 above, II, pp. 135-136.

[70] T. Dresner, *Similium juris poloni cum jure romano, centuria una* (Paris, C. Morelli, 1602). 69 p.

[71] P. B. Orzechowski, *Manuale fundamentorum juris civilis ac Poloni quatuor disputationibus juridico-historico politicis comprehensum: ad quatuor libros institutionum imperatoris Justiniani publico examine ventilatum in illustri schola Auriaca* (Breda, Joan. A. Wasberge, 1647).

[72] F. Bentkowski, *Historia literatury polskiey, wystawiona w spisie dziel drukiem ogloszonych* (Warsaw, 1814), II, p. 249.

[73] J. Lelewel, "Przypiski do dwu rozpraw Al. Mickiewicza i Franc Morze", in Lelewel, *Rozbiory dziel objemujacych albo dzieje, albo rzechy polskie roznymi czasy przez Joachima Lelewela ogloszone* (Poznan, 1844), p. 246.

[74] V. O. Bondaruk, Розвиток юридичної науки і освіти в Замойській академії (1594-1784 pp.) [Development of Legal Science and Education in the Zamojska Academy (1594-1784)] (Kyiv, 2016), pp. 146-147 (diss. kand. iurid. nauk).

[75] Ibid., pp. 147-149.

of the world;[76] Tomasz Zamojski (1594-1638) comparing Persia and Greek and Roman monarchies[77] and his explanation of the Institutions of Justinian and institutions of Polish Law (1612 r.); doctoral dissertations of D. Nico and V. Sczenski on judicial generalizations taken from canon and civil law (1778); W. Tepper on inheritance by decision of a court according to Roman, Austrian, and Polish law (1779); among others.[78] Also worthy of mention is that the Sejm of the *Rzecz Pospolita* in the context of a planned codification of law in 1768 decreed to "correct" legislation with the use of Prussian, Lithuanian, Roman, and "other various foreign legal norms".[79]

As for the period here considered, Tadeusz Czacki (1765-1813) asserted in 1808 that although one's own national law is undoubtedly an authority for a jurist, "foreign laws are evidence of respected ideas".[80] An earlier work by Czacki contained a requirement the comparison should seek "primary laws", the borrowing of which by other nations would lead to the formation of groups of legal orders. Czacki singled out at least two groups of European national legal orders: those whose law emanates from Roman law, and the other group.[81]

Bandtkie appealed for comparative historical legal studies to be undertaken, "to place the development of foreign law side by side with the development of the country". Knowledge of foreign law he considered to be one of the virtues of a jurist. He suggested study abroad in order to become familiar with foreign law and the invitation of foreign lecturers.[82] Critical and ironic with respect to

[76] B. Rudomicz, *Compendium monarchiarum mundi diuera regna, dominia, caeterorumque magistratuum regimina continens, eag: quam diu, sub quibus,et in quibus terrae partibus floruerunt, aut defecerunt declarans* (1648).

[77] T. Zamojski, *De monarchia et imperio Persarum et de republica Lacedaemoniorum, Atheniensium, Romanarum* (1612).

[78] See Bondaruk, note 74 above, pp. 145, 156, 158.

[79] A. V. Egorov, Теоретико-методологические основания сравнительного правоведения [Theoretical-Methodological Grounds of Comparative Jurisprudence] (Vitebsk, 2014), p. 17.

[80] T. Czacki, *Czy prawo rzymskie było zasadą praw litewskich i polskich? I czy z połnocnemi narodami mielismy wiele wspolnych praw i zwyczaiow? Rosprawa czytana w Krzemieńcu na otwarciu roku szkolnego 1808 w Gimnazyum Wołyńskiem* (Wilno, 1809), p. 122.

[81] Czacki, *O litewskich i polskich prawach o ich duchu, żrzódlach, związku i o rzeczach zawartych w pierwszym Sratucie dla Litwy 1529 r. wydanem* (Warsaw, 1800), I, p. 5.

[82] Bandtkie, note 15 above (1812), p. 3; Bandtkie, note 15 above (1814), p. 10, 17-18.

a priori philosophy, Bandtkie insisted that "knowledge, especially historical, of positive laws is incomparably more essential and useful than any, even the most perfected, systems of natural law".[83]

The historical and comparative legal approaches to the science of law Bandtkie integrated in the category of experience: "The life of a person is nothing in comparison with the life of mankind; all the skills of an individual have been limited and rest on the cognition or experience of generations past. What is some science if not the cognition of what experience of others succeeded or empowered them?" Without the generalization of one's experience and that of other nations, the essence of phenomena in their development is not understood, and therefore progress (or their improvement) is impossible.[84]

With assistance of comparative-legal studies, Bandtkie suggested the essence of compared phenomena be cognized, as well as the processes of reception in law.[85] In his view, experience (empirical) knowledge enables not only the cause-and-effect links to be understood in the function of law and the virtues and shortcomings of legal decisions, but also the ideals of law and justice to be formed on the basis for all people: the ideal (philosophical, natural) law should be formulated on the basis of comparative-legal studies.[86]

Bandtkie believe that the practical purpose of comparative legal studies was especially the improvement of national legislation by means of borrowing foreign experience: "The cognition of many foreign laws would blaze a trail for nations for own improvement if they would succeed to make a choice truly consistent with nationality".[87] Two specialists have noted that Bandtkie in his argumentation never turned to national legal tradition, but only to foreign law, Roman law, and aspects of contemporary law and logic.[88] Such a categorical proposition requires reformulation. In

[83] Ibid., note 15 above (1814), pp. 30, 33.

[84] Bandtkie, note 21 above, pp. 312-313.

[85] Bandtkie, note 15 above (1812), p. 3; Bandtkie, note 15 above (1814), p. 29

[86] Bandtkie, note 15 above (1814), pp. 33-35.

[87] Ibid., pp. 28-29; Bandtkie, "Myśli o zmianie prawodawstwa krajowego", *Rocznik Lubelski*, III (1960), p. 168; Bandtkie, note 23 above, pp. 39-40.

[88] M. Gałędek and A. Klimaszewska, "A Controversial Transplant? Debate over the Adaptation of the Napoleonic Code on the Polish Territories in the Early 19th Century", *Journal of Civil Law Studies*, XI, no. 2 (2018), p. 295.

the view of Bandtkie, not a concrete foreign model, but the "truth of law" (or a "correct law") was better for improving national law – a model of the better law identified by means of comparison of the available ones – because none of the last is perfect.[89] Another purpose of comparative legal studies, according to Bandtkie, was the preservation of identity, effectiveness, and dynamics of the "system of law of the country" by means of constant comparison, correlation, and approximation with the group of European legal orders based on Roman law.[90]

As noted above, Prince F. K. Szaniawski named among the means of cognition in the science of law: direct empirical cognition of law, interpretation, comparison, generalization of partial (individual) notions, systematization, and intellectual imitation.[91] Articles observed in the "physical sciences" might be measured, weighed, expressed quantitatively, and a study might be verified. Articles of the "moral sciences" are more relative and cognized *a posteriori*, and perfect precision in the expression of moral conceptions is impossible to achieve. Therefore, in the moral sciences the comparison of experience performs the role of research.[92]

The sense of comparison and generalization, according to Szaniawski, is that this is the sole and universal means with whose assistance general abstracted transcendental ideas (or concepts) are formed on the basis of the "observation of the similarities, differences, and links" between individual ideas, and these last are sensors, "emanate from the observation of articles which individually irritate our senses". From "individual truths" (empirical experience) and "material grounds" (reason) are extracted necessary and useful conclusions as a "general truth". These grounds themselves, and reason, are not eternal or natural; they also are formed by science, especially on the basis of comparison and comprehension of empirical experience. The means of empirical, sensory cognition for jurisprudence are provided by history: "How obvious is the observation of phenomena and study in physics, such becomes history in the science of law". A comparative approach is combined with the historical in the

[89] Bandtkie, note 15 above (1814), p. 34-35; Bandtkie, note 87 above (1960), p. 169.

[90] Bandtkie, note 21 above (1816), p. 320-321.

[91] Szaniawski, note 8 above, p. 2.

[92] Szaniawski, note 10 above, pp. 3-4.

comparison of the experience of centuries, connecting the past with the future.[93]

Szaniawski consistently required in the process of comparison: knowledge of all parts of the science of law; comprehensive consideration; and understanding of the socio-economic, natural-geographical, educational-intellectual, and historical contexts of legal norms and cause-and-effect links; and not absolutizing either the similarities or the differences in law.[94] When undertaking comparison, there must be in the center of attention not only institutions and legal decisions, but also the subject-matter of regulation in various nations or at different times; then the possibility emerges to "investigate well the causes of norms and the consequences arising from them; to cognize the spirit of the time, to judge properly the state of nations in the circumstances in which they happen to be".[95]

A distinctive feature of the comparative approach is that with the assistance of analysis and synthesis of empirical data it construes from elements and their interaction a "general image of the whole", but is always returning to empirical data for verification and supplementation of the last.[96] In the view of Szaniawski, the science of law thanks to the historico-comparative approach creates the foundations for real philosophy as a science of human reason: philosophy is above all the choice, on the basis of reasonable generalization, of the experience offered by history with a view to the improvement of people and bringing them closer to the happiness peculiar to them.[97] But individual philosophical observations in law should be subject to comparative analysis.[98] The comparison thereof makes it possible to "identify the difference between the bad and the good, to see different means of honesty, correctness, and humanism".[99]

93 Szaniawski, note 4 above, pp. 5-8; Szaniawski, note 8 above, pp. v-viii; Szaniawski, note 10 above, pp. 64-65, 74.

94 See for example: Szaniawski, note 10 above, pp. 9-10, 13, 73-74; J. Jakubowski, "Pierwszy wykład prawa na Uniwersytecie Warszawskim", *Palestra*, no. 3/2-3(14-15) (1959), p. 81.

95 Szaniawski, note 10 above, pp. 86-87; Jakubowski, note 94 above, pp. 82-83.

96 Szaniawski, note 10 above, p. 5.

97 Szaniawski, note 4 above, pp. 7-8; Szaniawski, note 8 above, p. vi.

98 Szaniawski, note 4 above, p. 9.

99 Ibid., p. 11.

Szaniawski was of the view that the practical need for comparative legal studies followed from the fact that "in not a single country could law be so perfected that everything was provided for, helped effectively in each instance", for only in experience are the virtues and shortcomings of legal decisions manifest.[100] One practical purpose of comparative legal studies is to provide scientifically for the reception and adaptation of law because "one should seek benefit in all provisions without distinction as to from where the provisions were taken"; but "ignorance, slavish and blind imitation of foreign examples is the source of endless mistakes between people".[101] Szaniawski believed that with the assistance of comparative cognition of historical and contemporary experience of the legal regulation of a certain subject-matter one might "achieve precision in the detailed adaptation of the prescriptions of law to contemporary requirements of the State which these prescriptions should serve".[102] The possible role of comparative legal studies in reducing differences in national law, the harmonization of national law, and the predictive function of comparative legal science were mentioned, but not very clearly.[103]

Ignacy Benedykt Rakowiecki (1782-1839) appealed in 1820 for comparison as a means of the cognition of the law of nations. He asserted that the history of foreign legal orders had become the subject-matter of studies by many scholars and attempted to trace the history of the study of the law of nations of the Slavic ethno-linguistic group at the end of the eighteenth and early nineteenth centuries.[104] Rakowiecki suggested that comparison be used, *inter alia,* in order to separate original elements (including those belonging to the ethnic-linguistic group) in national law from alien elements.[105] He advanced the idea of ethno-linguistic communities and groups of legal orders based on a single pra-language and

[100] Ibid., p. 5; Szaniawski, note 10 above, pp. 87-88.

[101] Szaniawski, note 4 above, p. 11; Szaniawski, note 10 above, pp. 72-74.

[102] Szaniawski, note 10 above, pp. 86-87.

[103] Ibid., p. 76.

[104] I. B. Rakowiecki, *Prawda ruska; czyli, Prawa wielkiego xięcia Jaroslawa Władymirowicza, tudziez traktaty Olga y Igora ww. xx. kiiowskich z cesarzami greckimi, y Mścisława Dawidowicza x. Smoleńskiego z Rygą zawarte, których texta, obok z polskiém tłomaczeniem poprzedza Rys historyczny zwyczaiów, obyczaiów religiy, praw y języka dawnych słowiańskich y słowiańsko-ruskich narodow* (Warsaw, 1820), I, pp. 228, 244, 246, 250, 252.

[105] Ibid., I, pp. 81-82; II, p. 315.

"primary" law. The purpose of comparative studies, in his view, was cognition of the "brotherly" languages and legal orders.[106] As noted in another context, Rakowiecki asserted on the basis of the presumption of the historical existence of a single indigenous law for each ethno-linguistic group of nations the possibility of the cognition of a single legal order by analogy with another.[107]

According to Hube, sufficient materials had accumulated and general interest had been inspired to carry on comparative legal studies.[108] He insisted that the law of each ancient and contemporary nation was important to the science of law and to the unjustified concentration on Roman law.[109] He noted that comparative historico-legal studies should be undertaken in a general context and on uniform historical foundations. Each legal system should be regarded in its own historical context, even Roman law.[110] The subject-matter of comparative legal studies should be first and foremost the conceptions and grounds of the law of various nations which influenced the general development of law (in the Hegel-Gans understanding of a nation as a step in the development of mankind).[111]

Hube considered it possible to obtain results of a philosophical character from large-scale comparative historico-legal studies: identification of the "spirit of ancient legislation taken with respect to new institutions".[112] Another purpose, or "objective result", of such a study was the comparative cognition of national law: "The key to the concept and an understanding of a national feature is the preliminary universally generalized intent".[113]

Hube considered the "comparison of related legislation" to be a means of cognition of the grounds of Slavic law. The reconstruction of the law of an individual Slavic nation has to be done by analogy with knowledge of Slavic law as a whole – on the

106 Ibid., I, pp. 81-82, 84; II, pp. 243, 246, 315-316.

107 Ibid., I, p. 81-82, 84; II, pp. 243, 246.

108 Hube, note 26 above (1827), I, p. 70.

109 Hube, note 26 above (1829), pp. 299-300.

110 Hube, note 26 above (1827), I, p. 71; Hube, note 28 above (1827), p. 8.

111 Hube, note 26 above (1829), p. 300; Hube, note 26 above (1830), I, p. 54.

112 Hube, note 26 above, I (1827), p. 70.

113 Hube, note 26 above (1829), p. 301; Hube, note 26 above (1827), I, p. 70; Hube, note 26 above (1830), p. 48.

basis of a presumption of the essential and substantive unity when possible formal distinctions.[114] Sobociński called Hube a "leading comparatist of a European scale".[115]

Karol Boromeuss Aleksander Hoffman(n) (1798-1875) noted that the active development of the science of law in the Kingdom of Poland should be facilitated by reception of law from many countries ("Poland in the eyes of the world may be considered to be a test country for new legislation"); the understanding and use thereof required comparative-legal knowledge by every jurist.[116]

For Maciejowski, comparative historico-legal cognition was fundamental in the science of law.[117] Explanation of the history of national law by analogy with others was one purpose of comparative historico-legal knowledge. In 1829 and later he pointed to the methodology for such research: to cognize the history of an individual "perfected" (more developed) foreign law – Roman law, for example – and understand the origin, development and improvement thereof, and then compare it with the law of one's own country, determine the similarities and differences, comprehend the distinctive features thereof[118] – which might be defined as the "central point" approach. Another more profound purpose is determining the autochthonic or received ("transplanted") origin of national law grounds and, in this latter instance, the foreign source thereof.[119]

[114] Hube, note 26 above (1829), pp. 335, 338; Hube, note 26 above (1830), I, pp. 37, 42-43; Hube, note 26 above (1827), pp. 70-72, 75-76; Hube, "O starożytnych zbiorach praw Czeskich", *Themis Polska*, V (1829), pp. 1-3; Hube, "Wywód praw spadkowych słowiańskich (Wywód spadków podług dawnych praw słowiańskich), *Themis Polska*, VIII (1830), pp. 425-426, 428, 430-431, 433, 436-437, 441, 444, 454, 467, 472-473, 475, 497-498; Hube, «История древнего наследственного права у славян» [History of Medieval Inheritance Law Among the Slavs], Сборник исторических и статистических сведений о России и народах ей единоверных и единоплеменных [Collection of Historical and Statistical Information on Russia and People of the Same Faith and Tribe], (1845), I, p. 87.

[115] W. Sobociński, "Prawo francuskie w Niemczech a w Polsce: nowe opracowania niemieckie recepcji I refleksje porównawcze", *Annales Universitatis Mariae Curie-Skłodowska, Sectio F: Humaniora*, XXXVII (1982), p. 184.

[116] K. B. Hoffman, "O stanie nauki prawa w naszym kraju", *Themis Polska*, I (1828), p. 29.

[117] Maciejowski, note 54 above, p. 419.

[118] Ibid., pp. 414, 417-418; Maciejowski, *Historya prawodawstw słowiańskich* (Warsaw, 1832-1835), I, p. 35.

[119] Maciejowski, note 54 above, p. 418; Maciejowski, "Uwagi nad artukułem 960 K.C.", *Themis Polska*, VII (1830), pp. 229-230, 232.

One should bear in mind that for Maciejowski, national law might mean either the law of a country or the law of a group of countries within a certain ethno-linguistic group (especially Slavic). That is why, for example, for Polish law the comparison and analogy with the law of other Slavic peoples performs an integrative role for identifying common foundations. An assumption operates of the community and therefore the reception is not considered at all (cognition within the limits of one ethno-linguistic group of a single people by analogy with others). Comparison with Roman law had a special mixed integrative-contrastive nature, and with the law of Germanic peoples – almost exclusively contrastive.

Maciejowski noted that the comparison of national legal orders should be undertaken "by way of parallels" – in accordance with certain subject-matter of regulation and basic legal concepts: "What notions at various times did the Romans, Slavs, and Germans have about what we now call the subject and object of law; what notions did they have about the classification of rights, of law proper (*jus*), and, finally, about justice".[120]

Maciejowski stressed that the significance of studying foreign law, including Roman law, lay not in establishing the authority or standard or in "suppressing the views of jurists of various nations", but in the cognition of foreign experience.[121] He pointed to the existence of universal and, so to say, regional (within the limits of a legal family), levels of comparative legal research and noted that his work on Slavic law belonged to the second level: it was devoted to "sketching the image of Slavic legislation", the "spirit of Slavic legislation". One of his research objectives was to explain the "mystery of the destiny of the Slavs".[122] He saw as one of the tasks of comparative legal studies the drawing together of Slavic legal orders, and the propaganda thereof.[123] Through comparative legal studies of the Slavic legal orders, Maciejowski sought to cleanse them of all borrowings and mixtures with other legal orders (to "deepen" them).[124]

120 Maciejowski, note 54 above, p. 423; Maciejowski, note 118 above, I, p. 35.

121 Maciejowski, note 118 above, I, p. v.

122 Ibid., I, pp. vi, 53-54.

123 Ibid., I, pp. 1, 11, 53-54.

124 Ibid., I, p. 2-4.

According to Heylman, the method, or regime, or means of a philosophy of positive laws that is comparative-legal by its nature – the "historical cognition of each legislation separately and the comparison of all cognized legislation, having regard to the initial reasons, stable grounds, duration of functioning, and consequences". Similar social relations should be compared which are the subject-matter of legal regulation.[125]

One aim of comparative legal cognition is "finding the limits of uniformity and diversity in all major social relations. In a word, the discovery of the stable order of nature and the thoughts and feelings of an entire species of mankind" is the subject matter of jurisprudence. But he further indicates that this discovery is not of uniformity in law, but of a universal dialectic of mutually opposed principles and ideas influencing law and the reflection in each concrete law the correlation and interaction of these principles (for example, the ideas of equality and subordination), and also the utopian nature of suggestions concerning the possibility of realizing only one of the principles in positive law.[126] By way of comparison a scale is established for evaluating law.

The second aim of comparison named by Heylman followed from the first and consisted of the cognition of relative substantive indicators of each national legal order according to a scale which he developed. This enabled the best foreign legal models to be determined in order to borrow them for their own national law and thereby "combine our life and aspirations with the feelings and enlightenment of the entire species of mankind".[127]

The practical use of comparative legal knowledge and the knowledge of an individual foreign law, and the developing of a methodology for such use during the period here investigated, were undertaken in the context of drafting legislation. The positions of proponents of the organic and socio-volitional visions of the development of law were widely represented in this process, including the advisability of using foreign experience, comparative studies were undertaken, and comparative judgments developed.[128]

[125] Heylman, note 57 above, p. 49.

[126] Ibid., pp. 50-51.

[127] Ibid., pp. 51-52.

[128] A. Kraushar, "Przedmowa wydawcy", in I. Daniłowicz, *Kodex Napoleona w porównaniu z prawami polskiemi i litewskiemi* (Warsaw, 1905), pp. 8-11; Daniłowicz,

In a draft instruction for a future codification commission in 1814, Bieńkowski insisted on the need to use foreign experience:

> ... not to use European codes, not to study universal principles while adapting them to the needs of our nation, and the mistakes of codifications would mean to ignore the wisdom which the work of such importance requires. The new code must be worthy of the century in which we live and, moreover, must be if not improved in relation to the others in force in Europe, then at least no worse than them.

The members of the Reform Committee were in a more skeptical frame of mind, but after a discussion, they all agreed to the need to "extract various issues from foreign legal sources". In Bieńkowski's view, foreign law represented a verified path which should be taken into account in lawmaking work. The criteria for choosing foreign law for practically-oriented comparison in Bieńkowski's opinion was either the universal importance thereof (Roman law) or the interlinkage and interaction thereof with national law (Prussian, Austrian, and French law). The norms of foreign law must be examined as to their compatibility with national law, legal culture, and morality, from which one may form a view as to their acceptability or advisability to preserve received French law.[129] Members of the Reform Committee in 1814 pointed to a number of issues concerning the acceptability of borrowing only that law which was based on the same confessional canon law and social ethic.[130]

The elements of the reception of law suggested by Wyczechowski and analyzed herein also contained the comparative methodology

ibid., pp. 65-66.

[129] H. Grynwaser, "Kodeks Napoleona w Polsce", in Grynwaser, *Pisma* (Wrocław, 1951), I, pp. 74, 86-87; M. Gałędek, "The Problem of Non-Adaptability of National Legal Heritage. Discussion on the Reform of Civil Law in Poland in the Course of Work of Reform Committee in 1814", *Romanian Journal of Comparative Law*, VIII (2017), p. 22, 26-27, 31; Gałędek, Klimaszewska, and Pomianowski, "Prace Komitetu Cywilnego Reformy nad przygotowaniem narodowej kodyfikacji prawa cywilnego i procedury cywilnej w przededniu utworzenia Królestwa Polskiego (1814-1815) – edycja źródłowa. Część I", *Krakowskie Studia z Historii Państwa i Prawa*, XII, no. 2 (2019), pp. 271-272.

[130] Gałędek, note 129 above, pp. 28-30; Gałędek, Klimaszewska, and Pomianowski, "Prace Komitetu Cywilnego Reformy nad przygotowaniem narodowej kodyfikacji prawa cywilnego i procedury cywilnej w przededniu utworzenia Królestwa Polskiego (1814–1815) – edycja źródłowa. Część II", *Krakowskie Studia z Historii Państwa i Prawa*, XII, no. 3 (2019), pp. 388, 392, 412, 416-417.

for legal research. The law of various countries must be compared according to an identical structure of questions. This structure does not necessarily coincide with the structure of their legislation and should be organized by subject-matter. Knowledge of each national legal order should be structured in accordance with a determined structure and then contrasted. Not only norms of law should be taken into account when comparing, but also legal doctrine and the political and socio-economic contexts of the development of law.[131]

It is noteworthy that Bieńkowski and Wyczechowski and certain of their colleagues repeatedly placed the emphasis when submitting their drafts to the Reform Committee on the fact that they were inspired by foreign experience. As Bieńkowski observed, "This norm rests on the science of the experience of all countries".[132] Also noteworthy was the counter response – the appeals of some members of the Committee to maximally reject foreign experience.[133]

The comparative approach to studying aspects of the reception of law was applied in the capital treatise by Daniłowicz devoted to a comparison of the French Code and Procedure adopted for several years before in Warsaw with ancient Polish and Lithuanian laws relative to the procedure for identifying which are the material difference in the spirit of those rights and what advantage is brought or might be brought to the country by the implementation of the Code and, *vice versa*, in what matters is the Code inconvenient, what ancient laws should be repealed and the introduction in place of them of local customary norms of another nation is detrimental, and what unpleasantness may this cause"? (1816), written at the request of the Council of the Wilna University as a qualification work for the right to occupy a Chair therein.[134] It should be noted that Daniłowicz relied to a significant degree on works of Montesquieu, Bentham, Filangieri, and Czacki and

[131] Grynwaser, note 129 above, p. 77, 101-102; A. Zarzycka, "Próby zmian prawa rzeczowego z Kodeksu Napoleona w Królestwie Polskim w latach 1815-1818", *Krakowskie Studia z Historii Państwa i Prawa*, II (2008), pp. 180-181.

[132] Gałędek and Klimaszewska, "Stosunek polskich elit do prawa francuskiego po upadku Napoleona – zarys problemu", *Studia z Dziejów Państwa i Prawa Polskiego*, XXI (2018), p. 78.

[133] Gałędek, note 129 above, pp. 22, 30-35; Gałędek, Klimaszewska, and Pomianowski, note 130 above, p. 410; Zarzycka, note 131 above, p. 180, 182-183.

[134] Kraushar, note 128 above, pp. 11-12.

critically evaluated German codification debates as filled with emotions and not an impartial comparative legal analysis. In the view of Daniłowicz, recourse by jurists to foreign experience for the purpose of improving national law in both the normative and doctrinal spheres without prior scientific research could violate the systemicity of legal regulation.[135]

Daniłowicz singled out (as subsections in his work) such elements of the comparative legal methodology of the reception of law as: the comparison of physical, political, and spiritual factors of the development of law in two countries; the individual normative and doctrinal (spirit) analysis of legal orders; comparison of individual institutes, norms, and experience of resolving problems – not only normative, but also with the use of information concerning the application of law and extra-legal regulators; determination of similarities and differences and the explanation of the reasons for these, including through the history of law, with the involvement of materials from an extensive range of legal orders and the philosophy of law; determination of the common virtues and shortcomings of two legal orders, the common virtues and shortcomings of each of the compared legal orders; consideration of the advisability of borrowing principles, institutions, and norms of law from one legal order into another, including the forecasting of the consequences of this.[136]

The works of Warsaw jurists during the period here considered presented the comparative approach as one of the basic approaches in the science of law. Foreign experience and their own national legal experience were considered in aggregate as the subject-matter, observation, and comparison of which were capable to some extent of performing a function analogous to an experiment in the natural and technical sciences, demonstrating the verification in practice of certain legal models.

The scientific and practical purposes of the use of comparison in the science of law were elicited, these of course being intertwined in part. One scientific purpose was the cognition of the essence of legal phenomena in their development, causal links, and interactions. The highest level of such cognition should be the forming of abstract concepts and the positivist philosophy of law. Such a philosophy should encompass both "universal truths" and

[135] Danilowicz, note 128 above, pp. 50, 56 .

[136] Ibid., pp. 32-33, 69-172.

the "material grounds" of law, provide for a reasonable choice from existing or the designing of new legal models, a doctrine on the spirit of the eras in the evolution of law, a determination of the principal factors of legal life and the dialectic of the correlation thereof, criteria for the evaluation of national law and the orientators of the development thereof. Its "universal image of wholeness" is dynamic and always unfinished, constantly returning to empirical comparative study for verification, supplementation, and improvement. Such a comparative in its grounds and essence positivist philosophy is relative because it does not absolutize either differences or similarities in legal development. The designated, but not further elaborated aim of forecasting legal processes was connected with all this.

Another scientific purpose of comparison in the science of law was proclaimed to be the cognition of the distinctive features of national law by means of determining the original and the borrowed elements therein, as well as the sources of borrowing. A third purpose of comparison was related to these – the search for the primary law of legal families in order to preserve and defend, so to say, the family identity of one's national law and clarify knowledge about the law peculiar to a legal family.

Among the practical aims of comparison in law the Warsaw jurists named: expert examination of legal decisions; improvement of law by means of reception (especially the choice of the better or most appropriate legal models) and adaptation of borrowed elements or the purification of national law from borrowings; the drafting of new law; the inner harmonization of complex national legal orders; the approximation of legal orders of one legal family.

The Warsaw jurists advanced a number of requirements for comparative legal research. The subject-matter of legal regulation must especially be at the center of attention of a legal scholar (certain social relations), and not the structure of a legal order. The subject-matter must be cognized in context (especially political, socio-economic, religious), its causal links and interactions in compliance with the principle of historicism. The last principle had special significance because a considerable part of comparative studies were historico-legal studies. Not only norms of legislation, but also judicial practice, extra-legal regulators, and scientific doctrine should be enlisted in comparison.

Depending on the need and object, integrative, contrastive, and mixed comparison should be substantiated and used; levels should be chosen – universal, regional, and binary. Other legal orders were chosen for comparison with national law either because of their general impact or because of linkages and interactions.

Several methods were formulated for undertaking comparative legal studies. The "method of parallels" made provision for the comparison of legal orders according to a certain subject-matter structure of questions. The "central point" method provided for an evaluation of national law in comparison with a certain model legal order (for example, Roman law). The methods of reconstruction and analogy were used to compare national legal orders within a single legal family, based on the presumption of their historical unity. Detailed and consistent methodologies of comparative legal research were set out in the works of Wyczechowski, Szaniawski, and Daniłowicz.

§2.3. Institutionalization of Comparative Legal Sciences

During the first third of the nineteenth century a certain pluralism may be noted in the European science of law in the organization of comparative legal knowledge – both the bases of the general doctrine on law within the limits of the creation of a respective scientific discipline and as one or a complex of scientific and instructional disciplines – comparative jurisprudence, comparative legal history, comparative branch legal disciplines.

Comparative jurisprudence was defined for the first time as a theoretical-methodological approach in 1800 and as a scientific discipline in 1810, being consciously elaborated during the first third of the nineteenth century primarily but not exclusively by the Germans. Comparative jurisprudence was regarded as one of the principal general legal disciplines (together with history (and/or encyclopedia) and the philosophy of law) whose subject-matter was national legal orders and the processes of their interactions. The object was their developmental trends, determination of the particular, special, and universal in their elements, and these in turn were the foundation for forming the general doctrine on law, concepts, and conceptions, the creation of theoretical-methodological grounds for branch legal sciences, legal country study disciplines, and the philosophy of law.

There are grounds for confirming the existence during this period, despite lengthy clarifying discussions, of unified theoretical foundations of comparative legal reasoning resting on a significant block of comparative legal studies, logic, and the motivation of scholars to organize comparative legal knowledge into a number of comparative legal disciplines, especially comparative jurisprudence. The forming of comparative jurisprudence was resolved virtually simultaneously with the disciplinary development of such disciplines as the history of law, philosophy of law, and the transformation in principle of the encyclopedia of law. The principles for singling out functional and disciplinary aspects of comparative jurisprudence were similar to those of other comparative disciplines, such as comparative autonomy, comparative linguistics, and others.

The origin of the comparative (general) history of law was linked with the requirement of scholars in those days for universalization of the subject-matter of the history of law actively underway and with the gradual separation of the politico-legal problem within general (universal) history throughout the eighteenth and early nineteenth centuries. The development of sources today enables the emergence of this discipline to be dated no later than 1818. The comparative history of law in its conceptualizations of the time was defined as a separate legal (and also comparative and historical) science which was forming at the juncture of the history of law, philosophy of law, and comparative jurisprudence, and should extract and generalize especially on the basis of comparative and chronological analysis knowledge about the history and contemporary state of law and legal thought of various nations as the basis for developing and clarifying concepts, cognition of the essence of legal phenomena.

The forming of a comparative approach to branch legal studies and respective scientific and instructional disciplines occurred over a lengthy period and was precisely separated out from the early eighteenth century at least, the first known conceptualization thereof being in 1800. This approach developed actively, including as the basis for separating out a complex of branch comparative legal instructional disciplines, during the first third of the nineteenth century; existing sources, however, do not make it possible to unequivocally confirm the conscious forming of the theoretical-methodological foundations of the respective scientific disciplines.[137]

During the period here considered, Warsaw legal scholars proposed several variants for the institutionalization of comparative legal knowledge in the context of the differentiation of the science of law. Bandtkie wrote that the study of foreign law, especially Roman and "each later [law] created on the basis thereof" required many "auxiliary sciences, great preparation, and devoted activity".[138] Among the components of the science law (actually referring here to general jurisprudence), he named Roman, German, French, and canon law, the history of law, and the philosophy of law; among the auxiliary sciences – languages, history, antiquity, and philosophy.[139] Philosophy, in his view, should be based on "truths verified by experience", and therein was the high purpose of positivist jurisprudence.[140] Bandtkie wrote about the history of laws (of various nations) as a sphere of scientific research.[141] But in his works published during the first third of the nineteenth century, the concept of the "general history of law" was not encountered, although authoritative authors mention this.[142]

In 1808 Hugo Kołłątaj (1750-1812) wrote about political geography as a sphere of research, if not a science. The context of his observation enables the legal augmentation of this concept to be confirmed, even though it was not sufficiently conceptualized.[143]

Prince F. K. Szaniawski believed the comparative approach to be fundamental in the science of law, just as in all other developed sciences. He constantly emphasized this beginning in 1808: "The science of law emanates from the comparison of observations about all nations".[144] Szaniawski is called the precursor of Polish comparative jurisprudence, for he presented an "account of the

137 Kresin, note 1 above, II, pp. 334-336.

138 Bandtkie, note 15 above (1814), p. 30.

139 Bandtkie, note 15 above (1816), p. 319.

140 Bandtkie, note 15 above (1814), p. 35.

141 Bandtkie, note 15 above (1812), p. 174.

142 Sobociński, note 19 above, p. 160.

143 H. Kołłątaj, *Uwagi nad teraźniejszem położeniem tej części Ziemi Polskiej, którą od Pokoju Tylżyckiego zaczęto zwać Księstwem Warszawskiem Lipsk* (1808), p. 141.

144 Szaniawski, note 4 above, pp. 5, 9; Szaniawski, note 8 above, pp. i-xii; Szaniawski, note 10 above, p. 5; Jakubowski, note 94 above, p. 81.

theory of legal comparativistics",[145] but we have not found an elaborated analysis of his respective theses.

In 1819 Szaniawski published a book on the static of law or the science of comparisons in law. He pointed to the naturalness of the differentiation of all sciences in the expansion of scientific knowledge: "The number of sciences in multiplying, especially in this century; in the broad sciences certain parts are being separated and comprise a new wholeness". He noted the differentiation of the science of medicine, literary studies, physics, natural history, mathematics, the formation of sections, "solitary parts", or new sciences.[146] The science of law is very broad, divided into "many partial sciences", and (although he did not expressly name them) into general sciences working with the data of all "partial" sciences".[147]

Szaniawski constructed science by analogy. Whereas static, which he considered to be a section of mechanics, engaged in the comparison of forces mutually operating on one another and hence derived the rules of equilibrium, then in jurisprudence one might have the science of legal statistics (statics of law) or the science of comparisons in law, which provide: "Comparison from different angles of vision of all information within the science of law; taking into account the various consequences which usually ensue when combining the application of various prescriptions of law, and from that the invention of intellectual means and useful grounds which may ensure permanent benefit in the management of people".[148] Szaniawski stressed the need to single out comparative legal science based on its, roughly speaking, special subject-matter, object, and a research approach: "The precise orientation of attention and creation of judgments of those who approve the laws and evaluate the quality thereof so that concisely and confidently they might proceed to the proper benefit of human societies".[149]

In proposing a new science, Szaniawski referred to the fact that in France in 1804 (actually in 1803) Mathurin-Louis-Étienne Sedillez (1745-1820) had offered to teach at the end of a cycle of

[145] Jakubowski, note 94 above, p. 82.

[146] Szaniawski, note 10 above, pp. 5-6.

[147] Ibid., p. 6.

[148] Ibid., pp. 3-4, 6.

[149] Ibid., pp. 11, 88-90.

university legal education "the science of the comparison of various legislation".[150] We note that reference was made merely to an instructional discipline, and the suggestion was never acted upon.[151] However, from Szaniawski's point of view, this strengthened his position: "Therefore a science of comparisons in law is needed in order to draw the attention of legislators, bureaucrats, and all individuals undertaking public services to the need to proceed always moderately in proposing means for the general good".[152] In Jakubowski's opinion, Szaniawski believed the science of comparative law to be one which could "cumulate in a system of theses and hypotheses in each state of legal knowledge".[153]

The Introduction to Szaniawski's book was structured as follows: (1) What I Understand by the Static of Law; (2) The Application of this Science; (3) Character; (4) Sources. The body of the work was divided as follows: (I) General View of Comparison; (II) Comparison with a Less General View; (III) Comparison of Various Subject-Matter Usually Desirable in Law; (IV) Afterword: Various Special Comments. By sources Szaniawski had in view the publication of legislation of various States and scholarly works. Among the authors of "close and direct sources" he singled out Montesquieu, Beccaria, Filangieri, Bentham, Thomas Robert Malthus (1766-1834), and Frederich Heinrich Jacobi (1743-1819).[154] But Szaniawski emphasized the lack of an integrated consideration of the science he proposed:

> Not a single author to date has collected everything together, not put in order and by a scientific means presented all the subject-matter which would encompass a whole or even the most important part of comparisons with respect to all information comprising the science of law which would not be mixed with side reflections and which together might

150 Ibid., pp. 6-7; his source was M. L. E. Sedillez, *Considérations sur l'organisation des écoles de droit, suivies d'un tableau de l'enseignement du droit, présentées au Tribunal par M. L. E. Sedillez: Séance du 21 ventôse an XI.* (Paris, [1803]).

151 G. Antonetti, "La Faculté de droit de Paris à l'époque où Boissonade y faisait ses études, *Revue internationale de droit comparé*, XLIII (1991), pp. 333-356.

152 Szaniawski, note 10 above, pp. 8-9.

153 Jakubowski, note 94 above, p. 82.

154 Szaniawski, note 10 above, pp. 10-11.

comprise an autonomous science of static or comparisons in law.[155]

It should be added that Feuerbach's view of German jurisprudence (1810) was published in a Polish language translation under the title "On Jurisprudence".[156] Possibly here for the first time the term "comparative jurisprudence" (porównawcza nauka prawa) appeared in one of the Slavic languages; "general jurisprudence" was translated as powszechne prawodawstwo.[157]

Rakowiecki was among the first to single out the "general history of legislation" (this designation emphasized several times in the text) as a sphere of research alongside the "history of legislation of a nation" in his *Pravda Russkaia*.[158] Modern legal scholars consider Rakowiecki to be the creator of comparative legal history.[159]

Hube noted that in his time the science of law acquired a universal character, having in view the cognition and mastery of the law of all nations. He noted that this occurred earliest in Germany. Hube welcomed such a "liberation of science from views limited by locality" might in the future raise the study and creation of law to a new level.[160] But, as noted above, the history of law and the philosophy of law were for him the two basic elements of jurisprudence and autonomous sciences of law, and the second rested on the first.[161] He named the "history of the institutions of new nations",[162] the "history of Slavic laws (or science of ancient Slavic laws)",[163] and the general history of legislation (law) as separate subjects of research.[164]

155 Ibid., p. 11.

156 P. J. A. Feuerbach, "O prawodawstwie", *Pamiętnik Warszawski*, II (1822), pp. 199-209, 301-315.

157 Ibid., pp. 301, 308.

158 Rakowiecki, note 104 above, I, pp. 135, 244, 252.

159 M. Iłowecki, *Okręty na oceanie czasu. Historia nauki Polskiej do 1945 roku* (Warsaw, 2011), p. 136.

160 Hube, note 26 above (1829), pp. 299-300, 306-307.

161 Ibid., p. 300.

162 Hube, note 26 above (1827), p. 69.

163 Hube, note 30 above, p. 3.

164 Hube, note 26 above (1829), pp. 300-301.

In a work of 1830 Hube pointed to the existence of the "science of the comparison of laws", which he perceived critically and devoted attention to the genesis of comparative legal knowledge. He especially noted works devoted to designing a system of universal jurisprudence whose purpose was "to link by an external order the heterogeneous grounds of Roman law, practice, and natural law; and the method was discovering similarities and differences". In Hube's view, the comparative approach in these works was "evidence of the great flexibility of mind and prepared a more general synthesis". But this approach remained rather limited as a consequence of the purely external and formal contrast of completely heterogeneous and non-comparable elements – "historical fantasies" (natural law) and positive law of various nations, because of which the last was not self-sufficient and was devalued, and extolled only universal abstract similarities in law. Given the dissemination of such works and the comparative approach in jurisprudence and despite the severe reservations expressed, he named the eighteenth century the "century of comparisons".[165]

Hube stressed that at the new stage of the development of jurisprudence connected with an era of political reaction and reconciliation of reason with real social life, it was inadmissible to mix comparative legal knowledge with the speculative philosophy of law (philosophy of natural law) because the last scorned the comparison of positive law. Science must perceive the law of each nation as individual and of equal value, relying not on external, but on internal comparison (which reveals the "internal value of the subject-matter").[166]

Therefore, Hube condemned the historical school for the fact that Hugo transferred the comparison of positive law and comparative legal knowledge into the philosophy of law (created a philosophy of positive law which simultaneously became the "science of comparing laws"),[167] and the history of law in the vision

[165] Hube, note 27 above (1830), pp. 47-48.

[166] Ibid., pp. 48-50, 54.

[167] "In carrying over the traditional notions of the historical school. Hugo also created the philosophy of positive laws, but the work which he named is rather a comparative and speculative account of various positive laws in which the early ideas of philosophy and basic instances of history are forcibly combined". On the contrary, in Hube's view, "philosophy, just as reason, may be only one or, in any event, should aspire to this". Ibid., p. 53.

and works of this school does not rest on comparative legal studies, except for the study of Roman law, and has no philosophical spirit. Instead, the historico-philosophical school which Hube identified with Gans and in which he included himself is based on a comparative legal approach ("universal-historical consideration") to the general history of law. The philosophy of law in his vision "rested on instances prepared thanks to natural law, but left the abstracted orientation" and occupies itself with that which "in a real society is prolonged and eternal"; that is, the reasonable grounds of law:

> The historical school considers philosophy both as a comparative science and as knowledge of the future anticipated perfection of the human species. The other school assesses philosophy entirely otherwise. In its view, this is a science which discovered in our time the grounds of the eternal being of human society.[168]

Together the general history of law and philosophy of law comprise an organic whole within the framework of the science of legislation (positive jurisprudence).[169]

In 1829 Maciejowski pointed to the existence of the general history of legislation as a science founded by Montesquieu. It was developed, however, only by a German scholar, Feuerbach; the others investigated only the history of Roman law.[170] Maciejowski wrote of his intention to take the first steps towards forming a comparative history of law which probably should have been another name for the general history of legislation.[171] It is appropriate to recall the four-volume history of Slavic legislation by Maciejowski, which provided a mighty impetus for the development of the regional comparative history of law.[172]

Heylman, with whom Hube had discussions, suggested that the philosophy of law in force be distinguished from the philosophy of all positive laws and the philosophy of ideal law as sciences

168 Ibid., pp. 49-57.

169 Ibid.

170 Maciejowski, note 54 above, pp. 414-415.

171 Ibid., p. 422.

172 Maciejowski, note 118 above, I.

which have common grounds but differ in their subject-matter.[173] Indicating the differences in his own positions from those of Hugo, Heylman thus additionally augmented the philosophy of all positive laws with comparative content. Heylman observed that the last discipline, despite its apparent character, "confined itself always to a consideration of the positive laws of a small number of nations", justifying this, following von Savigny (without citation) by the fact that the cognition of the law of less developed peoples does not much matter and that "it is impossible to substantively be familiar with an endless multiplicity of different and diverse laws". Therefore, he distanced himself from the "too frequent" definition of the philosophy of positive laws as universal and also called it the philosophy of diverse positive laws.[174]

Moreover, the philosophy and history of law in force in Heylman's vision also have a comparative character because the law of all nations of a determined linguistic group was relegated to the law in force.[175] The philosophy of ideal law by its nature is the highest theoretical science of law, but is based on the comparison and generalization of ideas, conceptions, "feelings" embedded in the positive law of "the whole human species". In this science the spirit of national law is encountered and finds harmony with a universal spirit, the line disappears between law and morality, the ideas of reason and justice in law are revealed, as is the supremacy of the purpose of man in comparison with the purpose of the nation and the State.[176] Other sciences of law besides the philosophy of law, namely the history and dogmatic of law in force, Heylman evidently rejected having a comparative character: they were lower in level of generalization and supply analyzed empirical material for the philosophy of law in all of its three hypostases.[177]

We also note that when the School of Law was refounded at Warsaw in 1808, part of its subjects had an implicitly (civil law, criminal law, public law – without limitation by the Duchy of Warsaw – which was the sole correct decision given the piecemeal character of its legal order) and explicitly (Roman law, Code Napoleon) character of comparative cognition of foreign and

173 Heylman, note 57 above, p. 40, 49.

174 Ibid., pp. 48-49.

175 Ibid., p. 49.

176 Ibid., pp. 52, 54.

177 Ibid., pp. 54-55.

Polish law. Only natural law stood apart in this list.[178] Considering the nomenclature of disciplines and on the basis of the content thereof, modern specialists assert that in Warsaw the historical-legal and comparative methods of teaching law were offered foremost to students.[179] In Warsaw University the nomenclature of subjects with a clear or implicit comparative legal component was expanded. At Krakow University when Western Galicia was part of the Duchy of Warsaw, as noted above, there was a Chair of the History of All Laws.

From 1825 Hube began to teach the history of law at Warsaw University and noted that his predecessor, Maciejowski, lectured only on the history of Roman law. Now he had been assigned to also teach the history of new laws, especially the laws of the Germanic States.[180] Hube's lectures, which suggested the approaches of the historico-philosophical school and especially Hegel, dissatisfied the authorities, as a consequence of which the Commission of Education attempted to liquidate his Chair. But it was retained thanks to active protests by the Dean of the Law Faculty, Bandtike, the lecturers, and the students.[181]

The policy of excluding the comparative element of education was characteristic in the Kingdom of Poland after the suppression of the November Uprising of 1830/31. As Sójka-Zielińska noted, beginning from 1831 the Tsarist authorities watched over whether legal education had a pure applied professional nature, and the "delving into theory or comparison with the legislation of other States" was strictly prohibited.[182]

[178] A. Oniszczuk, "Doświadczenia Księstwa Warszawskiego w zakresie edukacji prawniczej", *Krytyka Prawa*, VIII, no. 3 (2016), p. 76.

[179] Ibid., p. 86; A. Rosner, "Dzieje Wydziału Prawa i Administracji Uniwersytetu Warszawskiego w latach 1808-1831", in G. Bałtruszajtys (ed.), *Zarys dziejów Wydziału prawa I administracji Uniwersytetu Warszawskiego* (2d ed.; Warsaw, 2016), pp. 20, 22, 26.

[180] M. Paszkowska, "Romuald Hube (1803-1890)", in *Portrety uczonych. Profesorowie Uniwersytetu Warszawskiego 1816-1915* (Warsaw, 2016), p. 250; Польша и Россия в первой трети XIX века. Из истории автономного Королевства Польского. 1815-1830 [Poland and Russia in the First Third of the Nineteenth Century. From the History of the Autonomous Kingdom of Poland. 1815-1830] (Moscow, 2010), p. 434.

[181] Paszkowska, ibid., p. 251.

[182] K. Sójka-Zielińska, "Nauczanie historii prawa w czasach przemian ustrojowych", in A. Turskiej (ed.), *Humanizacja zawodow prawniczych a nauczanie akademickie* (Warsaw, 2002), p. 44.

From at least 1814 Warsaw legal scholars considered the advisability of differentiating the science of law within the complex of sciences. They say the reason for this in the expansion of legal knowledge, as a result whereof parts of the science were becoming separate. A separation was contemplated into "partial" (branch) and general, and sometimes legal country studies. All this, together with the imprecise delimitation between spheres of research, instructional disciplines, and sciences made understanding the list of the last rather complex.

The development of higher legal education facilitated the development of comparative legal disciplines in the Duchy of Warsaw and the Kingdom of Poland because the nomenclature of instructional disciplines as noted above correlated with the nomenclature of the sciences in the understanding of legal scholars. Another factor was the translation of foreign scientific works, among which the translation of Feuerbach's article in 1822 should be singled out.

From at least 1814 Bandtkie substantiated the history of laws (all) as a separate sphere of scientific research within the historico-legal cognition, and in 1820 Rakowiecki called it the general history of law. Hube in 1829 named two more spheres of a comparative historico-legal character – the history of the institutions of new nations and the history of Slavic laws. Finally, in 1829 Maciejowski called the general history of legislation a comparative history of laws and defined it as an individual science founded by Montesquieu and elaborated by Feuerbach.

When proclaiming comparison to be the basis of all sciences of law, Szaniawski in 1819 proposed a separate "legal static (statistic) or science of comparisons in law". The rather eclectic science should encompass both the comparative legal sphere and the problematic of the encyclopedia of law. National legal systems and the dialectic of their interaction comprised its subject-matter, as did the comparison of legal conceptions and concepts. And its purposes were the forming of a general doctrine on law and the finding or creation of the better law with a view to the improvement of the national legal order. Szaniawski was aware also that he was not the author of the idea of comparative legal science and that he for the first time proposed the grounds for a system thereof.

The major dispute concerning the institutionalization of comparative legal knowledge occurred in 1830. It summed up the development of the positions of the principal orientations of legal thought of the Warsaw legal scholars. Heylman, who manifested his adherence to the historical school of law but in fact synthesized the foundations thereof with the ideas of the historico-philosophical school, proposed a comparative legal vision of the philosophy of positive law in which the philosophy of all positive laws (or philosophy of diverse positive laws) encompassed the comparison of national legal orders within different legal families, the philosophy of law in force – legal orders within a single legal family, and the philosophy of ideal law – a comparison of ideas and conceptions. The history of law in his vision did not have a comparative character and should have only provided national materials for comparison and generalization within these three philosophies. Hube, on the contrary, who positioned himself as a proponent of the historico-philosophical school, criticized the "science of the comparison of laws" having roots in mixing the history of law with natural law philosophy typical for the eighteenth century. He placed comparative legal knowledge within the "general history of laws" based on a universal historical understanding of law. The philosophy of law should be based on comparative historico-legal generalizations.

The surveys of the literature of the eighteenth and beginning of the nineteenth centuries represented in the works of Prince F. K. Szaniawski, Rakowiecki, Maciejowski, and Hube may be regarded as the first attempts to reflect upon the history of comparative legal studies and the recognition thereof, one way or another, as an institutionalized sphere of scientific cognition.

Part Two
Comparative Legal Picture of Warsaw Jurists

Chapter 3
National Legal Order as the Particular in Law

§3.1. Theory of Positivist Social Law

The most fundamental problem of legal thought in the second half of the eighteenth and first third of the nineteenth centuries was the completion of the development of the new positivist and social worldview of jurists, which ultimately provided for the forming of a new special scientific picture of the world. It is appropriate briefly to show why the opposition of universal natural and social positive law was the basic axis for the development of European legal thought for a lengthy period. It also is important to understand in what context Polish legal thought developed during the period here considered.

The dualism of law as the subject-matter of the legal sciences throughout the centuries (natural and positive law) reflected the syncretic nature of the general doctrine on law with philosophy, proposed not only the absence of self-value of the existing positive legal orders, but also the incidental nature of their distinctive features and subordinated their pluralism to a monist metaphysical benchmark. The secularization of natural law was the essence of the gradual transformation of understanding the subject-matter of jurisprudence from the Reformation to the Enlightenment, which made possible the cognition thereof by means of philosophy without a theological dogmatic as well as recognition of the autonomy of human will in law – which increased the significance of positive law as a sphere of human rationality. But only in the eighteenth to the early nineteenth centuries was the non-universal, non-metaphysical, non-legal character of natural law proclaimed; it was considered to be the outcome of human thought and went beyond the subject-matter of jurisprudence. Natural law was deprived of any positive content and began to be regarded as a negative (determines the limits of law) or as a generalization of positive law.

In the first half of the eighteenth century the trend was the gradual erosion of the theory of natural law, especially through:

the idea not of its legal but of its ethical character; the denial of its normativity (at least direct, without the positivization thereof); the nationalization thereof, the denial of the universality thereof; the idea of its human origin as a generalization of the experience and ideals of a concrete society – the denial of its metaphysical nature; the assumption of its philosophical-worldview character; the development of the idea of cognition of natural law on materials of positive law (especially customs); the differentiation thereof into individual elements, part of which were positivized, and the sphere of natural law respectively narrowed; its historical vision – the idea of the gradually growing role and expansion of the sphere of positive law with the development of society (assertion of the gradual forming of the social nature of man together with the physical). Thinkers of this period gradually withdrew natural law from the subject-matter of legal cognition, leaving it in philosophy. Positive law was emancipated, and the spheres of positive and natural law were demarcated, but their dualism and the notion of the derivative nature of the first from the second were retained.

The works of Montesquieu have a special place in the development of the doctrine on the correlation of positive and natural law by reason of their depth of synthesis and their influence. Having cast aside the traditional metaphysics of natural law, Montesquieu declared the positive law of the people (in the modern understanding – national law) as an autonomous object of study, the non-incidental nature of diversity in law, and the subject-matter of research became not the conformity of this object to natural or Divine law, but the distinctive features thereof in comparison with the law of another people.

The process of squeezing out natural law from the subject-matter of jurisprudence intensified in the 1780-90s, including thanks to the exceptionally influential works of Filangieri, Hugo, Kant, Burke, Herder, Bentham and later Hegel, Puchta, Gans, Cousin, Lerminier, and other legal scholars. They proclaimed the philosophical, ethical character of natural law, and considered positive law to be a manifestation of social will and simultaneously the historically formed experience of regulating social relations; they acknowledged that it is an autonomous manifestation of human rationality, even if relative, non-universal, and non-eternal. The concept of natural law itself did not disappear from the works of many scholars, but it changed in principle and was often designated as either the generalized experience of the positive legal development of various societies which should be evidence of the general feature of human rationality or as conscious physical limitations of the effectuation of law as freedom of will, or the distinctive features of the development of politico-legal doctrines and legal consciousness of an individual people or as philosophy of law, logical forms and constructions which have no concrete positive content.

The social sphere, to which law belongs, was finally separated out among the physical and biological spheres of being. The will of God (or pure reason) and physical and biological nature generate man, but as a free, relatively undetermined creature. The social sphere is a sphere of the self-development of freedom as a constituent thereof (just as for romantics nature is the possibility of culture, pre-culture, but not culture proper) – God does not create any law. Natural law is moved from the legal map of the world to the world of philosophy and lacks any positive content – historical and territorial.

The theory of natural law was discredited in principle as a result of intensive public discussions at the end of the eighteenth and early nineteenth centuries, especially during the so-called "codification debates" in the German states in 1814 (in fact, at least from 1810 to 1817). Both sides, which were constituted as historico-philosophical and historical schools, acknowledged the impossibility of natural law as law proper and instead the exclusiveness of positive law.

The development of positivism at this time was greatly affected by the defeat of Napoleonic France, which undermined the universalist projects of the Holy Roman Empire of the Germanic Nation, *ius commune*, and the Code Civil, and confirmed the national positive legal orders as the sole possible systems of law. The exclusiveness of positive law (existing, empirically cognizable) transformed national legal orders into a self-sufficient subject-matter of research, enabled them to be regarded as manifestations of human legal experience, and their diversity as a non-incidental and stable phenomenon requiring scholarly comprehension.

The process of the transformation of the subject sphere of law and object of legal sciences also was a lengthy one; it began in the sixteenth century with the recognition of the autonomy of the social sphere of human existence and singled out the secular ethic of human relations, which did not coincide with the doctrine of the Catholic Church. This was gradually realized in the ideas of social integration, whose forms are society and the State, as well as of the autonomy of social law (created by society, including institutionalized in the State, and by groups therein). The ideas of the territoriality of societies and their localization in space were the prerequisite for the recognition of social and legal pluralism in the world, the equality of social legal orders. The gradual transformation of social philosophy into socio-political and socio-legal in their essence connected with the forming of the idea of State-centric legal development is expressed in the idea of the absorption of society by the State and makes it and its law total, but unstable, lacking a permanent link with the social foundation thereof.

The nation was gradually deemed to be a new subject of legal development, and the national legal order became the object of the science of law. The idea of the nation as a functional community by its personal and territorial embrace identical to society whose volitional State-building and lawmaking rests on a lengthy historical tradition and is one of the expressions of organic and spiritual-cultural development and collective rationality finally eliminates the individual, combines the subjective and objective will, legitimizes the national State and law, and simultaneously confirms the equality and pluralism of legal orders.

The process of the development of the doctrine of private and public national law from the sixteenth to the eighteenth centuries is responsive to this development of ideas, being founded on an expanded interpretation and interpolation of the doctrine of Roman law, the combining thereof with customary law, and the juridicization of the secular ethic of social relations. The contractual coordination of individual wills became the principled foundation thereof. The doctrines on the institutional and legal character of the State, the sociality of law, the social contract, sovereignty (State, people's, and others), nation, and others were manifestations of the objectivization of socio-political philosophy. A consequence of the objectivization of a significant part of the subjective political and inter-subjective private law, and also the transformation of objective canon law, were the narrowing thereof and the development of new relatively solitary spheres of legal regulation – public legal and international legal.

All these phenomena, in our view, are interconnected and may be regarded as facets of a single process of the gradual rejection of the theological and natural totality and overcoming the post-universalist worldview atomization. In place of this was the building of a new, distinctly empirical, social, and pluralist picture of the existence and interaction of multiple totalities or concrete universums. In our view, this process is key to understanding the development of the social sciences in general and the legal sciences in particular.

The destruction of a vertically determined dichotomy of God (relatively cognizable self-determined universal, general) – Man (determined by God, but relatively individual, particular) thanks to the said intellectual and social processes led to confirmation of the horizontal mutually determined triad of Social world (universal) – Supranational social communities (social particular – space of concrete interaction of the individual – civilization, legal family, and others) – Concrete collective social subjects (social individual, particular – State, society, nation). This in turn gradually formed the subject-matter and object of comparative legal studies concentrated on the cognition of pluralism of the social particular in its links with the other particular and with the special and the universal.[1]

One manifestation of the positivist understanding of law is the thesis of Kołłątaj concerning the submissiveness to law and power, the rule of law in a national State which at the same time must be combined harmoniously with liberties of people.[2] The thesis concerning the rule of law was repeatedly stressed by contemporaries of Kołłątaj. Suffice it to recall the view of the Minister of Justice, Łubieński: "there is only real freedom where law rules despotically".[3] Later Prince F. K. Szaniawski uttered the slogan "the rule of law in force".[4]

In an address by Szaniawski which opened the academic year 1808/09 on the positions necessary for the study of law at the Warsaw School of Law, the law was regarded as that which

[1] O. V. Kresin, *Comparative Legal Studies: 1750-1835. Approaches to Conceptualization*, ed. & transl. W. E. Butler (London, 2019), I, pp. 186-193; II, pp. 330-332.

[2] H. Kołłątaj, *Uwagi nad teraźniejszem położeniem tej części ziemi Polskiej, którą od Pokoju Tylżyckiego zaczęto zwać Księstwem Warszakskiem* (1808), p. 220.

[3] H. Konic, "Nowy przyczynek do dziejów kodeksu Napoleona w Polsce", *Gazeta Sądowa Warszawska*, no. 13 (18 March 1903), p. 195.

[4] F. K. Szaniawski, *Statyka prawa, czyli nauka porównywań w prawie* (Warsaw, 1819), pp. 22-24, 28.

is deliberately created by each society for itself according to its own notion of its requirements, distinctive features of evolution, and orientators for future development. The possibility of creating a perfect law suitable for all societies or States and for all times was rejected. Reason and rationality (as pure reason and practical reason in Kant) were a source of law, but these were the thinking of concrete people, of their consciousness and will lacking any metaphysical nature. Just as human morality influences the creation and application of law, so *vice versa* the last materially influences morality.[5]

Szaniawski linked natural law with the immutable nature of man and, following Kant, considered natural law not as binding norms but as an internal moral imperative. Positive law, on the contrary, was binding, social, and State-territorial; that is, only it was objective law proper.[6] In our view, the dualism of positive and natural law is not present in such opinions; this is pure positivism, and natural law is something linked with law but not law itself.[7]

In works published between 1817 and 1819, Szaniawski wrote about the laws of nature as physical possibilities and limitations in human life, universal, immutable, inevitable, perfected ("God is the first legislator") which constitute a certain necessity in the life of things and living essences, including people. Another category of laws is moral and simultaneously established by the will of people; they extend solely to the external behavior of people in society. They are social and territorial, are laws insofar as they are binding, and are the force that creates the necessity: "By the word 'law' we understand every prescription operating in a State" (1819).[8] Thus, the first were natural laws (which Szaniawski reduced to objective natural law), and the second were positive. Both groups create the

[5] Szaniawski, *O usposobieniach potrzebnych do uczenia się prawa. Rzech czytana przy otwarciu Szkoły prawa w Warszawie dnia 14 Października 1808 roku* (Warsaw, 1808), pp. 4-5, 7, 11, 13.

[6] J. Jakubowski, "Pierwszy wykład prawa na Uniwersytecie Warszawskim", *Palestra*, no. 3/2-3 (1959), pp. 77, 80.

[7] Another view is expressed in P. Pomianowski, "Glówne nurty ideologiczno-metodologiczne w środowisku warszawskich prawników przed wybuchem powstania listopadowego", *Zeszyty Prawnicze UKSW*, XI (2011), p. 406; P. Szymaniec, "Nauka prawa jako dzialalność pro bono. Uwagi na temat polskiej nauki prawa w latach 1807-1831", M. Marszal and J. Przygodzki (eds.), *Pro publico bono – idee i dzialalność* (Wroclaw, 2016), p. 114.

[8] Szaniawski, *Wiadomości początkowe w nauce prawa* (Warsaw, 1817), pp. 1-3, 6-8, 16, 19-20, 26, 28-29; Szaniawski, note 4 above, p. 12.

necessity, but only the second group is law proper: "Human laws we otherwise call positive laws".[9]

Reason, morals, morality, religion, and notions of people about natural law (that is, on the conformity of the social world to the natural world and taking account of natural necessity) influence our behavior and the establishment of law being a primary source thereof, but precisely are separated from it: "Righteousness and virtue are the subject-matter of morality; only justice itself, which is realized by external signs, concerns human laws; human power cannot effectively compel virtue, but it encourages this, inspires, inclines, directs".[10] All these factors, unlike objective natural laws, are mutable, dependent on place, time, and circumstances, and therefore positive law also is provisional, localized, imperfect, and the subject-matter of constant human lawmaking activity.[11]

The reason for the appearance of positive law is the desire for social links, for the creation of society for mutual good and improvement of itself and of mankind (therefore the author linked positive law as civil, and civilization as "changes, benefit, and the perfection of people caused by their combining into a society").[12]

Positive civil law encompasses all relations of members of a concrete society or of a State to one another; external law is the "relations of societies in the vision of societies"; the law of nations is relations between societies or States (mutual duties between individual communities, peoples, and States arising from customs between peoples, agreements; that is, from positive law, but may be based on a notion of natural law).[13] The forms of positive law F. Szaniawski named in 1817 are customary law (as "separate decisions" according to events and circumstances passed on through experience, that is, including judicial practice) and legislation (in the law of nations, an agreement); the first in history transforming by evolution into the second by way of the comparison of norms, the forming and generalization of grounds,

[9] Szaniawski, note 8 above, p. 29.

[10] Ibid., pp. 9-10, 16-17, 19, 21-23; Szaniawski, note 4 above, pp. 15, 88.

[11] Szaniawski, note 8 above, pp. 19-20; Szaniawski, note 4 above, p. 77.

[12] Szaniawski, note 8 above, pp. 14, 31, 34; Szaniawski, note 4 above, pp. 19, 26, 35, 58.

[13] Szaniawski, note 8 above, pp. 34-35; Szaniawski, note 4 above, p. 57.

or the borrowing of foreign law.[14] Therefore, Szaniawski related to the codification of law favorably.[15]

Feliks Słotwiński (1788-1863) published a work in 1812 on the history of the law of nature based on a post-critical analysis of the ideas of Kant and supported a precise separation of law and morality. Positive law is in force and binding irrespective of judgments relating to its conformity to the bases of practical reason, and any dictatorship of morality in law leads to subjectivism and unlawfulness.[16]

The views of Damazy Antoni Jan Dzierożyński (1783-1835) expressed in 1813 and 1828 are of interest. Natural law came down in his vision to the laws of physical nature, and also to God having granted to man the freedoms of reason and will. That is, the moral part of such natural law is freedom, and not prescription. People create societies by proceeding from their own needs, and each society has its own special social contract based on consent relative to the needs of people and the means of providing them, the rights and duties of members of society, and the freedom of their wills. And the law of society, consequently, is particular and not universal, volitional and contractual, and not prescribed, and the aim and application of law of different societies may differ. There is no place in such a vision for natural law proper, but merely for convictions and "rules of natural rationality" which have to be relegated to the domain of human psychology.[17]

The idea of natural law[18] as divine, or at least as a mixture of ethics and law, or as thrusting a law from without on society generated sharp condemnation from Bandtkie.[19] He also rejected the idea of natural law as pure reason: "there is nothing anywhere

[14] Szaniawski, note 8 above, pp. 30, 35, 54, 281-282.

[15] Szaniawski, note 4 above, p. 68.

[16] Szymaniec, note 7 above, p. 120.

[17] Pomianowski, note 7 above, p. 408; Pomianowski, *Początki polskiego czasopiśmiennictwa prawniczego. Seria pierwsza "Themis Polskiej"* (Warsaw, 2015), p. 112.

[18] For a different perception of Bandtkie as a natural lawyer, see W. Sobociński, "Jan Wincenty Bandtkie obrońca Kodeksu Napoleona", *Rocznik Lubelski*, III (1960), pp. 160-161, 164.

[19] J. W. Bandtkie, "Wywod historyczny praw mieyskich w Polsce dawney obowiązuiących", in J. W. Bandtkie, *Zbiór rospraw o przedmiotach prawa polskiego* (Warsaw, 1812), pp. 22, 48, 50; Bandtkie, *Uwagi o prtrzebie nauki prawa w naszym kraju w szczegolności, a o użytku onejże w ogolnością* (Warsaw, 1814), pp. 15, 23.

and will not be in human behavior a mathematical uniformity, a natural system"; he treated the ideas of Kant's critical period with irony without naming their author.[20] In general, Bandtkie considered the designing of any natural law systems to be an exercise of little value, reducing them to ideals of law and justice which are created by society and, being combined with experience, were embodied in positive law at various stages of the development of society.[21] But he did not object to the use in the future of the concept of "natural law" – in the sense of the "truths of law" which are a generalization of the experience of positive law.[22]

In works published between 1827 and 1830, Hube set out a completely positivist vision of law as the "legal order of society" and system of the positive law of the State.[23] He noted that "by system I understand the order and placing in order of individual subject-matter".[24] Hube condemned and ridiculed "abstracted ideas of laws of nature" and believed that different variants of natural law were merely historical pre-scientific types of ideas about law, an element of the idolatry of an infantile brain of ancient man in world harmony, a theological construct, an abstraction of the dogmatics of Roman law in the quest for a perfect law, a speculative intellectual structure.[25] Evaluating codifications elaborated on the basis of the idea of natural law as reason, Hube observed that they have an illusory elegance, but suppress the functioning and development of living law emanating from the needs of societies and destroy their legal diversity.[26] Therefore, a "reaction became absolutely necessary", abstract reason must subordinate itself to the evolutionary development of social order, merely transforming it from a mosaic into a system.[27] Reason no longer makes a claim to the creation of an objective natural law

[20] Bandtkie, note 19 above (1812), p. 72; Bandtkie, note 19 above (1814), pp. 33-34.

[21] Bandtkie, note 19 above (1814), pp. 33-34.

[22] Ibid., pp. 34-35.

[23] R. Hube, "Krotki rys historyi literatury prawa (1827)", in Hube, *Opera*, ed. K. Dunin (Warsaw, 1905), I, pp. 67, 71; Hube, "Niektore uwagi nad historya nauki prawa (1830)", in ibid. (1905), I, p. 42; Hube, "Uwagi nad systematem Kodexu cywilnego francuskiego", *Themis Polska*, V (1829), pp. 313-324, 331-332, 334.

[24] Hube, note 23 above (1829), p. 313.

[25] Hube, "O stanie nauki prawa w naszych czasach (1827)", in note 23 above (1905), I, p. 9; Hube, note 23 above (1830), pp. 37, 39, 46-48.

[26] Hube, note 23 above (1830), pp. 48-49.

[27] Ibid., pp. 49-50.

("the delirium of a state of nature has disappeared"), and it is becoming an abstracted form of the positive law of society.[28]

Zaborowski also shared a positivist and social vision of law in works published in 1829. The idea of natural law, including the law of reason uniform for all, everywhere, and for always, he considered to be anachronistic and rejected by the science of law.[29] He scornfully ridiculed natural law: "This fencing with ingenuity does not harm skills and thus merely demonstrates the triumph of truth over ingenuity and rhetoric".[30] He affirmed the existence in human reason of an innate idea of good and evil, of an "implicit feeling";[31] that is, certain elements of essentialism are manifested characteristic for all versions of the idea of natural law. But the development of the idea of justice is collective, originates in society, and is reflected in positive law and through political power.[32] Just as other Warsaw legal scholars at the time, Zaborowski emphasized the impermissibility of mixing knowledge and notions of the laws of physical nature (universal, necessary, immutable) with laws created thanks to the moral nature of man (changing, progressing, not subject to precise measurement and calculation).[33]Moreover, in his view, morality should not be mixed with law proper, although it influences the last and is broader in comparison.[34]

Heylman condemned as unsubstantiated, unproved, and outdated the idea of a reasonable natural law, for reason is not abstract or universal; and distinctive features of collective consciousness and culture are linked with the peculiarities of the development of concrete societies – therefore, the diversity of laws is inevitable: "The moment will come (just as with the question of whether the Earth revolves around the Sun, and not *vice versa*) when all jurists will be persuaded that reason is not the sole source of legislation and that there may be two, three, or more reasonable

[28] Ibid., pp. 51, 53.

[29] C. [Zaborowski], "Rozbiór krytyczny dzieła pod tytulem: Upominek pogrobowy ś.p. Kazimierza Pliszki Podlesianina; rzecz o sukcessii ...", *Themis Polska*, VI (1829), p. 213.

[30] Ibid., p. 213.

[31] Ibid., p. 214.

[32] Ibid.

[33] Ibid., pp. 229, 240.

[34] Ibid., pp. 229-230.

legislations".[35] The idea of human reason Heylman welcomes, but it is not universal and not abstract, just individual and lacks any metaphysical nature, is above all a creation, including of the surrounding world, but is not an autonomous creator and merely cognizes and to some extent, co-creates: "The relation between reason and the external world gives material grounds to legislation. Moral grounds which serve legislation emanate from the relation between reason and the spirit of the Creator".[36]

On the whole, Heylman condemned any natural law ideas: "The multitude of so-called natural laws which the semi-wise in philosophy and jurisprudence have proposed ... who instead of healthy grain gathered the shells".[37] Instead of this, he substantiated a philosophy of an ideal law as the *a posteriori* generalization of elements of positive law which received universal dissemination.[38]

The sole proponent of natural law whose work drew attention at the time, albeit in the form of crushing criticism, was Bieńkowski, the anonymous author of a monograph on the natural law of inheritance.[39] In his view, human reason discovers, and positive law should reflect natural law having universal extra-historical and an extra-local character: "Know, on one hand, that every legal prescription should contain within it a moral truth, and know also that each truth is uniform, identical everywhere, always, for every person, for all nations, and for the entire human species; know, finally, that every truth does not change anywhere, nowhere contradicts itself, and is always homogeneous".[40] That which conforms to natural human feelings is just, and deviations from such natural justice in the past and present are linked either with superstition or with the personal interests of the legislator.[41] In Bieńkowski's view, contemporary legislation should be reviewed, replacing therein that which is not consistent with "natural

35 A. Heylman, "Wywod zasad ogolnych nauki prawa i prawodawstwa", *Themis Polska*, VII (1830), pp. 6-8, 11.

36 Ibid., pp. 8-9.

37 Ibid., p. 53.

38 Ibid., pp. 52, 54.

39 [A. Bieńkowski], *Upominek pogrobowy Ś. P. Kazimierza Pliszki Podlasianina Rzecz o sukcesji, czyli uwagi nad prawem przyrodzonym do spadku* (Warsaw, 1827).

40 Szymaniec, note 7 above, p. 109; Pomianowski, note 7 above, pp. 405-406; Pomianowski, note 17 above, pp. 105-106.

41 Szymaniec, note 7 above, pp. 109-110.

reason".[42] Szymaniec and Pomianowski were of the view that Bieńkowski's natural law had a form typical of the Enlightenment.[43]

Bieńkowski had partially expressed his view earlier, when working in the Reform Committee. He supported the idea of universal natural civil law and insisted that civil law conform to morality, "which is immutable, uniform, and the same for always and everywhere for every person, for all nations, and for the entire species of mankind".[44]

In response to Bieńkowski, Stanisław Węgrzecki (1765-1845) noted that nature dictates only the primary grounds of positive law; the latter develops according to the development of societies. The abilities of people are natural, and therefore the positive law created by them, whatever it was, also is natural. Moreover, Węgrzecki noted that the proclamation of concrete norms to be natural or non-natural by Bieńkowski was arbitrary and subjective.[45] The positions of Bieńkowski's other adversary, Zaborowski, we have analyzed above with respect to natural law.

Modern specialists of Polish legal thought in the first third of the nineteenth century do not separate out the discussions concerning the relationship and character of positive and natural law among the "basic branches of the discourse".[46] This is no accident. The proponents of natural law did not offer at that time new conceptions except those already debunked and subjected to doubt. A course on natural law was offered in the School of Law curriculum, but it is unclear whether it was offered as objective law, an analogue of the philosophy of law, or in other mode.[47] The positiveness and sociality of law was declared and substantiated without encountering virtually any material resistance.

[42] Ibid., pp. 111-112.

[43] Ibid., pp. 109-110, 112; Pomianowski, note 7 above, p. 405.

[44] Pomianowski, "Postulat narodowego charakteru prawa w pracach kodyfikacyjnych doby Królestwa Kongresowego", *Czasopismo Prawno-Historyczne*, LXXI, no. 1 (2019), p. 122.

[45] Szymaniec, note 7 above, pp. 113-114.

[46] Ch. E. Mecke, "Dyskurs o zasadniczej myśli prawniczej w "Themis Polskiej" (1828-1830) na tle program historycznej szkoły prawa w Niemczech", *Forum prawnicze* (2018), p. 23.

[47] A. Rosner, 'Tradycja i nowoczesnośc w nauczaniu prawa. Doświadczenie Rzeczypospolitej szlacheckiej i Szkola Prawa w Księstwie Warszawskim", in H. Izdebski (ed.), *Nauka i nauczanie prawa. Tradycja i przyszlość* (Warsaw, 2009), p. 55.

That Polish jurists did not see any hostility in principle between the historical and historico-philosophical schools was not paradoxical, but completely normal; although they were demonstrably had coalesced with one another, in essence they were regarded as two branches of a single positivist (in the terminology of the time – historical) orientation of legal thought.[48] We concur (by analogy) with Mecke that the discussions concerning the history of the sources of positive law had not merely a historico-legal, theoretical-legal, or comparative legal scientific character, but also masked a discourse concerning the modern orientations of the development of the legal order of the Duchy of Warsaw and the Kingdom of Poland.

The natural law discourse was influential at the end of the eighteenth century (for example, for Kołłątaj moral laws were objective and immutable because they arose from the order of nature),[49] but in the early nineteenth century the discourse was in practice frozen. No doubt it was declared or perceived between the lines of scholarly works or addresses in lawmaking agencies, but not regarded as worthy of attention.[50] The exception was a discussion between Bieńkowski (anonymously), Zaborowski, and Węgrzecki in 1829 – and this merely confirmed the general trend.

Thus, a positivist and sociological discourse dominated in the thought of Warsaw jurists during the period here considered. The laws of nature as external conditions of human activity were separated out from the domain of natural law; these created the possibilities and limitations which are the necessity and framework for the development of law, but not law itself. Moreover, first, natural conditions are diverse, and second, freedom of will is natural for man, overcoming the determinism of nature in lawmaking. An essential difference between law and morality was determined, despite their mutual influence on one another: morality may perform the role of an internal imperative of human behavior, but this is subjective and not obligatory,

[48] Mecke, note 46 above, pp. 28, 32.

[49] M. Iłowiecki, *Okręty na oceanie czasu. Historia nauki Polskiej do 1945 roku* (Warsaw, 2011), p. 126.

[50] Pomianowski expressed the same thought. See Pomianowski, note 17 above, p. 64. For another view relating to dominance among Warsaw jurists before 1831 on the natural law understanding of law, see W. Witkowski, "Warszawa jako ośrodek polskiej nauki prawa w dobie zaborów", *Krakowskie Studia z Historii Państwa i Prawa*, VIII (2015), p. 48.

whereas law regulates external human relations and is objective and binding by virtue of its social conventionality. The emphasis was important, that not only was law conditioned by the influence of phenomena external to it (especially morality, social relations), but itself was capable of materially influencing the development of the last. Essentialist concepts about innate ideas were actually confined to the bio-psychological grounds of human thought; it was acknowledged that human reason fully or basically was not metaphysical, and was formed historically in the process of the development of man and society. The idea of natural law as law proper is primarily rejected and ridiculed, and instead became perceived as a conditional name for social ideals and/or generalization of legal experience.

Positive law in all its forms was perceived as that created by society while proceeding from perceptions of its needs. Therefore, unlike laws of nature, it is changeable and territorially localized, social. The normative character of natural law was denied. Individual works by scholars which repeated natural law ideas formed in the preceding eras could not cast doubt that there was no dualism of natural and positive law in the dominant discourse of Polish legal thought during the period here considered. One should speak of the positivist and social essence of the majority of works of legal scholarship.

§3.2. Socio-Volitional Theory of National Law

The socio-volitional theory of national-State law developed in European legal thought during the second half of the eighteenth and first third of the nineteenth centuries was based on the requirement for territorial-subject conformity of the legal order to a civil society, nation, and State – on their identical scope relative to the contemporary development of law despite their historical and functional delimitation, on the conviction that, thanks to the State, national law acquired a final and distinct institutional form and territoriality. The territoriality of national-State legal orders enabled the legal map of the world to be designed exclusively of them. The sociality of will and statehood enabled the legal order to be objectified, eliminated man as a subject of law and his subjective right, and transformed national law into a particular unit of legal development. The socio-volitional nature of law enabled the identity of the being with the ought to be proclaimed, and this signified the self-sufficiency and exclusivity of a positive legal order. The requirement of statehood for a national legal order finally separated law from other social regulators; consideration of national-State legal orders as based on social will enabled them to be considered as of equal value.[51]

An understanding of people/nation on Polish lands during the early nineteenth century was rather complex. The subject-matter of discussion was primarily linguistic-cultural/ethnic or the political understanding of a nation. The political idea of a nation-State coincided with the idea of a political society directly encompassing the idea of national State-building and lawmaking, and emanated from the politico-legal discourse of the *Rzecz Pospolita,* was comprehensible and evident. But with the loss of independence and changes in the social content of the concept of a nation after the French Revolution, the political understanding of the nation required fundamental rethinking.

According to the 1791 Constitution (Preamble, Article V), the indicia of a nation were proclaimed to be "political existence, external independence, and internal freedom" and the existence of a common will expressed in State-building and lawmaking. At the same time, actually this will was given to an insignificant social minority, to politically-subjected strata, and the peasantry, proclaimed to be part of the nation and comprising the majority of the population, according to the Constitution were not even liberated, although their dependence supposedly was to become contractual, and no longer unconditional (Articles II, IV).[52]

As Grynwaser noted, being supposedly the most scrupulous and authoritative specialist in legal history and legal thought of the first third of the nineteenth century, during this period on central Polish lands not one of the "material manifestations of collective Polish patriotism, radicalism, or progressivism" proposed a consistent resolution of the question of formal liberation from personal dependence, and then the real equalization in the rights of the largest part of the population – the peasantry.[53] We note that this question was unequivocally "placed edgewise" by the French Revolution and made relevant by the Constitution of the Duchy

[51] Kresin, note 1 above, II, p. 336.

[52] *Ustawa Rządowa. Prawo uchwalone dnia 3 Maia, Roku 1791* (Warsaw, 1791), pp. 4-6, 8-10.

[53] H. Grynwaser, "Demokracja Szlachecka. 1795-1831", in Grynwaser, *Pisma* (Wroclaw, 1951), I, pp. 181, 188.

of Warsaw and the received French codes, but did not become the subject-matter of extensive discussion and, most important, an expressed consensus of political forces. At the same time, this question attracted the attention of individual jurists and politicians – which only confirms the general thesis.

In a Report prepared by the Directorate of Justice in 1807 for Napoleon, the social reality of the Polish lands was deliberately or unconsciously distorted; the authors proclaimed that the idea of an identical law for all estates, for all members of society, had been realized.[54]

Bandtkie's sharp condemnation of estate inequality, we assume might have been directly connected with the idea of society as a unit, an all-estate-embracing State and law, the inadmissibility of the usurpation by one stratum of the prerogatives of the entire nation, including lawmaking powers:

> Where one class of the nation exclusively itself establishes laws, where as a consequence of the abuse of liberties the order of things is being overturned, there not only laws, albeit supra-human, do not receive general authority, but national laws will not be sufficiently perfected because the inferiority conditioned by laws is despised.[55] Kollątaj took the view that there was an insistent need for emancipation of the peasantry (as an indication of the highly civilized level of the nation), which might be directly linked with his understanding of a nation as a political, civil community, for a person who is not free cannot be a fully-fledged citizen, a member of the nation.[56]

The essence of the socio-volitional, political understanding of the people/nation is demonstrated by the well-known statement of Czacki in 1800 and later: law may be only national.[57] A people

[54] Konic, "Nowy przyczynek do dziejów kodeksu Napoleona w Polsce", *Gazeta Sądowa Warszawska*, no. 14 (22 March 1903), pp. 210-214; A. Kraushar, "W setną rocnicę Kodeksu Napoleona", *Gazeta Sądowa Warszawska*, no. 22 (28 May 1908), pp. 330-331.

[55] Bandtkie, note 19 above (1812), pp. 145, 148, 206-207; Bandtkie, note 19 above (1814), pp. 9, 19; Bandtkie, "Myśli o zmianie prawodawstwa krajowego", *Rocznik Lubelski*, III (1960), p. 169; Sobociński, note 18 above, p. 162.

[56] Kołłątaj, note 2 above, p. 184.

[57] T. Czacki, *O litewskich i polskich prawach o ich duchu, żródłach, związku, i o rzeczach zawartych w pierwczym statucie dla Litwy, 1529 roku wydanym* (Krakow, 1861), I, pp.

has a self-sufficient history, but the rise and decline thereof are absolutely linked with the State:

> When any people ceases to be self-governing, in just a few generations disdains unhappiness and indifference to a nonexistent country, consigns it to oblivion, and creates hatred to effacing it from among States, not forgiving weakness and former resistance ... Poland already is effaced from the peoples ... a Land whose name remained effaced from the list of peoples".[58]

These thoughts were reiterated in essence by Wawrzyniec Surowiecki (1769-1827) in 1807, together with the apprehension that even the word "Pole" would be forgotten in several generations.[59] A similar view, but already in the context of the "resurrection" of the Polish people in 1808, was expressed by Julian Ursyn Niemcewicz (1758-1841),[60] and in 1809 by the President of the Senate, Count Stanisław Małachowski (1736-1809) (Napoleon "wanted to place us in the political existence of peoples lost as a result of the partition of our land")[61] and the Roman Catholic Bishop and poet, Jan Paweł Woronicz (1757-1829).[62] Woronicz also noted that the existence of a people assumes a certain "political constitution", the creation of political institutions to defend the conscious freedom of this people and its culture, laws, and customs. In an address in 1831 Brodziński declared that a nation perishes together with the loss of statehood ("political existence"), but may be reborn together with the restoration of the last: "We recovered from the grave the light of our nationality, we are standing with a right in national life to act among co-nations ... Freedom will not be achieved without the independent existence of a people".[63]

vii, 7, 11, 16, 18, 19, 22, 29, 43-45, 49, 51-54, 56; II, pp. 292-293.

58 Czacki, ibid., I, pp. iii, vi, 10, 49; Czacki, "Mowa przy otwarciu Gimnazyum Wołyńskiego w Krzemieńcu d. 13 października 1805 r.", in *Wiek XIX. Sto lat mysli Polskiej. Zyciorysy, streszczienia, wyjatki* (Warsaw, 1906), I, p. 154.

59 A. Wierzbicki, *Europa w polskiej myśli historycznej i politycznej XIX i XX wieku* (Warsaw, 2009), p. 66.

60 [J. U. Niemcewicz], *Przestroga dla społziomków na rok 1809* (Wrocław, 1808), p. 7.

61 "Mowa, J. W. Małachowskiego, Prezesa Senatu przy otwarciu Seymu miana w Senacie dnia 10 Marca 1809", *Gazeta Korrespondenta Warszawskiego i Zagranicznego*, no. 21, Dodatek (1809), p. 297.

62 Wierzbicki, note 59 above, p. 66.

63 K. Brodziński, *O narodowości Polaków* (Warsaw, 1917), pp. 22-24, 27.

Kołłątaj put forward the same thesis of the destruction, the "effacement", of the Polish people together with the State. A political people is capable of being reborn if statehood is returned to it.[64] In his view a people may acquire the right to be itself in political and armed struggle, may fall as a victim of others, or may destroy its own statehood, cardinally transform itself, its character, as a result of the exercise of will towards political transformations (as during the French Revolution).[65]

Kołłątaj condemned the fractionalization of countries, the "breaking up" thereof between several States. He observed that a single country must correspond to one people and one State.[66] A political nation in Kołłątaj's vision is linked by the will of people, a "notion accepted among themselves", and love for their State system.[67] At the same time, a people become stable thanks to a single "language, thoughts, and customs": The "impermanence of States which, glued together of many heterogeneous parts, must collapse one after the other".[68] An indicator of a people, according to Kołłątaj, is the "freedom to establish laws" and their constant improvement.[69]

Stanisław Wawrzyniec Staszic (1755-1826) asserted in 1815 that the equality of nations is a normal state, and not the dominance of one over another. An attribute of a people is law and own administration; that is, statehood.[70]

An interesting vision of national law was set out in a Report prepared by the Directorate of Justice in 1807 concerning the possibility of introducing the French Code Civil into force in the Duchy of Warsaw. The adoption of law, original or received, must reflect the will of the people and be adjusted, take into account the consequences thereof for the development of society: the "legislator takes into account good and evil arising from laws". The lawmaker must find a balance between laws and the interests of man, other peoples, and States/societies. Law must be changed

64 Kołłątaj, note 2 above, pp. 6, 10-11, 146.

65 Ibid., pp. 11, 74, 94, 210, 220.

66 Ibid., p. 125.

67 Ibid., pp. 146-147.

68 Ibid., pp. 141, 146-147.

69 Ibid., pp. 205-206.

70 Pomianowski, note 44 above, p. 116.

depending upon the intellectual and socio-economic development of a nation: "Laws are created for the happiness of societies". The lawmaker also should take into account the tradition and customs of a people to the extent that they do not interfere with the development of the last and change the habitual when necessary. In essential instances a people undertakes political revolutions and adopts laws corresponding to the changes in social relations.[71]

Prince Czartoryski wrote about the unacceptability of imposing a foreign, albeit better, law on a people as a breakdown of public will.[72] In 1810 the Warsaw Council referred to the inadmissibility of "betraying a person to law" which is not a manifestation of the will of his society.[73] Wyczechowski in 1809 and Karol Diehl (1765-1831) in 1811 saw under these conditions a manifestation of national will in the adaptation of received law and in lawmaking in spheres which such law did not cover: "We take advantage of the freedom accorded to us in order to adapt the Code to the requirements and customs of the country where circumstances require this and in the major objects".[74] Bieńkowski noted in 1814 that law must change in order to conform to "public opinion", the "wishes and interests of the inhabitants".[75] Later he wrote that the branches of law (except the supposedly universal civil law) must develop and reflect the "various relations of each country".[76]

Wyczechowski approached the issue of eliciting the social will broadly; it meant taking into account the opinions of courts, educational institutions, center of academic science (Society of the Friends of Science), voivodship councils and commissions,

[71] Konic, note 54 above, pp. 210-214; Kraushar, note 54 above, pp. 330-331.

[72] Kraushar, note 54 above, p. 332; M. Gałędek, "The Problem of Non-Adaptability of National Legal Heritage. Discussion on the Reform of Civil Law in Poland in the Course of Work of Reform Committee in 1814", *Romanian Journal of Comparative Law*, VIII, no. 1 (2017), p. 16.

[73] Grynwaser, "Kodeks Napoleona w Polsce", in Grynwaser, *Pisma* (Wroclaw, 1951), I, p. 59.

[74] Ibid., I, p. 39; J. J. Litauer, "Przeciwnicy Kodeksu", *Gazeta Sądowa Warszawska*, no. 22 (28 May 1908), pp. 363-367.

[75] Gałędek, Klimaszewska, and Ponianowski, "Prace Komitetu Cywilnego Reformy nad przygotowaniem narodowej kodyfikacji prawa cywilnego i procedury cywilnej w przededniu utworzenia Królestwa Polskiego (1814-1815) – edycja zrodlowa. Część I", *Krakowskie Studia z Historii Państwa i Prawa*, XII, no. 2 (2019), p. 272.

[76] Pomianowski, note 44 above, p. 122.

and consideration by parliament.[77] In Wyczechowski's view, the most appropriate modern form of law was codified legislation, which should ensure the national and systemic character of law. He unambiguously rejected a purely organic model for the development of law, pointing out that the creation of legislation is a conscious process of combining tradition with new principles and institutions with a view to the development of social relations.[78]

A Report of the State Council to the Sejm in 1818 called the development and consistent application of national legislation the "primary grounds of happiness of each people". With regard to content, law must be "impartially weighed", internally consistent, and correspond to the contemporary level of European development and simultaneously the distinctive features and requirements of the people. Such law exerts a reverse impact on the people: "A system of laws ... is capable of advancing them in the direction of social virtues and improvements".[79]

Prince F. Szaniawski observed back in 1808 that an obligatory property of law must be its "applicability to every possible subject-matter, links, and changes which occur daily in the human community", and also that legislation cannot provide for and assist for everything in each instance.[80] And so law, especially legislation, must be constantly developed consciously with a view at least to preserving conformity to social relations.

These ideas were elaborated by Szaniawski in later works. He noted that positive law by its nature is "individual, temporary, and local"; it should be changed according to circumstances which influence people and their social links, and this may lead both to the improvement or to the deterioration of law. Ultimately, he defines human / positive / civil law in a purely socio-volitional manner, and this is the "common will of society, which is ascertained by respective power in society". This somewhat narrower definition is explained by the fact that Szaniawski believed custom – which

[77] A. Zarzycka, "Próby zmian prawa rzeczowego z Kodeksu Napoleona w Królestwie Polskim w latach 1815-1818", *Krakowskie Studia z Historii Państwa i Prawa*, II (2008), p. 181.

[78] Gałędek and A. Klimaszewska, "A Controversial Transplant? Debate over the Adaptation of the Napoleonic Code on the Polish Territories in the Early 19th Century", *Journal of Civil Law Studies*, XI, no. 2 (2018), pp. 283, 286-287, 292.

[79] Zarzycka, note 77 above, pp. 190-191.

[80] Szaniawski, note 5 above, pp. 4-5.

also is positive law, a form which disappears and cedes place to legislation and judicial practice, and these forms are will-established. But Szaniawski's doctrine on law also contains in part the idea of organic development.[81]

Despite having a linguistic-cultural understanding of a people, Szaniawski believed that, as a rule, a people, society, and country should coincide: "Often those three expressions – a country, nation, and State – are used to designate a single concept". He defined a State primarily through the population: "people who comprise a unified significant ordered community having its own power, its own laws, its own force are called a State".[82]

It is not easy to call Szaniawski a "statist", for the State in his works is subordinate to society: "An individual good is the purpose of law, and a public good may be called a means leading to this purpose".[83] Therefore, law in a State does not lose its social character: "Laws coordinate the freedom of all members of the State and indicate the boundaries in its use", and subordination is merely a medicine for instances when "the state of the stable health of society" is disturbed.[84] The State and the people and society are not central to an understanding of lawmaking; Szaniawski placed the emphasis on man and his will.[85]

The volitional vision of lawmaking corresponded to Szaniawski's confidence in the primacy of human convictions from which are derived "various types of occupations, education, passions, inspirations, and customs of peoples".[86] Legislators must adopt law on the basis of a comprehensive knowledge of the needs, "local experience", and "state in general of those people with every point of view".[87] Another important element in Szaniawski's socio-volitional understanding of law was his assertion that societies arise earlier historically than law is established, and it must correspond to the development of society, exist within its limits as unified, general, homogeneous – for which lawmakers must

[81] Szaniawski, note 8 above, pp. 14, 20-21, 26, 29-30, 34, 54, 282; Szaniawski, note 4 above, pp. 70, 72.

[82] Szaniawski, note 8 above, pp. 36-37.

[83] Szaniawski, note 4 above, p. 19.

[84] Ibid., pp. 22-24, 28.

[85] Ibid., pp. 19-20, 22-24, 26, 35.

[86] Ibid., p. 70.

[87] Ibid., p. 71.

aspire.[88] Szaniawski expressed the idea of the sovereignty of each society / State. It was based on the fact that the creation and form of a State expressed the will of a certain discrete society.[89]

Beginning at least from 1812, Bandtkie traced in his works individual indicia of a volitional vision of national law. He believed that the customs of a people might evolve on the basis, over a lengthy period of time, of decrees of the authorities, and by the same volitional means might thereafter develop (and not only by organic evolutionary means).[90] He favored unity and systemicity, the codification of national legislation, which can be achieved only by volitional means, and wrote of the need for the constant renewal of legislation as social relations developed.[91] Contemporary law must give maximal autonomy to man in society, for the creation thereof required profound scientific knowledge, unity of thoughts, and decisiveness. Bandtkie cast doubt upon, although he did not emphasize this, the idea that each people at every moment is capable of creating law: "It is more complex for us than anywhere else now; that is, at least for the present generation to make laws well".[92] Nonetheless, Bandtkie unambiguously declared his monarchism under which national law must have a volitional, but not a social, origin.[93]

Beginning in 1827, Hube used the concept "system of legislation" of a State or people and also pointed to the history of legislation as the subject-matter of research, a scientific discipline.[94] He set out his own vision of the elements of the development of law: material (eternal and immutable problematic of law) and

[88] Ibid., pp. 74-76.

[89] Ibid., p. 57.

[90] Bandtkie, note 19 above (1812), p. 85; Bandtkie, "O uprawnieniu dzieci przez zaszly zwiazek malzenski czynionem", in Bandtkie, *Zbiór rospraw o przedmiotach prawa polskiego* (1812), p. 216.

[91] Bandtkie, note 19 above (1814), p. 10; Bandtkie, note 54 above, pp. 168-169, 171, 174; Bandtkie, "Co stanowi prawnika", *Pamiętnik Warszawski*, VI (1816), p. 324; J. J. Litauer, *Memorial J. W. Bandtkiego o prawie hipotecznym z roku 1818* (Warsaw, 1915), p. 65.

[92] Litauer, note 91 above, pp. 50, 63-65.

[93] Bandtkie, note 19 above (1814), p. 10.

[94] Hube, note 23 above (1827), I, p. 71; Hube, "Wywód praw spadkowych słowiańskich (Wywód spadków podług dawnych praw słowiańskich)", *Themis Polska*, VIII (1830), p. 454.

technical (development of form thereof).[95] Hube supported the idea expressed by Gans, among others, that each people is at any time capable of creating law for itself (especially legislation) by mobilizing knowledge and a common will. The legislative organ must express the general position of society, otherwise the results will be useless.[96] Hube favored the idea of national codification, provided that legislation would correspond to legal consciousness and the requirements of the people and to the constant development of social relations.[97]

The link between social relations and positive law in Hube's vision remained primarily unidirectional, the first generating and determining the second.[98] Nonetheless, the gradual development of man led to self-contemplation, his reason departed from custom, formed concepts, and "the more the power of thought matured and general [concepts] amalgamated, the stronger that idea penetrated, that he in and of itself might be legislator";[99] lawmaking becoming a volitional act, and the principal form of law becoming legislation.

Hoffman set out in 1828 a political understanding of the people (it dies away together with the State). He pointed out that historically at a certain stage of the development of a people political institutions begin to emerge, and they make law which becomes the experience of the people and over time the subject-matter of research and improvement by science. Political institutions and the law created by them create the character of the people and national legal doctrine.[100]

Zaborowski noted in 1829 that law is established by the will of public authority and "depends on the form of government and the dominant conceptions", political changes.[101] The historical genesis of society is linked with the fact that "an individual will ceded to the common will", and the emergence of legislation – with material political changes, the lack of social homogeneity,

95 Hube, note 23 above (1830), p. 51.

96 Hube, note 23 above (1829), pp. 298, 310.

97 Ibid., p. 325; Hube, note 23 above (1830), p. 34.

98 Hube, note 23 above (1830), p. 36.

99 Ibid., p. 38.

100 K. B. Hoffman, "O stanie nauki prawa w naszym kraju", *Themis Polska*, I (1828), pp. 1, 16, 27.

101 Z[aborowski], note 29 above, pp. 214-216.

and the need for changes in law.[102] He observed that norms arise from social conditions and needs, but "power is an obligatory condition of society", authoritative lawmaking is fundamental in society. To retain power in a national society is possible only with the assistance of institutions corresponding to the conceptions of this society.[103] But legislation also is capable of exerting a reverse influence on the legal conceptions dominant in society.[104] Nonetheless, Zaborowski followed von Savigny and asserted that there are eras in the development of a people unsuitable for the creation of new law – especially under conditions of a foreign law not assimilated and not contemplated by legal scholars.[105]

Heylman adhered to an organic theory of law but believed the volitional establishment of law to be justified if it corresponded to thought-out customs and judicial practice, the needs and consciousness of the people, when the political and technical elements of law are combined with and form "people's-scientific legislation".[106] In his view, legislation may be an "instance of earlier laws and customs", and in some peoples it may become even the principal form of law, perform a revolutionary function (as in France), leading to the unity of national law, or become a decisive form in the event of conflicts of law.[107] In supporting von Savigny's idea that "a people does not have a disposition for legislation in every period", Heylman favored the retention of received legislation in the Kingdom of Poland so long as it will not be considered or formulated as the basis and notion of a national codification of law.[108]

In 1829 Maciejowski cast doubt on the ability to create codified legislation at any moment on national grounds, unlike individual norms, but on the whole believed it was an orientator for all peoples to be achieved at a certain level of development of legal

[102] Z[aborowski], "Jurysprudencya sądu kassacyinego Xięswa Warszawskiego i związek instytucyi kassacyinéy z ogólném życiem prawném w kraju", *Themis Polska*, VI (1829), p. 362.

[103] Zaborowski, note 29 above, pp. 216-219, 221-222, 225; Zaborowski, note 102 above, pp. 363, 366-367, 371.

[104] Zaborowski, note 29 above, p. 239-240; Zaborowski, note 102 above, p. 365.

[105] Zaborowski, note 102 above, pp. 368-369.

[106] Heylman, note 35 above, p. 5-6, 18-19, 26-29.

[107] Ibid., pp. 29, 33, 39.

[108] Heylman, "Myśli o nauce prawa i prawodawstwie w kraiu naszym", *Themis Polska*, VII (1830), pp. 111, 125, 130-131.

science and education: "Those individual parts to be gathered into a whole and linked by the node which creates the unity and, so to say, a harmony in the entire work; in fact this is a matter of art, and having command of such an art is neither easy nor rapidly achieved".[109]

One manifestation of the socio-volitional understanding of national law was an enthusiastic perception of the new paternalist State which, in the words of Węgrzecki in 1810, was comprehensively concerned about and improved society, "ensures that all evil in society was terminated".[110] Małachowski developed the idea of civil patriotism in an address to the Senate in 1809: "the zeal of the civil spirit devoted itself to serving the country".[111] Bieńkowski observed that, historically, with the transition from a state of nature to a national society people give away their freedom to power in order to defend personal and property rights.[112]

The socio-volitional understanding of State and law during the period here considered sometimes acquired an openly statist interpretation. Józef Maria Hoene-Wroński (1776-1853) wrote in 1818 about the supremacy of the State consciousness of a person over a national consciousness, about patriotism as "complete loyalty to the affairs of State" which is higher than the national spirit as love for the motherland, and also on the State as an individual.[113] Wojciech Bogumił Jastrzębowski (1799-1882) wrote in 1831 that peoples would gradually die out within the States.[114]

During the period here considered, the socio-volitional theory of national law was well developed in the works of Warsaw legal scholars. The basis thereof was the presumption of the conscious creation of a nation by a collective will which also provided the possibility of termination of the existence or the rebirth of a

[109] W. Maciejowski, "Ogłoszenie prenumeraty", *Themis Polska,* V (1829), pp. 417, 419-420; Maciejowski, "Uwagi nad artukułem 960 K.C.", *Themis Polska,* VII (1830), p. 324.

[110] Galędek, "Does War Deepen Distrust Toward the State? Reorientation of Polish Political Thought under the Influence of the Napoleonic Wars", *Del Siglio XIX al XXI. Tendencias y debates: XIV Congreso de la Associación de Historia Contemporánea, Universidad de Alicante 20-22 de septiembre de 2018* (Alicante, 2019), pp. 1754-1755.

[111] Mowa, note 60 above, p. 298.

[112] Gałędek, note 72 above, p. 24.

[113] Wierzbicki, note 58 above, p. 53.

[114] Ibid., pp. 55-56, 59-60.

nation by the respective absence or presence of the will of society. Without denying the objective prerequisites of national life such as language, customs, and others, the socio-volitional theory placed the principal emphasis on the targeted formation of political institutions and national law as the realization of individual and collective freedom.

This approach enabled one to assert the changeability and temporary nature of law, its dynamic, to advance the requirement of its constant renewal in order to ensure conformity to the development of social relations, queries, and ideals of the people or, on the contrary, to assist the development of these relations. The possibility was presupposed of both evolutionary and revolutionary modernization of law, a close or remote orientator becoming the codification thereof as a form of achieving systemicity and rationality. The volitional origin of law substantiated the equality of peoples as bearers of social will and the sovereignty of society / nation / State as the realization of this will, the unacceptability of the forced export of law because of the freedom of a people to autonomously determine its own legal life.

The requirement of the statehood of a people, the coincidence of people, country, and State, was integral to the socio-volitional theory of law. But the question of the subject of the realization of the social will in lawmaking remained open. For some legal scholars this was the State, absorbing society, and for others – the politically organized society itself. Ultimately, of importance in principle was the definition of national law – a creation of the common will of society – as a whole, a legal particular.

One of the issues most discussed during the period here considered was the correlation of the political and technical elements in law, which means in fact the correlation and interaction of will and tradition, volitional and organic factors of lawmaking. The socio-volitional and organic theories viewed the nomenclature of these elements and their correlation differently. From this followed different answers to the sacramental question of the capacity of a people for lawmaking under certain or any conditions. In the vision of proponents of the socio-volitional theory, law might always be created, whereas for proponents of the organic theory – only when harmony existed between the people's legal consciousness and lawmaking.

§3.3. Organic Theory of National Law

The organic theory of national law, just as the socio-volitional theory, developed in European legal thought during the second half of the eighteenth and first third of the nineteenth centuries. It also suggested a vision of national law as a unit of legal development, a totality which removed in itself the individual and the subjective law thereof. This theory was based on a consideration of the nation as a natural population, but also endowed with a number of social and ethno-cultural characteristics and a socio-psychological unity. Within the framework of such a vision, lawmaking is part of the life of a nation and always accompanied the development thereof irrespective of State-building, although the last was regarded as an indicator of maturity of a nation. This does not deny the idea of a social will, but makes the last derivative and determined, one manifestation and consequence of the vitality of a nation, and not constitutive thereof, rejects the social will and the State as a value in and of themselves, and subordinates the State to itself. The organic theory created more consistently the grounds for the consideration of national legal experiences as equal in character and individuality, and the respective national legal orders – as non-incidental phenomena and prolonged in time. To a great degree the organic theory provided not only for formal autonomy, but also a substantive distinctiveness of national legal experience, considering this in inextricable unity with the spiritual and cultural calling and development of the nation.[115]

As Rosner noted, after the Partitions of the *Rzecz Pospolita* the conviction was formed in the course of length debates that the people is not only a political community, but also a cultural-linguistic community and might develop also in the event of the loss of the State.[116] Wierzbicki believed that this view during the first third of the nineteenth century became "axiomatic for the majority of ideological-political currents" on Polish lands.[117]

115 Kresin, note 1 above, II, pp. 336-337.

116 A. Rosner, "'Nauka prawa ... stała się nieuchronnie potrzebną nie tylko przez swą użyteczność, lecz obowiązki, jakie nas łączą w obywatelskim stanie'. O tradycji i nowoczesności w nauczaniu i prawa w Księstwie Warszawskim i Królestwie Polskim (1807-1830)", *Krakowskie Studia z Historii Państwa i Prawa*, VIII (2015), p. 232.

117 Wierzbicki, note 58 above, p. 66.

The cultural-linguistic idea of the nation to a greater degree than the socio-volitional theory enabled the Polish-ness to be identified under conditions of non-statehood, and then non-sovereign statehood, proclaimed the immanence and continuity of lawmaking irrespective of its political institutionalization, but moved away from the said old understanding of the people and required reflection on the geographical and ethnographic limits of the Polish people. Once again we turn to Grynwaser, who alleged the absence of attempts to reflect on cultural-linguistic particularity and the fully-fledged character of "serf" cultures of the Lithuanians, Belorussians, and Ukrainians, whose ethnic lands were part of the *Rzecz Pospolita*: "only the elite of society were seen – the *szlachta*, and that was Polish and no national or religious differences were proclaimed: the existence thereof did not advance the nationality question". In Polish legal thought an unequivocal ideal was advanced of the restoration of the *Rzecz Pospolita* within its old boundaries before 1772, namely as the Polish State.[118] Kołłątaj regarded the Ukrainian, Belorussian, and even the Lithuanian lands as provinces of Poland: "A change of names of those parts will make it possible to happily forget all the ancient disagreement and perpetual anarchy: no one will be any longer a Lithuanian, Prussian, Volynian, Podolian, Kyivan, Rusyn, and so on – they will all be Poles".[119]

To be sure, such a "nationalization" of the common heritage was a step backward even in comparison with the practice of the *Rzecz Pospolita* itself, which consistently was regarded as the creation of the Polish and Lithuanian peoples, and also as the aggregate of historical States enumerated in the royal title. Moreover, the 1791 Constitution proclaimed in Article 1 that Roman Catholicism was the dominant religion in the State, which concisely pointed to the preservation of an exclusive understanding of the Polish people and its culture and the absence of any aspiration to integrate any representatives of other confessional ethnic-religious groups therein.[120] Later this position was reflected in an explanatory memorandum to the draft Book One of the Civil Code of the Polish Kingdom, where the Tatars were recognized among the ethno-religious groups as fully assimilated and "equal participants in the

[118] Grynwaser, note 52 above, I, p. 195.

[119] Kołłątaj, note 2 above, pp. 180, 183.

[120] Note 51 above, p. 4.

exercise of civil-law, political, and civil rights", and the rights of Jews were to be determined by the policy of the State with respect to them and subject to special administrative regulation.[121]

We illustrate the in essence cultural-linguistic organic understanding of the nation from notable works whose authors were not jurists. Samuil Bogumił Linde (1771-1847) in an introduction to volume one of his Dictionary of the Polish Language, wrote in 1807 about the "renewed national spirit", the most valuable hallmark of which was the Polish language.[122] Kazimierz Brodziński (1791-1835) wrote in 1831 that the national spirit, an "innate idea", and a calling were given by God to the nation when it was emerging. All members of the people are part thereof as a living organism or, at least, a unified family, united by aspirations, ideas, and feelings, and also historically forms a unified character and abilities. But Brodziński reiterated the well-known thesis of the death of a people together with the loss of statehood.[123]

Maurycy Mochnatski (1803-1834) noted that the nation is above all a moral community, the "aggregate of all its notions, concepts, and feelings correspond to religion, political institutions, legislation, and laws", and its historical existence is a "continuous process of self-awareness".[124] Adam Z. Czarnocki (1784-1825) (the pseudonym of Z. Ia. Dolenga-Khodakovskii) observed that the sole bearer of a nationality is the simple people who preserve the spiritual link with the pre-Christian era – the time when the nations were born, and only folk culture may be considered to be national.[125]

Czacki pointed in 1800 to the value of preserving national law, which over time should pass from the form of customary law to legislation: "The merit of retaining, thinking over, or establishing laws is the fruit of a higher illumination and profound

[121] K. Sójka-Zielińska, *Wielkie kodyfikacje cywilne. Historia i współczesność* (Warsaw, 2009), p. 263.

[122] S. Dubisz, "Samuil Bogumił Linde 1771-1847", *Portrety uczonych. Profesorowie Uniwersytetu Warszawskiego 1816-1915* (Warsaw, 2016), p. 331.

[123] Brodziński, note 63 above, pp 14-28.

[124] Польша и Россия в первой трети XIX века. Из истории автономного Королевства Польского. 1815-1830 [Poland and Russia in the First Third of the XIX Century. From the History of the Autonomous Kingdom of Poland. 1815-1830] (Moscow, 2010), pp. 420, 445.

[125] Ibid., pp. 443-444.

intelligence".[126] In 1807 J. K. Szaniawski called for "identifying the indicia inherent in our nationality, as well as their primary embryo from which our tribe has to develop in evolutionary and the natural way directed to its further callings", to quests for the national spirit.[127]

Elements of an organic approach to national law are visible in 1808 in the work of Kołłątaj. He drew a parallel, widely practiced in those times, between the life of a people and human life: peoples in their development pass through periods of childhood, adult life, and old age, after which supposedly death ensues. This overlaps with the idea of the historical development of the enlightenment of peoples and mankind as a whole. There are universal similarities in the development of peoples, especially the movement of all people towards freedom. But each people has individual primary customs, a dynamic and direction of development determined by its allocation. The gradual development of the customs of peoples correspond to these social changes. Customs historically are the principal source of law; they are linked inseparably with the language, law consciousness (thought), and character of the people. This link is inextricable and must be preserved irrespective of the forms which law acquires. The failure of legal and other reforms to conform to these phenomena leads to the degeneration of a people. Attempts to create a multinational State in the long term are futile.[128] Radical changes in the life of a people, however, may lead to its rebirth, in which the language is preserved, but a new character and initial group of customs, law, and political institutions may be formed.[129]

Prince F. Szaniawski defined a people through language, customs, and the continuity of people living on a single territory. He pointed to the normalcy of the coincidence of the scope of a people, country, and State, but emphasized the different significance and role of these concepts. He appealed to the idea of the stages in the development of law put forward, in particular, by Hugo and Savigny. Szaniawski stressed the positive character of customary law, its development begins from from individual

126 Czacki, note 56 above, II, p. 290.

127 J. K. Szaniawski, *Korespondencja w materiach obraz kraju i narodu polskiego rozjaśniających* (Warsaw, 1807), I, pp. 1-2; Wierzbicki, note 58 above, p. 69.

128 Kołłątaj, note 2 above, pp. 98-99, 114, 119, 141, 143, 147, 184, 205, 207, 209.

129 Ibid., pp. 146-147, 220.

decisions and thanks to experience, the comparison of individual prescriptions leads to the formation of general principles from which contemporary norms are extracted.[130] But he denied the existence of innate popular customs and believed that these arose in the process of social development. With the development of a people, the volume of law necessary for the regulation of social relations grows. Law always should correspond to the level of enlightenment of a people, its customs, experience, and socio-economic development. Therefore it is desirable that a State be national, for this enables the State to form a unified law.[131]

Bandtkie no later than 1812 set out a theory of the customary origin of law independently of the State ("often custom once embedded ... has an authority higher than any laws and, squeezed out from its home, returns by stealth along another road"), and also its evolutionary development with the gradual generalization of customary law and judicial practice is in the legislation of the State with later codification thereof. Customary law he postulated to be absolutely positive and social; that is, belonging to a concrete *socium*, derivative from its experience and way of thinking, and also not as the past and hardened, but as dynamic and renewable through judicial practice and prescriptions of the authorities accepted by society and passing into custom: "custom, which is long-standing and often renewed, acquires a customary binding force and becomes essential".[132] Bandtkie was of the opinion that law grows from socio-economic development of the *socium* and simultaneously determines the development thereof.[133]

All the same, in Bandtkie's view, historically the complexity of social relations and the professionalization of legal activity gradually led to judicial practice becoming an autonomous source of law having scientific grounds, although it remained linked with custom.[134] Bandtkie supported the professionalization of

[130] Szaniawski, note 8 above, pp. 30, 36-37, 54.

[131] Szaniawski, note 4 above, pp. 16, 23-24, 59, 70-76.

[132] Bandtkie, note 90 above, pp. 251, 258; Bandtkie, "O karze śmierci na kradzież stanowionéy rzecz podług praw kraiowych uwazana", in J. W. Bandtkie, *Zbiór rospraw o przedmiotach prawa polskiego* (Warsaw, 1812), p. 276; Bandtkie, note 19 above (1812), pp. 23, 28-29, 43-44, 46-48, 50-51, 85, 90, 120; Bandtkie, note 19 above (1814), pp. 28-29; Bandtkie, note 91 above, p. 311-312.

[133] Bandtkie, note 19 above (1814), pp. 28, 34; Bandtkie, note 91 above, p. 324.

[134] Bandtkie, note 19 above (1814), pp. 5-6, 14; Bandtkie, note 91 above, pp. 324-325.

legislative activity and emphasized the need for stable and ordered legislation.[135] Just as many other jurists of his time, he upheld the idea of the stages of the development of law – customary, academic, and legislative.[136]

Bandtkie underscored that the subject-matter of the history of law should be above all the law of the people and only as a last resort the law of the authorities; he accentuated the "consistency uninterrupted over the centuries of the state of national administration, laws, and customs" and the cultural-linguistic vision of the people.[137] He used anthropological discourse to explain the development of the peoples as individuals: "Peoples, as individual personalities in society".[138] In his view, law to a great extent was derivative from the character of the people, the national spirit.[139]

Bandtkie pointed out that the systematization of the law of a people might be conditioned historically by various circumstances: external threats, need to defend against foreign impacts or influence already undertaken, material changes in the world, legal doctrine, and so on.[140] However, as we mentioned in another context, Bandtkie noted that customary law may arise on the basis of decrees of the authorities: "Laws may fully become customs of a people and achieve the final purpose of any legislation".[141] Moreover, he believed that the content of will-established national law (including received) may thereafter be transformed by customary means – through doctrine and judicial practice.[142]

[135] Bandtkie, note 19 above (1814), pp. 10-13; Bandtkie, "O poważaniu dawnieyszém w Polszcze prawników uczonych", *in Posiedzenie publiczne Królewskiego-Warszawskiego Uniwersytetu, na uczczenie pamiątki uczonych mężow, a mianowicie polakow, odbyte dnia 15 lipca 1825 roku* (Warsaw, 1825), pp. 36, 39-40.

[136] Bandtkie, note 91 above, pp. 311-312.

[137] Bandtkie, note 19 above (1812), pp. iii, 1, 145.

[138] Ibid., pp. 55, 174; Bandtkie, note 19 above (1814), pp. 5, 7; Bandtkie, note 91 above, pp. 311-312.

[139] Bandtkie, "O karze", note 132 above, pp. 287-289.

[140] Bandtkie, note 19 above (1812), pp. 48, 90, 120; Bandtkie, note 91 above, pp. 215-217, 248, 251; Bandtkie, note 54 above, pp. 173-174; Bandtkie, note 135 above, pp. 39-40.

[141] Bandtkie, note 54 above, pp. 173-174; Bandtkie, note 91 above, p. 312; Litauer, note 91 above, pp. 52-53, 62, 64-66.

[142] Bandtkie, note 19 (1812) above, pp. 85, 94, 112, 116, 118, 141, 173-176, 198; Bandtkie, note 90 (1812) above, pp. 216, 264; Bandtkie, "O karze", note 132 above, pp. 274, 285-286; Bandtkie, note 54 above, pp. 170-173.

In a Report of the State Council to the Sejm in 1818 it was noted that national law should be the "fruit of experience, conscious need, and long contemplations and analysis", and the imposition thereof is inadmissible; this violates the "path of improvement of own national laws" peculiar to the people.[143]

Rakowiecki observed that the people is the subject of legal development, and law is part of its culture and reflects the character thereof and the national spirit in the development thereof.[144] Law, just as other elements of culture, develops organically and is part of the undertaking of a special mission determined by God for each concrete people.[145] The primary basis of law, so to say, primeval law, emanates from the people as a whole, is customary, and cannot be the result of the activities of the authorities. Thus, legislation from the outset represents the ordering of customary law, its adaptation to certain times and circumstances. Law exerts a reverse influence on social links and also acts as a factor in nation-building.[146]

Hube pointed out that law has always had and has a social, national character (together with inter-subject lawmaking). A people, in his view, is a natural union, arises by way of the combining of families and clans, grows, matures, declines, and then disappears; the preservation of the people and its law is an absolute value.[147] The people is an organic whole, dominates the individual, and national law dominates the inter-subjective and particular.[148] But ultimately a people and the law thereof are

143 Zarzycka, note 77 above, pp. 190-191.

144 I. B. Rakowiecki, *O stanie cywilnym dawnych slowian. Rzech czytana na publiczném posiedzeniu Towarzystwa Królewskiego Warszawskiego Przyiacoł Nauk dnia 3 Maia 1820 roku* (Warsaw, 1820), pp. 2-3, 15; Rakowiecki, *Prawda ruska; czyli, Prawa wielkiego xięcia Jaroslawa Władymirowicza, tudziez traktaty Olga y Igora ww. xx. kiiowskich z cesarzami greckimi, y Mścisława Dawidowicza x. Smoleńskiego z Rygą zawarte, których texta, obok z polskiém tłomaczeniem poprzedza Rys historyczny zwyczaiów, obyczaiów religiy, praw y języka dawnych słowiańskich y slowiańsko-ruskich narodow* (Warsaw, 1820), I, p. i, viii, 81-82, 139, 198, 227-228, 242-243, 245, 253; II, 315.

145 Rakowiecki, O stanie, note 144 above, pp. 7, 15-16.

146 Rakowiecki, Prawda, note 144 above, I, pp. 135, 137-138; II, 156.

147 Hube, «История древнего наследственного права у славян» [History of Medieval Inheritance Law Among the Slavs], in Сборник исторических и статистических сведений о России и народах ей единоверных и единоплеменных [Collection of Historical and Statistical Information on Russia and Peoples of the Same Faith and Tribes] (1845), I, pp. 61-63, 73, 76-77, 80, 82-83.

148 Ibid., I, pp. 61-64, 77.

formalized as a result of national State-building (transition from a family to a civil order). Without losing its national essence, law is transformed materially and exerts a reverse influence on its creator – the people, uniting and developing it.[149]

In Hube's view, the historical development of law is an evolutionary and gradual process of cause and effect generated by the development of society/people and determined by the entire aggregate of its life, the "mutual requirements of all individuals", their ideas, spirit, "common feeling": "Positive law should emanate from the life of the people and return to the path of [its] life".[150] Even during an era of revolutionary changes, law retains its connection with national tradition, customary law, national spirit, character, and morality. Hube set out a theory of the evolution of regulatory forms, beginning with theological prescriptions to custom and to scientifically-substantiated legislation, but namely custom (together with judicial practice) in his doctrine is the first form of law proper and does not disappear, although cedes somewhat to the "authority of understanding" embodied in legislation.[151] The political essence of legislation is virtually ignored in this theory.

Custom is the principal historical form of positive law, a "product of joint human activity relating to the ordering of social links" which in the contemporary world is embodied as judicial practice, namely an expression of the legal life of the people and a source of the creation of legislation – the legislator generalizes the grounds thereof on a scientific basis without disturbing the link of norms with the "legal relations of the people".[152] As Hube affirmed, customs are the simple "slow appropriation" of the fundamentals of the life of society as its "common booty", without reliance on the force of the inner conviction of people, although they "have the authority of time and general recognition of usefulness"; they generate a "profound feeling of adherence", and judicial practice

[149] Ibid., I, pp. 64, 92, 100, 104.

[150] Hube, note 25 above (1827), I, p. 10; Hube, note 23 above (1829), pp. 297-298, 302, 308, 310-312, 325, 335; Hube, note 23 above (1830), I, pp. 36-38.

[151] Hube, note 25 above (1827), I, pp. 7, 10; Hube, note 23 above (1829), pp. 309-310; Hube, note 23 above (1830), pp. 35, 37.

[152] Hube, note 25 above (1827), I, p. 12; Hube, note 23 above (1829), pp. 298-299, 301, 303-304, 311, 335; Hube, note 23 above (1830), pp. 37-38, 42.

and especially legislation are a product of the awareness of these fundamentals.[153]

Therefore, legislation is not arbitrary because it "also rests upon customs, but on customs understood and thought through"; a "code is the mirror of the legal life of a people", whereas customs lose their authority after the creation of legislation.[154] Legislation brings an abstract form and system to the law of society.[155] Legislation is derivative and should fully reflect national grounds; otherwise it will not enter the legal life of the people and the last will proceed along its own path and be embodied in judicial practice, and it will adapt, ignore, or conflict with the legislation.[156]

Judicial practice does not lose its importance with the emergence of legislation; it constantly develops and is even capable of rectifying a situation under conditions when laws prove to be arbitrary (for example, certain received laws): "after all, the social life of a people remains independent of the acceptance thereof virtually the same as before. Judicial practice follows life".[157] In any event, the social legal order of which customs and judicial practice are expressions is primary, self-sufficient, and preserves its dominance after the creation of the State: "Common social life does not ask about laws, it follows its inherent path, and only then can laws cope with it or ennoble it, if they correspond to the general feeling and affect it".[158] Hube affirmed that each people is capable of creating laws for itself at any time, but for this the join efforts of scholars, courts, and legislators are essential, and reliance on national legal experience and concepts.[159]

Zaborowski concisely declared an organic vision of the development of law which he considered to be undoubted and accepted by representatives of the historical and historical-philosophical schools: "law, just as human language, has its own beginning, growth, and is improved in accordance with the requirements and civilization of a country". In his view, legal

153 Hube, note 23 above (1829), p. 304; Hube, note 23 above (1830), pp. 37-38, 51.

154 Hube, note 23 above (1829), pp. 304, 325.

155 Hube, note 23 above (1830), p. 43.

156 Hube, note 23 above (1829), pp. 307-309, 312, 325; Hube, note 23 above (1830), p. 36.

157 Hube, note 23 above (1829), p. 308; Hube, note 23 above (1830), p. 44.

158 Hube, note 23 above (1829), pp. 308, 311-312; Hube, note 23 above (1830), p. 38.

159 Hube, note 23 above (1829), pp. 298-299, 310.

life "pours out in a people and, just as in the physical existence of an individual, has its own organs in courts, legislation, and legal scholars". At the same time, despite mention of an "imiplicit feeling" innate in a people of good and evil, he believed that law is born and is gradually developed by society (especially through social power), is inextricably linked with all elements of the consciousness of a people and its political institutions, arises from social conditions, requirements, and aspirations, and is embodied primarily in customs that the legislator should take into account. If they are not taken into account, the adopted legislation is ignored by society so long as the courts by their decisions do not adapt and assimilate it. Zaborowski believed that a people is not capable of lawmaking at every period of its development.[160]

Zaborowski defined legal life as the aggregate of legal conceptions of society/people which developed in an evolutionary way.[161] Judicial practice, legislation, and legal doctrine are sources of law and manifestations of legal life.[162] Social and legal life, in his view, historically arose simultaneously and were linked with the origin of courts: "When courts work, it is evident that the will of one cedes to the common will".[163] He described political power not as State power, but as social power.[164]

Legislation emerged later, when political changes and social conflicts also required changes in the law. Finally, the need for a rethinking of law, the generalization and systematization thereof, lead to the creation of scholarly doctrine.[165] Both legislation and scientific legal doctrine did not sever the link with the people's legal consciousness (or common conviction), but merely formalized it:

> It seems that what the people is convinced of and what lives in its conviction, only this does the legislator give the seal of continuity and power; that the thoughts taken from among the people, digested by the legislator, sanctified by

[160] Zaborowski, note 29 above, pp. 213-216, 219, 221-222, 238-239; Zaborowski, note 102 above, pp. 361-368, 371, 373.

[161] Zaborowski, note 102 above, pp. 361, 370; Zaborowski, note 29 above, p. 213.

[162] Zaborowski, note 102 above, p. 361.

[163] Ibid., p. 362.

[164] Ibid., p. 366.

[165] Ibid., p. 362.

> the manifestation of the common will, return anew to the people, seeking a new sanction in its impressions.[166]

One element of progress is the reverse impact which legislation and scientific legal doctrine render (thanks to which law "harmonizes with the spirit of the time") on legal consciousness and the legal practices of the people/society.[167]

Dramatic events in the life of peoples (especially political and foreign legal influences) disturb the harmony of such complex legal development. In this event legislation may be ignored by society, judicial practice, and legal scholars, for coercion in and of itself does not generate moral consequences but may also be gradually "assimilated". But harmony in each instances sooner or later is restored each time.[168]

Judicial practice remained, in Zaborowski's view, a key element in the support and restoration of harmony in the legal life of society and a major source of law. It must be stable and uniform, harmonized, response to the convictions of the people, and enliven legal life – this is the highest purpose of courts.[169]

Zaborowski followed German jurists and in one year developed with Lerminier his vision of the elements of positive law. In Zaborowski's the political element of law encompassed the part of law arising directly from the life of the people/society (for example, family law) and the political development thereof, and the technical element "is formed more by the works of legal scholars and experiences less the influence of political changes in the country" (for example, the doctrine on obligations).[170]

In articles published between 1829 and 1830, Heylman wrote about the people as an organism which has its own mission. He pointed to the innateness of customary law in each people (together with language and social order), which is indestructible and develops, *inter alia,* in the form of judicial decisions in an evolutionary manner and irrespective of the State as an "organic whole". A professionalization occurs after the customary era

166 Ibid., pp. 363, 366, 371.

167 Ibid., pp. 365, 370.

168 Ibid., pp. 363-365, 367-369, 371.

169 Ibid., p. 373.

170 Ibid., p. 366.

in law (not only in the law of an individual society, but in international law), and lawmaking passes into the hands of jurists and later, thanks to them, legislation arises (or, respectively, contractual regimes). He stressed that the grounds of legislation and scientific legal doctrine should rest on customs, requirements, convictions, aspirations, morality, the spirit of the people (all these factors evolve). National scientific doctrine should be the basis of legislation, which personifies a carefully thought over customary law. If legislation does not correspond to thought over customary law, it exists in parallel with the last and is gradually transformed and assimilated by courts. At the same time, thanks to legislation and doctrine, the law of a society is reconsidered and modernized, gradually becomes a whole, systemic. The people are not capable of creating their own legislation in each period. Custom and judicial practice as sources of law do not lose their significance. In particular, the "practical development of positive law occurs daily in the courts".[171]

Of interest is Heylman's idea that the political element of law (law in the people's conviction, according to Savigny) may in the doctrine of the historical school be considered to be a variation of the idea of natural law but at the same time customary law created on the basis of this element is positive by virtue of its being binding.[172] Heylman also embodied the political element in parliament as a lawmaking agency, and the technical element (law of jurists) – in courts; he believed that these elements in the law of each people correlate variously. In his view, a new instance of legal life is observed in post-revolutionary France, where the political and technical elements combined; the political element performed a revolutionary function, having made the law of the people uniform, legislation became "popular-scientific", and the technical element became uniform by means of introducing the court of cassation and its interpretation of law, which led to a "continuous and full life of mutuality between the people and a court proceeding".[173]

In 1829 Maciejowski wrote about cognition in the history of an individual national law of the birth, development, and

[171] Heylman, note 35 above, pp. 2-6, 12-21, 25-29, 33-34, 44-45, 51; Heylman, note 109 above, pp. 111, 117, 122-125, 128, 130-132.

[172] Heylman, note 35 above, pp. 15-18.

[173] Ibid., pp. 27-29, 33-35, 39, 48-49.

improvement of its spirit and "grounds".[174] Legislation is the highest form of the development of national law, but it must to derivative from and subordinate to the people's legal life.[175]

In his history of Slavic legislation, Maciejowski advanced as a subject of legal development solely a people, to be sure in connection with the legal family to which it belongs (this will be considered by us separately).[176] Despite the possibility suggested by Maciejowski of the existence of national law before the formation of the State, he constantly emphasized that the national State and national-State law were the sole possible path of legal development, and legislative positivization of law is a natural function: "to give law not only to oneself, but also to others, is natural". Therefore, the history of law which is born of the spirit of the people, in Maciejowski's view, begins with its codification and adoption by the State. This process merely deepens its national character: without the sanction of the State, law is powerless. General and recognized legislation with the limits of an entire people positively affects its further development, the courts do not simply apply it, but they discover therein shortcomings for further rectification by the legislator and perform an educational function. In and of itself the consistent use by Maciejowski of the terms "prawodawstwo" and "ustawodawstwo" (both we translate as legislation) instead of "prawo" (law) and the definition of national law as the law of a country unambiguously point to its positive, territorial, and State character, and not only to its ethnic and customary character.[177] The combining of positiveness and the "nationality" of law Maciejowski defined thus: monuments of law "are not the matter of arbitrariness of the lawgiver, but arise from legal images and [level of development] of the enlightenment of the people".[178]

Thus, the notion of the nation as a moral essence, a natural union, and at the same time a metaphorical organism similar to the human organism, an "organic whole" absorbing man and embracing his interests and aspirations was characteristic of the organic theory of State law in the works of Warsaw legal scholars

174 Maciejowski, note 108 above (1829), p. 414, 416-417, 419.

175 Ibid., note 108 above (1830), p. 234.

176 Maciejowski, *Historya prawodawstw słowiańskich* (Warsaw, 1832-1835), I, pp. iii, vi, and others.

177 Ibid., I, pp. vi, vii, viii, 6, 36-37, 43.

178 Ibid., I, p. 51.

during the period here considered. Social order and public power generate a State; it is an essential stage in the development of the nation. But the State always is subordinate to national society.

The determinative characteristics and simultaneously the factors of the development of a people are the language thereof, psychology (character, spirit, mentality, legal consciousness), and customs. The view of scholars relative to their origin differ. Some asserted that all these characteristics were acquired in the process of the self-development of the people. In the vision of others, they are innate; this presupposes a certain essentialism of their ideas approaching a metaphysics of natural law.

In the vision of proponents of the organic theory, the development of the law of a people is evolutionary. Even revolutions may not terminate the dependence of positive law on national legal consciousness. Just as in the case of a living organism, the development here has a certain succession from birth to death. The stages of the development of lawmaking and systems of sources of law are identical for all peoples and correspond to the stages of national development. The doctrine on these was perceived by Polish legal scholars initially from the works of Hugo even before the formation of the German historical school of law by Savigny. According to the Polish interpretation of Hugo, the gradual acquisition of experience and the generalization thereof is the basis of evolutionary development. Accordingly, from the outset law existed in customary form, subsequently it is generalized, and the sphere of legal activity is professionalized, and judicial practice, scientific doctrine, and legislation emerge.

New sources of law always remain derivative from national legal consciousness, generalized and contextualized by legal science. Therefore, judicial practice and scientific doctrine are more important than legislation; they are a contemporary form of customary law, a rethinking of custom. Legislation should be generated by the social will and also reflect the aspirations of the people. In this event it is capable of exerting a reverse impact on the people, and legislative norms are transformed into customs. If it has a self-willed character – for example, when foreign law is imposed – it remains inactive so long as judicial practice and scientific doctrine do not transform the content thereof in the process of application. No doubt the organic theory to a greater degree than the socio-volitional assumed the distinctiveness of national law, and not only its formal solitariness from others.

§3.4. Distinctive Elements of National Law

The formal solitariness of a national legal order, determined on one hand by the will of national society and, on the other, by international law, does not explain the substantive lack of identity of legal orders – they might have been regarded as deeply utilitarian, functional divisions of a law common to all people (irrespective of origin and character – divine, natural, reason). The question arose of the substantive individuality (or distinctiveness) of each national legal order – its unique elements and peculiarities of its common elements (disseminated in more than one legal order).

The notion of the distinctiveness of national law derived primarily from the organic theory of national law, emphasizing the essential role of self-development in the evolution of a people. During the period here considered, legal scholars advanced the thesis of the insufficiency of the influence of immutable natural and climatic conditions and to a significant degree the requirements and economy of peoples derivative therefrom which act as a framework of the possible in the process of the development of a people whose culture and self-awareness these limitations cognize and are juxtaposed thereto. Social life was regarded as free and self-determined, and law, as an integral element thereof within the framework of a cultural tradition and manifestation of its consciousness and comprehension.

The grounds of principle in understanding distinctiveness in law of legal scholars then were: the historicity of distinctive elements in national law determined by social development in concrete conditions, fully or basically rejecting their substantionality; the impossibility at least with respect to their own societies and States of the existence of absolutely autochthonic law in the contemporary world, the insufficiency of the distinctive, and also in principle the openness of legal systems to interaction; the dependence of the expansion or the narrowing of the sphere of distinctive elements in national law on the will of society and other factors, the possibility of alternative variants of development of this sphere; the impossibility of national law being completely deprived of its distinctive elements without the termination of its existence, and the necessity thereof.[179]

[179] Kresin, note 1 above, II, p. 337.

One of the topics that attracted Warsaw jurists during the first third of the nineteenth century was the distinctiveness or uniformity of the content of national legal orders. The significance of this topic was clearly felt in the words of Prince Czartoryski: the originality of law is linked with the qualities of a people; when losing legal distinctiveness, a people partly loses itself.[180] A Polish dictionary from those times most correlated distinctiveness with the word "nationality" (narodowość), understood as a "national peculiarity which distinguishes one people from another".[181]

Czacki noted in works published between 1800 and 1809 that the sources of individuality in national law are the spirit thereof (including the spirit of government), customs, and special conscious requirements, but the development of law in significant measure was the same as the development of the language of a people.[182] He had an organic view of the people, which individually pass through all stages in its development.[183] Law is an integral part of the culture of a people (not only something derivative from culture, but in mutual connection therewith).[184] In his view, the arising of law "from the cradle of the customary existence of peoples" and the gradual self-improvement thereof "with a change of the requirements and opinions". And the evolutionary transition from customary law to legislation was a normal path of law.[185] Czacki believed that the legislator should be oriented towards custom and judicial practice formed within the people but, to be sure, doubted the originality thereof, pointing out that often they were borrowed.[186]

Preservation of the individuality of national law, in Czacki's view, might, *inter alia*, be connected with a practical conflict of the national spirit – for example, the Poles and the Scandinavians could not accept the unlimited authority of the ruler in Roman law,

[180] Kraushar, note 53 above, p. 332.

[181] Wierzbicki, note 58 above, p. 69.

[182] Czacki, note 56 above, I, pp. vi-viii, 7, 51-54; Czacki, *Czy prawo rzymskie było zasadą praw litewskich i polskich? I czy z połnocnemi narodami mielismy wiele wspolnych praw i zwyczaiow? Rosprawa czytana w Krzemieńcu na otwarciu roku szkolnego 1808 w Gimnazyum Wołyńskiem* (Vilno, 1809), p. 85.

[183] Czacki, note 56 above, I, pp. iii, vi, 10, 49.

[184] Ibid., I, pp. vii, 7, 11, 16, 18, 19, 22, 29, 43-45, 49, 51-54, 56; II, pp. 292, 293.

[185] Ibid., II, p. 290.

[186] Ibid., I, p. 11.

as well as with other practical reasons, especially the complexity and lengthy time needed to study Roman law.[187] According to Czacki, the era of feudalism (evidently up to the eleventh or twelfth centuries) was a time of original national legal orders.[188] Despite the later coercive reception of Roman law, original elements did not disappear in national legal orders, and the Scandinavian ("northern") countries retained absolutely pure national law which gradually passed from customs into legislation ("they wrote statutes consistently with the spirit of their government").[189]

Kołłątaj believed that a common/national spirit, common feelings, character, language (or dialect), customs and habits, thought, and also a distinctive special mission, were inherent to each people. The political system of State and law must be adapted to the character of the people, but the character itself may change in an evolutionary manner or as a consequence of political tremors. The level of civilization of the people may coincide or not with other peoples. However, Kołłątaj suggested and even considered desirable the rapprochement of pollitical systems and political law of peoples connected with a uniform level of their civilization, which would not mean the loss of other elements of distinctiveness. Kołłątaj's ideas on the distinctiveness of national law were rather inconsistent, beginning with the declaration of cultural and linguistic factors and the proclamation of the existence within the boundaries of the former *Rzecz Pospolita* of only the Polish people, and continuing with the declared complexity of national distinctiveness and the possible existence of a supranational political and legal community immanent to different peoples.[190]

Niemcewicz believed that the distinctiveness of national law emanated from the geographical position and natural conditions of a country, but on the whole noted the predominance of the common features of peoples at the same level of civilization.[191]

Prince F. Szaniawski believed that "all laws are an expansion of natural law: human reason follows an innate order", but the positive law of a people must be adapted to the time, place,

[187] Czacki, note 182 above, p. 77.

[188] Czacki, note 56 above, I, p. 16.

[189] Ibid., I, pp. 18-19, 25, 28; Czacki, note 182 above, p. 121.

[190] Kołłątaj, note 2 above, pp. 73, 78, 90, 92, 98-103, 110, 114, 119, 141, 143, 146-147, 182, 184, 205, 207, 209, 220.

[191] Niemcewicz, note 59 above, pp. 16, 18.

human notions, and peculiarities of socio-economic development. In addition, the laws of peoples "do not always correspond to the original intention, for people do not always adhere to the material grounds of an innate law, often make mistakes, or use things and their own forces for the worst". However, the general natural foundation of law is universal, perfected, immutable, and distinctions in positive law are relative and changeable. Szaniawski at the same time acknowledged that the distinctions between the law of various nations are formed historically by way of experience, and connected with language and customs, and by comprehension of this experience, own lawmaking, and the selective reception of foreign law.[192]

In a later work, Szaniawski's emphasis relating to the distinctiveness of national law changed somewhat: although the natural law discourse was retained (to a significant degree the respective fragments were copied from earlier works), distinctiveness was presented not as the relativity of the adaptation of rejection, but as a historical law of societal development of "local experience" and a non-transitional phenomenon. Szaniawski asserted that law and the peculiarities of State-building should arise from the level of intellectual development and distinctive features of socio-economic development, customs, mode of thought, and the needs of the people. In a work published in 1819, Szaniawski structurally singled out in the Contents the problem of the originality and imitation in national law, and also the uniformity and diversity in law. In his view, "there is little useful originality in all human laws, and much imitation". But distinctiveness appears not only in the autochthonic origin of legal norms; Szaniawski wrote of the distinctiveness of the selection, alteration, adaptation, and assimilation of law, but not about blind imitation. Ultimately, Szaniawski concluded the national distinctiveness of law was inevitable and corresponded to the diversity of the physical nature of the Earth and to the particular and individual historical development of each society.[193]

Bandtkie was of the view that peoples "in the early embryos of society" are rather similar, and the uniqueness of national law, although linked with the language of a people, is form in the

[192] Szaniawski, note 5 above, pp. 4-5; Szaniawski, note 8 above, pp. 19-21, 36, 54, 281-282.

[193] Szaniawski, note 4 above, pp. 16, 23, 57-59, 70-76.

process of its historical continuous development which also may provide for the reception of law. Differences in the law of peoples are inevitable and ineradicable. Bandtkie wrote about the national spirit in law, but the last was not seen as immanent and should have been cognized and preserved by investigating the customary and other law of ancestors. He also mentioned national character, which, judging from the context, was formed historically. All the same in Bandtkie's works, especially from 1815 onwards, the preservation of the historical uniqueness of national law does not act as an end in itself. On the contrary, he substantiated modernization through the search for the better law among those in Europe, but having regard to imprecisely determined national grounds of law: "In the nineteenth century one could not think about experience, having so many models and so much expensive own and foreign experience; one should consult only with past history".[194]

Wyczechowski noted in 1815 that law, irrespective of its origin, becomes national when it is known to and recognized by citizens.[195] According to Wyczechowski, law should correspond to the level of development of social and economic relations, interests, and concepts of society, and therefore changes therein are completely logical: "There are no more interests, no more relations, no more notions, no more customs to which those [old] laws applied ... It is evident that contemporary relations were unknown to old Polish and Lithuanian laws, simply did not contain them because the previous legislators could not foresee the future socio-economic relations".[196] The aim of the lawmaker, Wyczechowski noted, was the rational creation or selection of existing legal acts most perfect in form and content and these should comprise a single mutually linked "system of law": "national laws are those which will be deemed to be such, which most correspond to contemporary civilization and are best suited to the stable happiness of the inhabitants of the Kingdom of Poland irrespective of the source

194 Bandtkie, note 19 above (1812), pp. iii, 53, 55, 60, 72, 172; Bandtkie, "O uprawnieniu ...", note 90 above (1812), pp. 215-216, 218; Bandtkie, "O karze ...", note 132 above, ibid., pp. 263-264, 280, 285-288; Bandtkie, note 19 above (1814), pp. 5, 7; Bandtkie, note 54 above, III, pp. 170, 173-174; Bandtkie, note 91 above, p. 311-312; Litauer, note 91 above, pp. 52, 62-66; Bandtkie, note 134 above, pp. 39-40, 42.

195 Zarzycka, note 77 above, p. 179.

196 Ibid., p. 180.

from which they were drawn".[197] However, he pointed to the desirability of the "stabilization of law" and not allowing too frequent changes therein.[198]

Rakowiecki noted in works published between 1820 and 1822 the integral and organic unity of religion (pre-Christian pagan), customs, language, character, and law of peoples which were preserved throughout centuries and together acted as the communicative foundation for the preservation and development of peoples (and, consequently, law exerted a reverse influence on society).[199] The source of the people's spirit was knowledge of traditions, customs, laws, and languages of ancestors; the national character derived from that.[200] Even the form of government derives from the distinctive features of the national spirit.[201] At the same time, the traditions and customs which are constitutive of law may originate from requirements and the way of life of national society, and the individual historical development of a people has a concrete causal character and becomes a factor in the evolution of law.[202]

Rakowiecki believed that a disturbance of the individuality of law and culture as a result of foreign impact might also disturb the course of development of a people and proclaimed the possibility of the purification thereof.[203] However, he allowed the possibility of preserving the individuality of cultural and legal development of a people even under conditions of that people's subordination to another people or to a foreign ruler.[204]

Hube pointed to the "individual and distinctive character" of each national law, including its concepts and grounds, its inextricable unity with the spirit or common feeling, character, morality, and customs of the people. The distinctiveness of national law is retained even during a period of revolutionary legal reforms:

197 Ibid., pp. 180-181; Pomianowski, note 44 above, pp. 118-119.

198 Zarzycka, note 77 above, p. 179.

199 Rakowiecki, O stanie, note 143 above, p. 2, 3, 15; Rakowiecki, Prawda, note 143 above, I, pp. viii, 81-82, 198, 227; II, pp. 156, 312-313, 315.

200 Rakowiecki, Prawda, note 143 above, I, pp. i, 139, 227; II, 243.

201 Ibid., I, pp. 242, 253.

202 Ibid., I, pp. 134, 228, 252; II, pp. 246, 254, 315.

203 Ibid., I, pp. 82, 84, 128; II, p. 315.

204 Ibid., I, p. 129; II, p. 255.

"That which once in the development of peoples had significance does not disappear, but rather becomes useful materials that becomes part of the later formation of a higher level". Any borrowing disturbs this distinctiveness and should be avoided. If it occurred, the autochthonic elements gradually squeeze out the received law and it ceases to be applied. However, in national law there are some elements which may be replaced and, consequently, are not material from the standpoint of distinctiveness.[205]

According to Zaborowski, the law of a people is as individual as its language. This depends on forms of government, conceptions, convictions, thoughts, customs inherent to the people. The distinctive law of a people in the form of the "aggregate of legal notions" appears already during the formation of the people and thereafter remains primarily a special mode of thought. It comprises the grounds of law, and norms of the last change and are modernized. Distinctiveness of law, however, is present primarily in its political element (the respective norms must be of autochthonic origin), and another element – the technical – encompasses norms of scientific origin which are similar in various countries and may be borrowed and assimilated.[206] But Zaborowski applies all this only to national States; in multi-national States law emanates from speculative constructions alienated from customs, realities, and aspirations of society – and this has negative consequences.[207]

Heylman wrote about innate language, customs, ideas, convictions, and public order being distinctive in each people. But, although supposedly immanent, these elements constantly evolve together with the development of social relations and the enlightenment of the people. The distinctive elements are most fully expressed in customary law and court decisions. The political element of law (or law in the national conviction) remains autochthonic, and the technical element (law in the hands of jurists) may have autochthonic or foreign origin. The authentic elements of law are more stable than the borrowed elements; the two groups may coexist eclectically. The first group over time may prevail and

[205] Hube, note 25 above, I, pp. 7-8; Hube, "O starożytnych zbiorach praw Czeskich", *Themis Polska*, V (1829), pp. 1-2; Hube, note 23 above (1829), pp. 298-299, 308-311, 329; Hube, note 23 above (1830), I, pp. 35, 38; Hube, note 147 above, pp. 61-63, 73, 76-77, 80, 82-83.

[206] Zaborowski, note 29 above, pp. 213-225, 229, 234, 238-240; Zaborowski, note 102 above, pp. 361, 363, 365-371.

[207] Zaborowski, note 29 above, p. 221-222.

squeeze out the second with the assistance of judicial practice, but the interests of the development and modernization of the legal order require balancing and gradual synthesis of these groups. The intellectual expression and result of the contemplation of the distinctiveness of national law, in Heylman's view, is the science of philosophy of the law in force separate from the philosophy of positive laws and the philosophy of ideal law. Reflecting on the problem of the distinctiveness of national legal orders in the world, Heylman concludes that there is "an eternal order of stable uniformity and infinite diversity", an "endless diversity of uniformity", and a "competition between the old diversity and the new uniformity".[208]

Maciejowski in 1832 pointed to the existence of national character and national spirit as factors of the development of law, the organic nature of the development of law as an element of culture (together with language and others), the conditionality of the modernity of tradition, the indestructibility of the individual element of culture, and the special mission of each people. The national spirit Maciejowski precisely concretized as political and legal.[209] The national spirit, national character, and the politico-legal institutions derived therefrom are not eternal, but develop historically; the absence of foreign influence plays a material role in their fully-fledged development.[210] In addition to culture, the distinctive features of the development of law are inextricably connected with the entire life of a people (especially with the nature of power, political relations between people and the authorities, structure of the church, national economy, requirements of defense) and rest on physical geographical conditions (location, climate, quality of the soil).[211]

The transition from customary law to legislation domination, which in Maciejowski's view was key in the history of the law of a people, was not accompanied by a loss of national individuality of law; legislation is not a manifestation of arbitrariness, but emanates from "legal images" and the peculiarities of the development

[208] Heylman, note 35 above, pp. 3, 12-15, 19, 26-28, 30-31, 44-52; Heylman, note 107 above, pp.114, 117, 122-123, 128-134.

[209] Maciejowski, note 175 above, I, p. iv, vi-viii, 2-3, 5,11, 53-54,70.

[210] Ibid., I, pp. 35, 54, 67-69.

[211] Ibid., I, pp. 4, 51, 56.

of the people (degree of its enlightenment).[212] In his view, the efforts of legal scholars and legislators might not only reflect the national distinctiveness of law and culture as a whole, but also strengthen and deepen this, as well as partially restore the lost organic nature of law by means of creating new legislation on the basis of customary law (the process of "deepening legislation"). Maciejowski believed that national law is capable of renewal and modernization on an own basis, with preservation of a complete individuality. Law exerts a reverse influence on a people, including with regard to the preservation of its distinctiveness, acting as one of the communicative factors.[213] The notion of the distinctiveness of legal orders and the gradualness of their development enabled Maciejowski to single out the history of national law as an individual subject-matter of legal research.[214]

The question of the distinctiveness of national law during the period here considered was constantly in a political context and repeatedly became topical in documents of agencies of power and debates in legislative organs of the Duchy of Warsaw and Kingdom of Poland. A Memorial of the Directorate of Justice in 1807 addressed to Napoleon noted that the distinctiveness of Polish law was determined by the peculiarities of the historical development of the economy and socio-economic relations and influence of religion and was expressed in "innate convictions" and customs of the people.[215] It was noted in various petitions, drafts, and addresses in the Sejm that the distinctiveness of law is determined by physical-climatic conditions of the country, distinctive features of socio-economic relations, and the morality of the people.[216]

212 Ibid., I, p. 51.

213 Ibid., I, pp. iv, vi, viii-ix, 2-4, 36, 51, 53-54.

214 Ibid., I, pp. 43, 52.

215 Konic, note 54 above, pp. 210-214; Kraushar, note 54 above, p. 331; Grynwaser, note 73 above, I, pp. 16, 55; M. V. Syrko, Цивільний кодекс Франції 1804 року та його вплив на цивільне законодавство країн Європи (на прикладі Польщі та Румунії) [1804 Civil Code of France and its Influence on Civil Legislation of the Countries of Europe (The Examples of Poland and Romania)] (Lviv, 2015), p. 88 (diss. kand. iurid. nauk).

216 See, for example, "Mowa J. W. Ministra Sprawiedliwości miana w Izbie Poselskiey 15 Marca 1809 roku", *Gazeta Korrespondenta Warszawskiego i Zagranicznego*, no. 25 (1809), p. 361; Grynwaser, note 73 above, I, p. 64; M. Gałędek, A. Klimaszewska, and P. Z. Pomianowski, "Prace Komitetu Cywilnego Reformy nad przygotowaniem narodowej kodyfikacji prawa cywilnego i procedury cywilnej w przededniu utworzenia Królestwa Polskiego (1814-1815) – edycja

However, the impossibility of the fully-fledged preservation of respective distinctive provisions of national law, their gradual disappearance, and the need for a pragmatic search for the better legal models was substantiated by Wyczechowski in his drafts and speeches by using the same factors: the development of socio-economic relations and the development of legislative technique. He noted that distinctiveness in law is an illusion: "no Christian nation no longer has its own original laws and customs"; even customary law may contain not original, but borrowed, norms.[217]

In addresses to sessions of the Reform Committee in 1814, Bieńkowski advanced the idea which correlated with the widely disseminated theory of political and technical elements of law: "the subject-matter of diversity" is the political, criminal, and police law of peoples, and civil law is "embedded in the nature of things and man" and "is the same everywhere, without distinctions". The other members of the Committee did not agree with this position, asserting that the civil law of peoples also contains distinctive and general elements, and ultimately Bieńkowski himself withdrew his remarks. But in later works he again emphasized that "nationality" in civil law is an "incidental creation".[218]

A Report of the State Council to the Sejm on the activity of the Government and the state of the country in 1818 noted that national law should simultaneously correspond to the "contemporary light of Europe" and to the character, customs, and requirements of the inhabitants.[219] The idea of preserving the historical distinctiveness of Polish law connected with obsolete social and political relations was rejected in the introduction to a draft Book One of the Civil Code of the Kingdom of Poland submitted by a deputation of the Sejm in 1823. Given the need for the modernization of law, it was suggested to form this distinctiveness pragmatically, having regard to the distinctive features of the political system

zrodlowa. Część II", *Krakowskie Studia z Historii Państwa i Prawa*, XII, no. 2 (2019), p. 417; Zarzycka, note 77 above, p. 179.

[217] J. Kodrębski, "Prawo rzymskie a Kodeks Napoleona w Polsce XIX wieku", *Acta Universitatis Lodziensis. Folia Iuridica*, XXXVIII (1988), p. 164; Zarzycka, note 77 above, pp. 179-180; Galędek and Klimaszewska, note 78 above, pp. 283, 286-287, 292; Pomianowski, note 44 above, pp. 118-119; Gałędek and Klimaszewska, "Stosunek polskich elit do prawa francuskiego po upadku Napoleona – zarys problemu", *Studia z Dziejów Państwa i Prawa Polskiego*, XXI (2018), p. 80.

[218] Grynwaser, note 73 above, I, p. 74; Gałędek, note 72 above, p. 23; Pomianowski, note 44 above, p. 122.

[219] Zarzycka, note 77 above, p. 191.

and administration, economy, and so on. The autochthonic or foreign origin of legal norms had no material significance if they corresponded to or would be adapted to the distinctive conditions of Poland.[220]

We partially concur with Pomianowski that the appeal to the nationality of law in the process of the Warsaw codification debates was linked not with a return to the operation of Polish law or with transforming customs into positive law, but rather with the discovery in legislation of foreign origin in force on Polish lands of norms similar to old Polish law or corresponding to social convictions and the Polish tradition: "The creation of national law in the Kingdom of Poland constituted rather turning to alien models meeting local expectations and outwardly connected with our tradition than a return to life of ancient norms".[221] Of interest is the view of Gałędek and Klimaszewska concerning the supposition by Bieńkowski, Wyczechowski, and other jurists of a possible new formation and formulation of the distinctiveness of national law.[222]

We turn in passing to the vision of the distinctiveness of national law held by Warsaw scholars who were not jurists. Staszic wrote about the individual national characteristics which might be natural or acquired. He relegated law to the natural indicia of a people; that is, evidently received by a people when it emerged. But this view was not metaphysical and proceeded from Staszic's idea about the origin of peoples from supranational linguistic communities (for example, Poles as a chip off the Slavs). But Staszic also wrote about the inevitability of the modernization and uniformization of national legal orders.[223] Jastrzębowski wrote in his projects about the gradual disappearance of differences and the distinctiveness of peoples, first in Europe and then through the entire world.[224]

In the view of Lelewel, every people has its own innate "leading idea" which has a precisely expressed politico-legal element that reflects the distinctiveness of the people and is embodied at various

[220] Grynwaser, note 73 above, I, pp. 132-133.

[221] Pomianowski, note 44 above, pp. 122-124.

[222] Gałędek and Klimaszewska, note 216 above, p. 81.

[223] T. Matlęgiewicz, "W kręgu myśli słowianofilskiej Stanisława Staszica", *Wschodni rocznik humanistyczny 2010-2011*, VII (2011), pp. 169, 171; Wierzbicki, note 58 above, p. 70.

[224] Wierzbicki, note 58 above, pp. 55-58, 60.

periods of it, s history in its law.[225] A more radical Romantic vision of the distinctiveness of national law was advanced by Brodziński. He said that the source of the distinctiveness of national existence is a completely unique national spirit given by God, an "innate idea", a mission. The national spirit is transmitted to members of the people genetically; they direct their efforts to its preservation and realization. The character of the people also is distinctive, formed in the process of historical development under the influence of religion, distinctive features of the economy, and others.[226]

We add that Daniłowicz in 1818 noted the individuality of the spirit of each national law (an analysis of which is the "most complex issue in jurisprudence"), and that underlying distinctiveness of the last are immutable causes (climate, peculiarities of the soil, physical location) and mutable (nature of administration, religion, customs).[227]

The doctrine on the distinctiveness of national law (narodowośc) was elaborated in the legal thought of Warsaw jurists during the period here considered. The problem of the originality and imitation, uniformity and diversity, in law was singled out and conceptualized. The respective ideas may be roughly divided into two orientations. Roughly, because we summarize two theoretical extremes, but in fact within the works analyzed they are mixed in varying proportions, which allows us to speak only about the dominance of one or the other vision.

The first orientation may be called culture-centric. It emphasized the inalienability of distinctive elements in national law personified above all in the national spirit (including the special spirit of law) and customs. The natural geographical conditions of the birth and development of the people may act as the prerequisite of distinctiveness. Distinctiveness may be substantive, innate, part of the special mission and "leading idea" of a people and merely disclose its properties during the people's life. It is transmitted communicatively or even genetically. Law is an inalienable element of the culture of a people and in permanent mutual linkage with other elements thereof. Distinctive elements

[225] Wierzbicki, "Joachim Lelewel 1786-1861", in *Portrety uczonych. Profesorowie Uniwersytetu Warszawskiego 1816-1915* (2016), pp. 321-322.

[226] Brodziński, note 63 above, pp. 14-21, 26-29; Wierzbicki, note 58 above, p. 70.

[227] Daniłowicz, *Kodex Napoleona w porównaniu z prawami polskiemi i litewskiemi* (Warsaw, 1905), pp. 26-27, 40, 46,67, 69-70, 173.

determine the character and direction of the development of law. In origin they are autochthonic, but by dissemination they may be distinctive or inherent to all peoples of a certain linguistic group.

The possibility is assumed of the existence of a "pure" national law – absolutely original, without borrowings. The preservation of distinctive elements in law is an absolute value; the modernization of law is possible of the basis of rethinking one's own law, and borrowings are not needed and even harmful. The coexistence of original and received law is eclectic and does not create a single legal system. In the event of the loss of distinctive elements, the original qualities of the people also are lost, the course of development is disturbed, and the very existence of the people is endangered.

But even in this event the possibility exists for the purification of law and the return to the foundations thereof in autochthonic sources. The autochthonic elements are more stable by virtue of their interlinkage with other elements of the spiritual and material life of the people, and therefore more influential than received elements lacking a local root. Autochthonic elements squeeze out the received elements, and the distinctiveness of national law is restored. The lawmakers should understand the distinctive grounds of national law and "deepen" them. The existence of multinational States is condemned because the law in them is alienated from the distinctiveness of the people. The distinctiveness is inevitable and immutable.

The second orientation may be defined as constructivist. It acknowledges the existence of distinctive elements in national law, but asserts that they in any event are not substantive and even immanent. They are "local experience", formed historically, derive from the conditions of the development of the people and an awareness of its special needs. By origin they may be original but chiefly are borrowed and later identified as distinctive. The distinctiveness of national law is manifest not in originality, but in distinctive features of the selection, alteration, and adaptation of legal models. It is rational insofar as law is oriented towards the needs and aspirations of a concrete society, is appropriated, and is acknowledged by the last.

Distinctiveness is not eternal. At one level of civilization, peoples come together and the distinctiveness of their law is reduced. The rationality of the creation or selection of the better law and the rejection of obsolete elements narrows the sphere of distinctiveness progressively. Individual legal scholars even allowed the gradual disappearance of distinctiveness of national law as a result of modernization processes.

Many ideas of that time provided for the possible synthesis of these polar orientations. The aforesaid idea of two elements of law was disseminated: political (law in the people's legal consciousness) and technical (the law of jurists, scientific law). Of these, the first is primarily distinctive irrespective of original or borrowed origin. The second element may be a sphere of conscious choice or the creation of distinctive or common legal norms and institutions, neutral, and not linked with the distinctive features of the people. In addition, the idea was advanced of the inevitable evolution and transformation of even immanent distinctive elements of law. Finally, individual legal scholars noted that the need for the modernization of law causes the need to balance and synthesize the distinctive and common elements of law.

Chapter 4 The Universal and the Special in Legal Development

§4.1. Content of Principal Discussions on Received Law

The practical problems of the further development of Polish law generated sharp and lengthy discussions among the Warsaw jurists. By virtue of real circumstances, the possibility of the reception and the fate of receipt blocks of foreign national law (especially French), supranational canon law, and Roman law which was general European in significance proved to be in focus during these discussions.

The reception of French codes and court organization in the Duchy of Warsaw, initially as a question and then as a fact, acted as one of the strongest irritators for the development of legal thought among Polish jurists and a major factor in the formulation of their positions with respect to the key problems of legal development and their worldview embodied in the special scientific picture of the world.

Among some of the Polish intellectuals the French codification of law generated sincere admiration and the wish to disseminate it to the Polish lands. The Polish Jacobites in particular who consolidated around the *Gazeta Warszawska* saw in the French enactments the basis for the undertaking of socio-political reforms; individual Polish figures proposed to Napoleon the introduction of the French codes in the Polish territories which had acceded to the Duchy.[1] The leading Polish public figure and jurist, Hugo

[1] K. Sójka-Zielińska, *Wielkie kodyfikacje cywilne. Historia i współczesność* (2009), p. 258; H. Grynwaser, "Kodeks Napoleona w Polsce", in Grynwaser, *Pisma* (Wroclaw, 1951), I, p. 23; M. Gałędek, "Does War Deepen Distrust Toward the State? Reorientation of the Polish Political Thought under the Influence of the Napoleonic Wars", in R. F. Sirvent and R. A. G. Lloret (eds.), *Del siglo XIX al XXI. Tendencias y debates: XIV Congreso de la Asociación de Historia Contemoránea, Universidad de Alicante 20-22 de septiembre de 2018* (2019), p. 1752; Gałędek, A. Klimaszewska, and P. Z. Pomianowski, "Prace Komitetu Cywilnego Reformy nad przygotowaniem narodowej kodyfikacji prawa cywilnego i procedury cywilnej w

Kołłątaj, called the Code a "universal book of enlightened peoples" and Napoleon himself a "virtuous Legislator who just wanted to bring us closer to unity with many enlightened peoples".[2]

But the most influential circles in the central Polish lands of large landowners and Catholic clergy, including the President of the Governmental Commission, Stanisław Małachowski, opposed possible reception of the Code. As Sójka-Zielińska noted, both groups were apprehensive of revolutionary transformations being sanctioned through the reception of French legislation: the first – social changes; and others – loss of control in the sphere of family law.[3] One of the Polish Memorials presented to Napoleon, "Observation Relating to the Revival of Poland" written in 1806 by some on the Department of Foreign Affairs of Poland, requested that the 1791 Constitution and Polish law be left in force on the Polish lands.[4]

Polish representatives in the Governmental Commission and a significant part of society after the return of the operation of private law of the *Rzecz Pospolita* hoped to further develop the tradition of the last and preserve its social and society-church relations with certain changes.[5] The Directorate of Justice headed by Łubieński in 1807 before the meeting of the Governmental Commission with Napoleon prepared reports on the inadvisability of the reception of French legislation and court organization, especially a Report entitled "Some Fragmentary Thoughts Expressed on the Question of Whether the Code of the Great Napoleon is Appropriate for Our People". Among the arguments mentioned were: the different level of intellectual development of the two States; the different type of economy and respective legal relations; the incompatibility of the Polish estate and new formally estate-less French law; and the significant function of the church in the legal life of Poland: "Poland is a country completely different from France". It was averred in the document: "if we want to be just, one should respect certain relations, otherwise we may generate much unhappiness from which material good will not follow"; the French legislation

przededniu utworzenia Królestwa Polskiego (1814-1815) – edycja ***źródłowa. Część** I"*, *Krakowskie Studia z Historii Państwa i Prawa*, XII, no. 2 (2019), p. 240.

[2] Sójka-Zielińska, note 1 above, p. 258.

[3] Ibid.

[4] Grynwaser, note 1 above, I, p. 21.

[5] Ibid., I, pp. 17, 25.

should not be carried over to Polish lands without the necessary adaptation.[6]

Among the Polish specialists there is no unequivocal view as to the influence of the reception of the Napoleonic codes on social relations. Rundstein pointed to the "discovery of the crucial achievements of the Great Revolution, proclamation of equality in law, liquidation of feudal traditions",[7] and in Posner's vision of a socio-legal revolution among those principles were the unity of law, individual freedom and equality before the law, secularization of law and court proceedings, independence of court proceedings from executive power, a new concept of law (not a privilege, but justice).[8] Dunin held a similar view.[9] Grynwaser, on the contrary, wrote about the "apparent Jacobinism" of this legislation, which in fact did not abolish feudal relations in the countries which were attached to France.[10] Nonetheless, it may be asserted that in the vision of Polish jurists during the first third of the nineteenth century the consequences of a possible and then actual reception were significant, as the aforementioned Report by Łubieński pointed out.

Whatever the case, the Constitution of the Grand Duchy of Warsaw dictated by Napoleon (Section IX, Article 69) provided for the reception of the French Code Civil, and Section I, Article 4(19) eliminated the personal dependence of peasants and proclaimed the equality of inhabitants before the law – despite the view of the

[6] H. Konic, "Nowy przyczynek do dziejów kodeksu Napoleona w Polsce", *Gazeta Sądowa Warszawska*, no. 14 (22 March 1903), pp. 210-214; Kraushar, "W setną rocnicę Kodeksu Napoleona", *Gazeta Sądowa Warszawska*, no. 22 (28 May 1908), pp. 330-331; Grynwaser, note 1 above, I, p. 17; J. J. Litauer, "Przeciwnicy Kodeksu", *Gazeta Sądowa Warszawska*, no. 22 (28 May 1908), p. 365; M. V. Syrko, Цивільний кодекс Франції 1804 року та його вплив на цивільне законодавство країн Європи (на прикладі Польщі та Румунії) [1804 Civil Code of France and its Influence on Civil Legislation of the Countries of Europe (The Examples of Poland and Romania)] (Lviv, 2015), p. 88 (diss. kand. iurid. nauk).

[7] S. Rundstein, "Kodeks Napoleona w Niemczech", *Gazeta Sądowa Warszawska*, no. 22 (28 May 1908), p. 355.

[8] S. Posner, "Dziś a przed stu laty. Nasz stosunek historyczny do kodeksu", *Gazeta Sądowa Warszawska*, no. 22 (28 May 1908), pp. 361-362.

[9] K. Dunin, "Jubileusz Kodeksu Napoleona", *Gazeta Sądowa Warszawska*, no. 22 (28 May 1908), p. 328.

[10] Grynwaser, note 1 above, I, pp. 17-18.

Polish Governmental Commission relating to preservation of the law of the *Rzecz Pospolita*.[11]

Thereafter, both the unconcealed opponents of the reception of French legislation such as the Chairman of the Council of Ministers and State Council of the Grand Duchy of Warsaw, Małachowski, in his respective public remarks and possibly more flexible officials such as the Minister of Justice, Łubieński, came willy-nilly to become involved in the introduction of such legislation.[12]

Commencing from 1808, various law-drafting commissions were created in the Grand Duchy of Warsaw, one of their principal issues being the introduction, adaptation, or change of the French codes. They became the platform for heated discussions in which and around which members, experts, and politicians, in order to substantiate their positions, had recourse to fundamental theoretical and practical questions of the development of law. The principal problems which generated these discussions were: emancipation of the peasants from personal dependence, equalization of all estates and ethno-religious groups in rights, ownership of peasant allotments; mortgage, land surveying, transition from estate to general courts, distinctive features of execution proceedings, participation of the church in administrative activity (registration of acts of civil status), secular marriage and freedom of divorce.

In general, the positions of the active social groups were predictable: the privileged did not want to lose their privileges; the landowners did not want to allow the emancipation of the peasants and especially to lose the lands which had been consolidated to those peasants; and they endeavored by any means to preserve ownership in the pledged estates; representatives of the titled nationality did not want equalization in rights with ethno-religious minorities; the clergy did not want to lose influence in society and the sources of their earnings. By 1809 the positions of the landowners had changed when it was understood that they in accordance with the Civil Code received the right of absolute ownership to peasant lands.[13] Virtually each of these pragmatic

[11] Ibid., I, p. 19.

[12] Ibid., I, pp. 24-29; Litauer, note 6 above, p. 365.

[13] Klimaszewska and Gałędek, "The Implementation of French Codes on the Polish Territories as Instruments of Modernization – Identifying Problems with Selected Examples", in A. Albarian and O. Moréteau (eds.), *Le droit comparé et / Comparative Law and …: Actes de la conference annuelle de Juris Diversitas* (2015), p. 76.

motives was connected with certain social convictions and traditions, and the proponents of the new legislation relied on new socio-political and legal doctrines.

In any event to openly propose the abolition of the operation of received law before the defeat of Napoleon was virtually impossible. Thus, proposals relating to adaptation, to the "appropriation to themselves" of French law were submitted rather extensively. Niemcewicz noted in 1808 the anachronistic nature of the "funny rag" of the ancient law of the *Rzecz Pospolita* and the incomparable superiority of the Code Napoleon as an expression of the new stage of nineteenth-century civilization. He pointed out that the old law did not reflect the new social relations provided by the Constitution of the Grand Duchy of Warsaw. Therefore, the reform of the law was inevitable, the received law should be respected, and "the aimlessness should be despised of those who for their own popularity either do not attempt to comprehend the Code adequately or commit sacrilege against it". But it should be adapted "to the situation and nature of our territory".[14]

In 1809 Łubieński substantiated the need for changes in the Code Napoleon to have regard to local historical and geographical distinctive features of the Polish lands and that the changes would lead to a fuller realization of the Code without disturbing the spirit thereof: "adapting to the country all that may ease for its subjects the exercise of those rights which may ensure their happiness".[15] Proposals similar to those made by Wyczechowski in 1809 (to prepare a "draft for the adaptation of the Code [Napoleon] to the Grand Duchy of Warsaw") or analogous to that made by Karol Diehl in 1811 might have been sincere or coerced and concealed a more radical program.[16]

The upheavals of the law drafting battles are not so important for the present study as is a formal analysis of the actual provisions of codes and draft legislation. Of interest to us are the arguments of the parties reflecting their legal world outlook. Attention should

14 [J. U. Niemcewicz], *Przestroga dla społziomków na rok 1809* (1808), pp. 16-18.

15 "Raport ministra sprawiedliwości Feliksa Łubieńskiego w sprawie zmiany niektórych artykułów kodeksu Napoleona, dotyczących hypoteki", in J. J. Litauer, *Memorial J. W. Bandtkiego o prawie hipotecznym z roku 1818* (1915), p. 78; "Mowa J. W. Ministra Sprawiedliwości miana w Izbie Poselskiey 15 Marca 1809 roku", *Gazeta Korrespondenta Warszawskiego i Zagranicznego*, no. 25 (1809), pp. 360-361.

16 Grynwaser, note 1 above, I, p. 39; Litauer, note 6 above, pp. 363-367.

be directed above all to the *a priori* hostility to the French code as being an alien one. Wyczechowski described this position in 1815 as follows: "no one law may be fully suitable for another country".[17] The members of the Reform Committee in 1814 demanded that "both in legislation and in administration national character and customs shall be adhered to", "local circumstances", and the national spirit shall be restored.[18] The question of the urgent replacement of the received legislation by national codes was a matter of principle for this group. One representative of the group, which dominated the early work of the Reform Committee, was Grabowski, who in September 1814 had declared that a rough draft was ready of a new civil code.[19] In fact, however, he referred not to polished drafts, but to individual changes: "to rewrite the main rules in a national spirit, leaving everything else to practice".[20] In 1818 the courts declared their position relative to the need to repeal the operation of the Code Napoleon.[21]

To this hostility was juxtaposed the pragmatic position represented especially by Bieńkowski, another member of the Reform Committee, in 1814: yes, a future national codification there will be, this is correct, but for the moment the specific provisions of the borrowed legislation should be considered from the standpoint of their usefulness for the development of social relations and those few should be changed which are unsuited, contrary to public opinion, and are burdensome, contrary to the Catholic faith and ownership relations in the country. It should be noted that this position was supported in October 1814 by a majority of Reform Committee members.[22]

[17] Gałędek, Klimaszewska, and Pomianowski, note 1 above, XII, no. 2 (2019), p. 242.

[18] Ibid., p. 265. Gałędek, "The Problem of Non-Adaptability of National Legal Heritage. Discussion on the Reform of Civil Law in Poland in the Course of Work of Reform Committee in 1814", *Romanian Journal of Comparative Law*, VIII, no. 1 (2017), pp. 21-22.

[19] Gałędek and Klimaszewska, "Stosunek polskich elit do prawa francuskiego po upadku Napoleona – zarys problemu", *Studia z Dziejów Państwa i Prawa Polskiego*, XXI (2018), pp. 76-78.

[20] Ibid., p. 78.

[21] Kraushar, note 6 above, p. 332.

[22] Gałędek, Klimaszewska, and Pomianowski, note 1 above, p. 272; Gałędek, note 18 above, pp. 21, 27; A. Zarzycka, "Próby zmian prawa rzeczowego z Kodeksu Napoleona w Królestwie Polskim w latach 1815-1818", *Krakowskie Studia z Historii Państwa i Prawa*, II (2008), p. 176.

Another position was formulated somewhat later – to retain and adapt the received French legislation. Wyczechowski noted that received law should not be rejected only because it was foreign and revolutionary in origin; one should "know of it and investigate it more closely", having determined (and obviously adapted) those principles therein which are unsuitable.[23] Later he also pointed out that any amendments to the Code Napoleon were risky, for they might disturb the "spirit of the integral system of the law" behind which there is "unity, experience, and available literature". Only prolonged application of the Code would enable one to formulate possible changes therein".[24]

The State Council in a Report on the activity of the Government and the state of Poland in 1816-1817 submitted to the Sejm on 28 March 1818 expressed gratitude to the Emperor: "Those who are now alive bless your Royal Highness and bless will future generations because, having become the Lord of this country, in equal degree by arms and by laws, you have permitted the half-ruined order and law not to be abolished, but propped up by your wisdom, quiet the chaos caused by the careless use of changes. You do not repeal the French code, but adapt it and make it fully native".[25] Ultimately, a certain critic of the received legislation, Kajetan Koźmian (1771-1856), during the discussions in the State Council in 1829 proclaimed the civil code to be a national code, the "spirit and prescriptions of which had been assimilated", with which other members of the Council agreed.[26] Kantorbery (Tomasz) Tymowski (1790-1850) noted that a national code is that which for a long time had been deemed to be such by the people, namely the Code Napoleon.[27]

The equivocal positions of the representatives of Polish society and the lack of a precise answer regarding the fate of the received legislation was well illustrated by Prince Czartoryski:

> To cast aside the remarkable law already introduced and to lose that which is useful and good therein in order to return to past laws without purifying them of all the

[23] Zarzycka, note 22 above, pp. 179-180.

[24] Grynwaser, note 1 above, p. 156.

[25] Zarzycka, note 22 above, p. 192.

[26] J. Kodrębski, "Prawo rzymskie a Kodeks Napoleona w Polsce XIX wieku", *Acta Universitatis Lodziensis. Folia Iuridica,* XXXVIII (1988), p. 163.

[27] Grynwaser, note 1 above, p. 156.

> numerous shortcomings would not be advisable. But no less regrettable for every country is the path when it should receive imposed legislation, even if it was perfect. It is better gradually to rectify, adding one's own institutions, than suddenly foreign to be adopted by another's force.[28]

The position of the Russian Imperial Government on the issue of immediate repeal, temporary retention, or change of French legislation received in the Kingdom of Poland was rather equivocal and unstable, we have set it out above.

Another important moment was the question of the sources of a future national code. Bieńkowski proposed to the Reform Committee in an Instruction to a future codification commission on 20 November 1814 in which he noted: "not to use European codes, to learn from general principles, adapting them to the requirements of our people, and from the mistakes of codifications, would be to ignore the wisdom which work of such significance requires". But after discussion, the Committee changed this part of the Instruction: "to draw various questions from foreign legal sources", but only if their adaptation would be responsive to "national customs and other local circumstances".[29]

Just as Bieńkowski, Wyczechowski supported the idea of the need to rely on existing received legislation and foreign experience, pointing to the anachronistic law of the *Rzecz Pospolita* as uncodified and connected with feudal estate historical realities.[30] Ultimately, on 27 November 1814, the Committee approved another text of the Instruction prepared by Aleksander Linowski (c. 1759/60-1820), according to which it was proposed to draft a code of civil law and procedure based not on foreign, but on Polish and Lithuanian law as verified experience developed and adapted to the needs of the country: "Only if there proves to be shortcomings will we turn for assistance to the book of laws which suggests provisions most suitable for our country".[31] However, as Gałędek noted, during the discussions in the Committee on various issues the members rarely turned to the law of the *Rzecz Pospolita*, a gradual consolidation occurred in 1814-1815 of opposition to a return to the norms of this

[28] Kraushar, note 6 above, p. 332.

[29] Grynwaser, note 1 above, p. 74; Gałędek, note 18 above, p. 22.

[30] Gałędek and Klimaszewska, note 19 above, p. 80.

[31] Gałędek, note 18 above, p. 26.

law in a future national code, the idea being generally accepted that the modernization of that law was impossible.[32]

When submitting his own draft Instruction for the legislative deputation in 1817, Czartoryski suggested to rely primarily on the law of the *Rzecz Pospolita,* but also on European codes and Roman law.[33] In counterbalance to this draft, the Governmental Commission proposed: "to take existing codes as an example and only during the discussion draw attention to Polish laws, the Lithuanian Statute, and the codes of other peoples".[34]

The draft fundamental principles of national codification proposed in 1818 by the Governor of the Kingdom of Poland (in all likelihood the author was Bieńkowski) the principle source was to be the law of the *Rzecz Pospolita,* and the auxiliary source – the "ancient and contemporary foreign codes" even without reference to those received and in force. But the Governmental Commission insisted that the most important source was to be the French codes in force in the State – which was approved by the Governor on 14 August 1818: "With the reservation simultaneously that the books of civil law should attempt to preserve all possible present prescriptions of the Civil Code, the preservation of which would not be contrary to the amendments which already have been made in them or those which new laws of the country or circumstances arising from the state thereof might require".[35] And in 1819 the State Council indicated to the editor of the draft Civil Code that the last should correspond as fully as possible to the received law in force.[36]

The Introduction to the draft Book One of the Civil Code prepared by the deputation of the Sejm indicated that the received French Code was deliberately chosen as the basis of the draft, for "Polish laws have become alien, for the most part the presently living" not corresponding to the realities of life; the Austrian and Prussian law operated only in individual parts of the State, and only the Code Napoleon has national operation; new social relations are developing under its influence, and numerous

[32] Ibid., p. 36.

[33] Zarzycka, note 22 above, pp. 182-183.

[34] Ibid., pp. 183-184.

[35] Grynwaser, note 1 above, opp. 117-118, 167-168.

[36] Ibid., pp. 123-125.

administrative prescriptions have been adapted to it. Moreover, this Code requires adaptation to political, economic, and other conditions of the Kingdom of Poland, but it would be premature to do so: "At first the new law must be understood uniformly, executed uniformly, and as a result of the influence of significant time become a concept common for all inhabitants of the country and acquire the features of habit, thereby achieving the degree of maturity necessary for its improvement". Therefore, the aim of the draft law was proclaimed not to be the adaptation, but the "application of the French code to the country".[37]

The Sejm ultimately in 1825 approved Book One of the Civil Code of the Kingdom of Poland. Calculations made by Pomianowski are eloquent: of 521 Articles, 348 were taken from the Code Napoleon or drafted on the basis thereof; twelve Articles from Austrian law; several from Prussian, and less than 30% of the Code may be regarded as Articles based on the law of the *Rzecz Pospolita* or an original elaboration of Polish jurists at the time.[38] The draft Book Two of the Code was prepared on the basis of Prussian and Austrian law, but during the consideration by the State Council was approximated to the Code Napoleon. It did not enter into force, and instead the Sejm in 1830 adopted amendments to the respective Book of the French Code.[39] As Pomianowski noted in this regard, "the overwhelming majority of proponents of the adoption of a national codification saw this as an improvement of the French prescriptions", extending this conclusion not only to the participants in the drafting work, but also to the writings of legal scholars.[40]

These positions of various political forces and jurists in the Kingdom of Poland were significant, especially taking account that in the majority of German states the received French law had been

[37] Ibid., pp. 132-133.

[38] Pomianowski, "The National Codification of Civil Law in Poland at the Beginning of the 19th Century. Sources and Inspirations", in V. Amorosi and V. M. Minale (eds.), *History of Law and Other Humanities: Views of the Legal World Across Time* (Madrid, 2019), opp. 238-240, 243.

[39] Zarzycka, "Rola organów władzy Królestwa Polskiego w pracach legislacyjnych nad narodowym prawem rzeczowym w latach 1815-1830", *Studia z Dziejów Państwa i Prawa Polskiego*, VIII (2003), pp. 132-133; Pomianowski, *Początki polskiego czasopiśmiennictwa prawniczego. Seria pierwsza „Themis Polskiej"* (Warsaw, 2015), p. 208. For a different view, French norms as the basis of the draft, see Grynwaser, note 1 above, pp. 147-148.

[40] Pomianowski, note 39 above, pp. 64-65, 250.

rejected back in 1814, and in France itself a rejection had occurred of individual provisions of the Code Civil, among them those relating to freedom of divorce.[41] Unlike the German states, where by virtue of nationalist moods the provisions of French legislation were reworked in order to conceal their origin, in the Kingdom of Poland, as Sobociński noted, "the national existence was under threat", and therefore the idea of preserving a liberal legislation no longer linked with French imperialism rather rapidly acquired a national-liberation hue".[42] The present study shows that this conclusion is closer to reality and to a great extent reflects the political realities of the Kingdom of Poland after the 1815 Congress of Vienna than is the view of Pomianowski, who believes that "a stronger link to French law" as an important element of separation from Russia was felt by Polish legal elites in connection with its modification between 1818 and 1825.[43]

Draft codifications based on Napoleonic legislation were submitted several times to the Legislative Commission of the Russian Empire (1809, 1813-1814, 1821).[44] In that case the motives probably were the modernization and liberalization of law; that is, the question of borrowing French models in each instances had a different meaning.

The fate of the received legislation was actively discussed by legal scholars. Bandtkie in 1815 and later wrote about the baseless appeals for the complete repeal thereof, for it was one of the best of the existing and based on the extensive use of Roman and foreign law, was systemic and harmonious, precise, refined, and did not mix norms of civil law with scientific doctrine and administrative prescriptions. Its virtue was the maximal freedom of legal relations and the private life of the individual. Bandtkie also believed that French law was close to the needs and character of the Poles.

[41] W. Sobociński, "Prawo francuskie w Niemczech a w Polsce: nowe opracowania niemieckie recepcji I refleksje porównawcze", *Annales Universitatis Mariae Curie-Skłodowska, Sectio F: Humaniora*, XXXVII (1982), p. 181; Pomianowski, "Postulat narodowego charakteru prawa w pracach kodyfikacyjnych doby Królestwa Kongresowego", *Czasopismo Prawno-Historyczne*, LXXI, no. 1 (2019), p. 119.

[42] Sobociński, note 41 above, pp. 182, 185-186. Also see Kodrębski, note 26 above, p. 157. For a different view, that received French law began to be regarded as national law by its opponents only after 1831, see W. Witkowski, "Warszawa jako ośrodek polskiej nauki prawa w dobie zaborów", *Krakowskie Studia z Historii Państwa*, VIII (2015), p. 49.

[43] Pomianowski, note 38 above, p. 243.

[44] Grynwaser, note 1 above, p. 81.

Nonetheless, the received Code Civil contained shortcomings subject to rectification. On the contrary, to return to the operation of the law of the *Rzecz Pospolita* was not worthwhile; this would mean a return to disorder in legislation or, in the case of the Lithuanian Statute, to an anachronistic law, for "that which was good for the sixteenth century was not appropriate for the nineteenth century, and not a single part of ancient fatherland legislation was better than the law now in force". Therefore, one should either make changes in the codes in force or draft new ones. But for the last a highly developed science of law was necessary, experience, and – most important – an urgent need, and this did not exist. Therefore it would be better to retain the received law for an extended period and even not change it, not allow legislative experiments with doubtful consequences, and develop legal education.[45] Sobociński asserted that Bandtkie in his address of 1812 even more clearly upheld the idea of not changing the received codes, but in a later publication these passages were cut out.[46]

Hube offered a larger vision of the received legislation. He believed that the Code Napoleon was a synthesis of new ideas and old jurisprudence (it combined principles of Roman and customary law).[47] It was embedded in French traditions (together with Germanic and Roman), was deeply national, and as such was even more localized by a new judicial practice.[48] French legislation was of high quality, and its reception on Polish territories was easy because the "entire old order of things no longer existed". But "foreign grounds were less consistent with local ideas", the national spirit, the distinctive features of social relations, and therefore the implementation of national codification was a priority on the basis of the "collection of observations of the country's [judicial] practice".[49] In addition, the preservation of the received codes made Polish doctrine constantly dependent on the French, the level of whose development Hube did not consider to be high.[50]

[45] Bandtkie, "Myśli o zmianie prawodawstwa krajowego", *Rocznik Lubelski*, III (1960), pp.168-169, 173-174; Litauer, note 15 above, pp. 50, 53, 62-66.

[46] Sobociński, note 41 above, p. 164.

[47] Hube, "O stanie nauki prawa w naszych czasach (1827)", in Hube, *Opera*, ed. K. Dunin (Warsaw, 1905), I, p. 7.

[48] Hube, "Uwagi nad systematem Kodexu cywilnego francuskiego", *Themis Polska*, V (1829), pp. 309-310.

[49] Ibid., pp. 297, 299, 301-302, 308, 310.

[50] Ibid., p. 329.

From the moment of the appearance of the Code, legal science had subjected it to consideration and discovered material problems. French legislation in particular, following Roman law and the old codes, considered the individual to be an independent entity, but according to contemporary doctrines should be regarded as mutually-dependent in society. By reason of such manifestations of imperfection, in Hube's view, this legislation must not be left without changes in the Kingdom of Poland.[51]

Heylman noted instead that the French codes and their realization were a "people's-scientific legislation", a new instance of the harmony of the political and technical elements in the development of law, a "continuous and lively mutuality between the people and judicial proceedings". The most important virtue of the French legal order he considered to be the achievement of a national unity of legislation, judicial practice, and legal science.[52] Therefore, Heylman believed it to be inadvisable to reject the received codes and court organization in the Kingdom of Poland, the more so because in the contemporary position of the country they were the basis of the unity of its law, court procedure, and doctrine.[53]

In his anonymous work of 1827, Bieńkowski noted that the received legislation, just as other codifications of that period, was farther from natural law than the law of the *Rzecz Pospolita*. But he did not call for casting aside the French codes – merely certain inappropriate norms.[54] Węgrzecki also insisted in a reply to this work upon the received legislation was of quality and reflected the principles of natural law, but in a form corresponding to the modern day.[55]

To the contrary, Zaborowski asserted that the introduction of French legislation by Napoleon occurred "in order to strengthen political advantage and moral impact", was directed towards the

[51] Ibid., pp. 302-307, 310-311, 313-324, 332-333, and 338-339.

[52] Heylman, "Wywod zasad ogolnych nauki prawa i prawodawstwa", *Themis Polska*, VII (1830), pp. 27-28, 30-31, 35, 39, 48-49.

[53] Heylman, "Myśli o nauce prawa i prawodawstwie w kraiu naszym", *Themis Polska*, VII (1830), pp. 111, 117, 122-123, 125.

[54] P. Szymaniec, "Nauka prawa jako działalność pro bono. Uwagi na temat polskiej nauki prawa w latach 1807-1831", M. Marszal and J. Przygodzki (eds.), *Pro publico bono – idee i działalność* (Wroclaw, 2016), pp. 111-113.

[55] Ibid., pp. 113-114.

further destruction of the "nationality of legal life". Preservation of the operation of the received codes was contrary to national notions and did not enable the fully-fledged legal life to develop, and these norms themselves remained dormant, unneeded by society. Zaborowski, however, averred that their rapid replacement was impossible because of the inadequate development of the Polish science of law, and therefore they should be adapted with the assistance of judicial practice.[56]

* * *

Issues of family law, especially relating to marriages, divorces, and registration of acts of civil status considered in connection with the received French legislation, were a somewhat specific discussion. In essence, these issues concerned the correlation between secular and canon law. Three models were suggested: (1) leaving all these issues to the jurisdiction of the State, secular marriage, and freedom of divorce; (2) return to the jurisdiction of the church, as was the matter under the *Rzecz Pospolita*; (3) various mixed State-church models.

One of the major material issues discussed at the time was the secular or religious character of marriage. The secular understanding of marriage was subject to severe critique in the Sejm at the time of the Duchy of Warsaw.[57] Some members of the Reform Committee in 1814 proposed the experience of Austria as a Catholic country, where the dissolution of marriage was considered in secular courts, and this did not lead to an increase in the number of divorces. Other Committee members insisted that marriage has solely a religious character, the social order and customs of the country are based on the sacredness of this tie, and therefore the respective issues should be within the exclusive competence of the church.[58] In June 1814 Committee members in general agreed

[56] [S. Zaborowski], "Rozbiór krytyczny dziela pod tytułem: Upominek pogrobowy ś.p. Kazimierza Pliszki Podlesianina; rzecz o sukcessii ...", *Themis Polska*, VI (1829), p. 231; [Zaborowski], "Jurysprudencya sądu kassacyinego Xięswa Warszawskiego i związek instytucyi kassacyinéy z ogólném życiem prawném w kraju", *Themis Polska*, VI (1829), pp. 365-368, 371-373.

[57] S. Godek, "'Już Napoleon w swoim Kodeksie rozwody upoważnia'. Kilka uwag w związku z książką Piotra Zbigniewa Pomianowskiego, Rozwód w XIX wieku na centralnych ziemiach polskich. Praktyka stosowania Kodeksu Napoleona w latach 1808-1852", *Czasopismo prawno-historyczne*, LXXI (2019), p. 377-378.

[58] Gałędek, Klimaszewska, and Pomianowski, "Prace Komitetu Cywilnego Reformy nad przygotowaniem narodowej kodyfikacji prawa cywilnego i procedury cywilnej w przededniu utworzenia Królestwa Polskiego (1814–1815) –

that the secular character of marriage did not correspond to the national distinctive features of the Poles.[59]

In June 1814 the Reform Committee decided by a majority vote that matters relating to marriages and the registration of acts of civil status should be returned to church jurisdiction, but secular arbitrators should become part of church courts. It was asserted that marriage has a civil and a spiritual nature that should not be separated. In the context of the present study we consider the following assertion to be important:

> Where is the order and good of society so that court proceedings are uniform, independent, and effectuated by offices determined for this purpose; it is impossible therefore to create a separate spiritual court for divorce cases but leave them under a single legal proceeding in the country, adding only clergy thereto. ... otherwise they would be given an exaggerated impact, which would awaken a long-standing apprehension of appropriation and abuse that generated mistrust, reproaches, and fear of the clergy and led in time past to religious reforms.[60]

But the majority of Committee members argued in favor of preserving church jurisdiction given the negative consequences of secular consideration of issues of marriage for public morality and the distinctive features of Poland. The Committee adopted draft law on marriage in October 1814. But the decision had no consequences, and the model provided by the French Code Civil remained in force.[61]

In his address at a session of the Reform Committee on 25 October 1814, Koźmian supported limitations on the church with respect to entering into marriage depending on degree of kinship and set out a classification of canon law: "(1) that which emanates from natural and divine law and which even the Highest Spiritual Authority cannot abolish; (2) from norms of the Church, where instances have been described from which spiritual authority may

edycja źródłowa. Część II", *Krakowskie Studia z Historii Państwa i Prawa*, XII (2019), p. 392.

59 Gałędek, note 18 above, pp. 27-28.

60 Gałędek, Klimaszewska, and Pomianowski, note 58 above, pp. 388-391, 393.

61 Gałędek, note 18 above, pp. 28-30.

exempt; (3) from civil norms which the Church respects, applying the obstacles to marriage specified by them".[62]

Wybicki protested during the discussions that Poland "always remained under the withe of the clerical and political oath, so that the spiritual authority would write us laws from behind the Alpine mountains", suggesting that issues of canon law be subject to executive power.[63]

As a result of the discussion, on 25 October 1814 the Reform Committee decided to preserve the conformity of civil law to canon law, but in order to change the provisions relating to the degree of kinship which are an obstacle to marriage the Government of the Kingdom of Poland should apply to the Pope in Rome.[64] At a session on 30 October 1814 it was decided to retain the conformity of civil law provisions to the confessional law of other confessions in the State and to acknowledge the primacy of religious prescriptions with respect to secular norms and the jurisdiction of spiritual courts (with the addition of secular arbitrators) on matters of the conclusion and dissolution of marriage, for "otherwise the prescriptions of law might prove to be unsuitable to some confession and in this event would not be respected, for the duties arising from religion are foremost and not from civil law, and therefore the legislator should avoid any inconsistency with the former".[65]

It is important to note, following contemporary Polish observers: despite the fact that all members of the Committee, including Bieńkowski, were conservative and considered the law of marriage in connection with religion, when considering the respective issues here they with rare exception did not turn to the content of canon law.[66] Ultimately, Book One of the 1825 Civil

[62] Gałędek, Klimaszewska, and Pomianowski, note 58 above, pp. 411-412; Gałędek and Klimaszewska, "A Controversial Transplant? Debate Over the Adaptation of the Napoleonic Code on the Polish Territories in the Early 19th Century", *Journal of Civil Law Studies*, XI, no. 2 (2018), p. 279.

[63] Grynwaser, note 1 above, p. 97.

[64] Gałędek, Klimaszewska, and Pomianowski, note 58 above, p. 413.

[65] Ibid., pp. 416-417; Gałędek, note 18 above, pp. 32-33.

[66] Gałędek and Klimaszewska, "The Work of the Civil Reform Committee on the New Regulation of Catholic Marriages in 1814", *Krakowskie Studia z Historii Państwa i Prawa* (Special issue; 2018), pp. 200-201.

Code of the Kingdom of Poland consolidated a mixed model of jurisdiction: civil courts with the participation of clergy.[67]

We add that Daniłowicz pointed to, in his view, the unsuccessful historical examples of the *Rzecz Pospolita* borrowing norms of feudal, canon, and Roman law which were not adapted to the living conditions of society and the spirit of the people.[68] He also noted the value of retaining the "purity" as one of the major advantages for the development of national law, and this is defined as the "elimination of all possible heterogeneous materials, alien mixtures – in a word, that which is not a simple expression of the will of lawmakers and cannot be called law".[69] But in the context of other assertions by Daniłowicz, the last should be understood not as an appeal for the purification of law and its limitation to the elements of autochthonic origin, but as a formal nationalization thereof – only that to which society has given consent through empowered institutions has force, and the autochthonic or borrowed nature of particular norms or institutions is not considered in this event. Undoubtedly, reference was being made to the elimination from national law of elements of supranational origin, including canon law.

* * *

The oldest legal discussion in the period here considered in the central Polish territories was linked with the historical influence of Roman law on the law of the *Rzecz Pospolita*. Some even consider this discussion to be the most important at the time.[70]

In his dissertation *De studio juris Polonici* (1806), Bandtkie wrote with regret that in the *Rzecz Pospolita* "Roman law might have much less authority that this in western countries", as a consequence of which there was a "shortcoming of theoretical science".[71] But back in 1812 he had noted that in the old Kingdom of Poland and the *Rzecz Pospolita,* Roman law in the version of the Justinian Code

[67] Gałędek, Klimaszewska, and Pomianowski, note 58 above, p. 389.

[68] Daniłowicz, *Kodex Napoleona w porównaniu z prawami polskiemi i litewskiemi* (Warsaw, 1905), pp. 38, 46, 51, 67.

[69] Ibid., p. 52.

[70] Ch. E. Mecke, "Dyskurs o zasadniczej myśli prawniczej w 'Themis Polskiej' (1828-1830) na tle program historycznej szkoły prawa w Niemczech", *Forum prawnicze* (2018), p. 23; Szymaniec, note 54 above, p. 107.

[71] F. Bentkowski, *Historia literatury polskiey, wystawiona w spisie dziel drukiem ogloszonych* (1814), II, p. 205.

was extended from Prussia to city law and had become "auxiliary or was considered referential" and likewise had become the basis of legal education.[72] In addition, Roman law was the foundation of collections of old Polish law, canon law, customs of judicial procedure, and influenced legal doctrine.[73] This influence of Roman law he proclaimed to be thereafter still real – relative to instances not encompassed by new legislation.[74] A competition was held during the Deanship of Bandtkie at the Law Faculty of Warsaw University during the 1825/26 academic year for the best scholarly work devoted to the reception of Roman law in ancient Poland.[75]

Lelewel in 1827 attempted to sum up the discussion. He emphasized the need to structure positions and, especially, to demarcate the question relative to the operation of Roman law on Polish territories from its role in the development of legal science. Various types of influence and operation needed clarification.[76] Lelewel noted that complete denial of the influence of Roman law (as Czacki stressed) was not productive, pointing out that legal scholars had proved such influence on city law, together with the role of Roman law as an auxiliary law in Royal Prussia (province of the Kingdom of Poland in the *Rzecz Pospolita*) and the Duchy of Courland and Semigallia (an autonomous part of the *Rzecz Pospolita*).[77] But this influence on Polish territories proper, Lelewel emphasized, was purely referential: "Roman law in a Polish court

[72] Bandtkie, "Wywod historyczny praw mieyskich w Polsce dawney obowiązuiących", in J. W. Bandtkie, *Zbiór rospraw o przedmiotach prawa polskiego* (Warsaw, 1812), pp. 175-176.

[73] Ibid., pp. 173-176, 197-199. Bandtkie, "O uprawnieniu dzieci przez zaszly zwiazek malzenski czynionem", in J. W. Bandtkie, *Zbiór rospraw o przedmiotach prawa polskiego* (Warsaw, 1812), p. 218; Bandtkie, *Uwagi o potrzebie nauki prawa w naszym kraju w szczegolności, a o użytku onejże w ogolnością* (Warsaw, 1814), pp. 32-33; Bandtkie, "O poważaniu dawnieyszém w Polszcze prawników uczonych", *in Posiedzenie publiczne Królewskiego-Warszawskiego Uniwersytetu, na uczczenie pamiątki uczonych mężow, a mianowicie polakow, odbyte dnia 15 lipca 1825 roku* (Warsaw, 1825), pp. 37, 42.

[74] Bandtkie, note 72 above, pp. 204-205.

[75] A. Rosner, "Jan Wincenty Bandtkie 1783-1846", in *Portrety uczonych. Profesorowie Uniwersytetu Warszawskiego 1816-1915* (2016), p. 65.

[76] J. Lelewel, "Prawo rzymskie w Polsczce w sprawach kriminalnych, z powodu rozpraw J. N. Janowskiego (1827)", in J. Lelewel, *Rozbiory dziel obejmujacych albo dzieje, albo rzechy polskie roznymi czasy przez Joachima Lelewela ogloszone* (Poznan, 1844), pp. 253, 257.

[77] Ibid., pp. 255-256.

proceeding had no force and authority"; we "did not like Roman law, loathed it, and did not want it to be binding". It had "no authority or even favor among the people"; Roman law "was in no way binding in Poland".[78]

Maciejowski acknowledged some, but insignificant, influence of Roman law on Polish and other Slavic laws manifest in legal education.[79] Hube wrote about the material influence of Roman law in 1827, but in 1829 clarified that on Polish territories it did not have binding force.[80] Zaborowski[81] and Heylman[82] denied such influence almost completely.

One of the few who upheld the binding force of Roman law in the past on Polish territories was Jan Niepomucen Janowski (1803-1888), a student of Bandtkie. He cited passages from the chronicles and descriptions of court cases which might testify to the use of the Justinian Code in courts but could not persuade contemporaries and was criticized in a well-argued review by Lelewel.[83] Bieńkowski in 1827 undertook to prove that a regional collection of laws – the Prussian Corrector (1598 Ius Terrae Nobilitaits Prussiae Correctum, Prawo Ziemskie Szlachty Pruskiej poprawione) – on the creation of which the Justinian Code exerted significant influence, operated throughout all of the *Rzecz Pospolita*. But this view was criticized by Węgrzecki[84] Also of importance was the position taken by Wychechowski:"that which we now call Polish national law is merely a codification of Roman and canon laws which were formed because of a mixture of those laws with folk laws and customs".[85]

78 Ibid., pp. 257, 263, 265, 267, 275; Lelewel, "Przypiski do dwu rozpraw Al. Mickiewicza i Franc Morze", in Lelewel, *Rozbiory dziel obejmujacych albo dzieje, albo rzechy polskie roznymi czasy przez Joachima Lelewela ogloszone* (Poznan, 1844).

79 Maciejowski, "Ogłoszenie prenumeraty", *Themis Polska*, V (1829), pp. 418-419. Also see Pomianowski, "Główne nurty ideologiczno-metodologiczne w środowisku warszawskich prawników przed wybuchem powstana listopadowego", *Zeszyty Prawnicze UKSW*, XI (2011), p. 411; F. Ochimowski, "Dawne prawo polskie prywatne a Kodeks Napoleona", *Gazeta Sądowa Warszawska*, no. 22 (28 May 1908), p. 335.

80 Hube, "Krotki rys historyi literatury prawa (1827)", in Hube, *Opera*, ed. K. Dunin (Warsaw, 1905), I, p. 70; Hube, note 48 above, p. 309.

81 [Zaborowski], note 56 above, p. 231.

82 Heylman, note 53 above, p. 137; Heylman, note 52 above, pp. 4, 27.

83 Pomianowski, note 39 above, pp. 139-142.

84 Ibid., pp. 144-145.

85 Kodrębski, note 26 above, p. 164.

No doubt on the whole the positions of those who supported the significant historical influence of Roman law on Polish law during the period here considered were weaker than those of their opponents. One must, however, agree with Mecke that the positions of the participants in the discussion did not differ materially.[86] It should be added that here one should speak of a discourse within whose framework a discussion arose several times.

All the works of the Polish legal scholars here considered during the first third of the nineteenth century acknowledged the material, if not determinative, influence of Roman law on the development of the legal orders of western European States. And it was generally recognized that Roman law was the basis of the development of the categories and conceptions of the science of law. Assessing the significance of rethinking Roman law in the works of Warsaw jurists during the period here considered, Kodrębski wrote: "an awareness that the norms in force of the Code Napoleon rested on Roman law, on one hand, strengthened the authority of the Code as a symbol of the civilization of the West and heir to the classical tradition and, on the other, was evidence of the actuality and vitality of Roman law".[87] Pomianowski observed: "The ascribed binding force to Roman law in Poland before the Partitions was something in the nature of writing a local metric for the Code Napoleon".[88]

In the present writer's view, the discussion of the introduction and further fate of French law in the Duchy of Warsaw and the Kingdom of Poland gives reason to consider that discussion to be the longest and most intensive in legal thought during the period here considered. From today's perspective, the reception left an exceedingly positive influence on the development of Polish society, especially by liberating personally depending peasants and equalizing the population in rights, and also modernization, unification, and systematization of law. During the introduction thereof, however, it was perceived variously, because the interests were disturbed of influential social groups, traditional notions changed, and the national dignity of the Poles was affected.

[86] Mecke, note 70 above, p. 28.

[87] Kodrębski, note 26 above, p. 173.

[88] Pomianowski, note 39 above, p. 144; also see Mecke, note 70 above, pp. 23, 28-29.

A vast spectrum of views relating to the fate of the received law was advanced: preservation, abolition, reworking, adaptation, and supplementation. But after 1814-1815, together with the defeat of Napoleon, this law lost its imperial sovereign and ceased to be perceived as a manifestation of foreign domination. And over time in the face of a repressive policy of the Russian Imperial Government, it acquired the character of national law, protecting the separateness and uniqueness of Polish society under conditions of statehood not fully realized.

Moreover, the virtues of French law gradually were recognized, and issues that generated the sharpest disagreement of various groups of the population were decided by making changes in legislation. Of course, socio-economic relations evolved under the influence of the received law. All this together led to the view dominating of the temporary preservation of French law until the undertaking of a new national codification. Polish legal scholars emphasized the high quality of this law, and also deemed it to be a factor in preserving the affiliation of Poland to western European intellectual space. But the views of legal scholars differed substantially on the conformity thereof to the conditions of Polish society.

Nor was there unity among Polish legal scholars regarding the sources of a future national codification. The view predominated that the complete rejection of French law was impossible, taking into account at least the impossibility of relying solely on the old law of the *Rzecz Pospolita*, which was obsolete, not unified, and not codified. It was suggested either to take French law as the basis with particular changes, or to synthesize the new law on the basis of French and other foreign codes, or to supplement with norms of French origin that which was lacking in the law of the *Rzecz Pospolita* or did not conform to the modern stage of development. But the most important codification outcome, in the present writer's view, was rather eloquent: two-thirds of the norms in Book One of the Civil Code of the Kingdom of Poland adopted in 1825 came from the Code Napoleon.

The position expressed in 1814 by proponents of a return to the operation of canon law and spiritual courts (and not only Roman Catholic) with a precise articulation of the significance of this issue should be perceived as opposition to the idea of the integrity of a national legal order. The influential nature of the idea of the supremacy of confessional norms in relation to national law is evident in the decision of the Reform Committee of the same year on preserving the conformity of civil law to church law, the decision concerning issues of changing church law through recourse to the Pope of Rome. And, on the contrary, in the position of individual members of the Reform Committee in 1814 against returning to spiritual courts jurisdiction with respect to the secular population can be seen as the idea of the wholeness, the universality, of national law, which did not provide for the existence of a competing legal order. To some degree the compromise decision of the Committee with regard to mixed spiritual-State courts on matters of family law corresponded to this idea, and, moreover, the carrying over of these cases according to Book One of the 1825 Civil Code to the jurisdiction of State courts, but with the participation of clergy, did so as well.

There is every reason to agree with the view of a number of legal scholars that the discussion of the historical influence of Roman law on Polish territories did not only have a historical-legal character. Directly or indirectly, it concerned an assessment of the contemporary state of and determination of the priorities for the further development of the law of the central Polish territories and attitudes towards the received French legislation.

§4.2. The Universal in Legal Development

The proclamation by legal scholars in the second half of the eighteenth and first third of the nineteenth centuries of the exclusiveness of national legal orders on the legal map of the world was accompanied by rethinking in principle the essence and role of the Universal in law. The bankruptcy of the idea concerning the possibility of formalizing any Universal in law in the form of a separate legal order was cognized and proclaimed by many legal scholars then, who pointed to the absence of normative space for this under conditions of recognition of the territoriality and sovereignty of States, and also the inappropriateness thereof – for each concrete nation this speculatively constructed legal order proves to be nil and alien simultaneously. This was demonstrated by assessments then of the possibility of an extra-national legal order, manifested in views on the nature of international law and the dominance of some nations over others.

Legal scholars concluded that the formalization of the Universal in law was impossible outside the framework of national legal orders: the dominance always of the essential, territorial, and socially limited and led to limited substantive changes, and the Separate could not be overcome without the complete destruction thereof, and international law acted as an external confirmation of the nation-State legal order and had only concrete-national material expression. The Universal in law, in the view of legal scholars at the time, should have been embodied in the nation-State legal orders, and only the procedural might be outside them.

Given the general convention of legal scholars then relative to the insuperability and totality of the form of the Particular – the national legal order – searches for the Universal in law were manifest in attempts to reflect on the substantive similarities in the development of legal systems through ideas of their substantive identicalness or relative substantive similarity. During the period here considered, legal scholars concluded that the substantive identicalness of legal systems was impossible, as also was a single invariable progress in the legal sphere, which always was affected by a number of distinctive features and factors of specific societies at a specific time. Accordingly, there was not and could not be a universally suitable positive law which might have been accepted by all legal orders.

Less radical than uniformity and more acceptable for legal scholars at the time was the idea of the relative substantive similarity of legal orders. Scholars referred to whether, given the conditions of the multiplicity and uncoordinated nature of the substance of national legal systems, the essential unity and stadiality of the world development of principles of positive law were possible. Legal scholars acknowledged the limited acceptability and relativity of the idea of such development – as one of the immanent trends towards doctrinal convergence (together with trends towards the preservation and deepening of individuality), having criticized its possible teleological implications. The grounds for such a vision were ideas that the Universal in law, which had not proper form, correlated only with the Distinctive within the framework of the Particular (national law), and the transfer of social legal experience is historical and concrete – from one Particular to another.

Another approach to the study of the Universal in law during the period here considered was the doctrine on the dialogue of legal systems. Legal scholars singled out two inter-connected but distinct spheres of this dialogue: within national legal systems and between them. The internal dialogue, which rested on the idea of the non-selfsufficiency of distinctive elements of national law in the world at the time, consisted of singling out, identifying, and being aware of certain elements as substantively general (and their form was always national-distinctive). Moreover, the aggregate of general and distinctive elements of national law was not the simple sum thereof, but represented a struggle and balancing, and the result and components thereof consequently might be determined only *a posteriori*. The dialogue becomes an internal interaction of the singled out and cognized distinctive and general elements, and legal scholars or lawmakers, depending on their position, might make a choice to the benefit of the priority development of the first, second, or both – understanding the inevitability of the internal pluralism of any national legal order.

The conception of external dialogue of legal orders had in view the generalization of the processes of the arising of similarities in law being also a result of borrowing, correlation, and competition of legal orders. Although a general element may emanate from the unity of the biological, physical, and anthropological nature of man, it, unlike this nature, is developed and transformed in the process of human interaction in society and between societies. Legal scholars were agreed that during the interaction of the Particulars between themselves, they act as an integral (the unity of the general and distinctive elements), and as a result of such interaction there is growth in the role and extent of general (disseminated in more than one Particular) elements which, nonetheless, do not lose their immanent (within the confines of national legal orders) character. In the conception of the external dialogue, the General is perceived not as the Universal and irreversible, but as a concrete-social (disseminated within a certain limited group of legal orders) and changeable, as a variable aggregate of interactions which is, above all, not material, but a procedural reality and may be materialized outside national legal orders only in a scientific text – as an analytical unity. At the same time, the idea developed of the procedural character of national distinctiveness in law – as distinctive features of the dialogue with others and participation in the creation of an era.

The recognition by legal scholars of the inevitability of national diversity and non-totality, non-transcendentalness, non-materiality, procedural, and immanent character of the social General in law placed its own national law in dialogue with others. This dialogue might have primarily a positive (exchange of experience) or negative (the other is a negative indicator of us) character. But the emphases did not change the recognition that this is not two dialogues, but merely two facets of a single dialogue, the result of which is the perception by the parties (lawmakers and scholars) of individual elements or principles of law – the Universal, General, and Common are conventional.[89]

Czacki denied the existence of Universal law in Europe during the Middle Ages and pointed out that the similarity of national legal orders may arise in the process their self-development and not testify to the existence of an institutionalized General in law.[90] He pointed to the possibility of the situation of interaction lacking in law – neighboring peoples might hate one another, not perceive or not understand other law and not borrow anything from one another. He categorically denied the reception of Roman law in Poland.[91] Czacki pointed to elements of universality in the development of law which are determined by various eras of civilization,[92] but this view was not emphasized.

Czacki partially even rejected the direct operation of Roman law in Europe of the Middle Ages: "inherited hatred of the Oracle of Justinian".[93] The theses concerning the non-universal, but national, character of Roman law and the naturalness of the nation-State form of law were reiterated by Czacki in 1809: "It is sufficient for me in order to show that Roman law is not the basis of our law" only the "law of the country is an Oracle for us, and foreign law is [merely] evidence of respected ideas".[94]

However, Czacki pointed to a completely normal phenomenon of the acquisition by one people from another of "primary customs" (for the recipient this fund may signify entering

[89] O. V. Kresin, *Comparative Legal Studies: 1750 to 1835. Approaches to Conceptualization*, ed. & transl. W. E. Butler (London, 2019), II, pp. 338-340.

[90] T. Czacki, *O litewskich i polskich prawach o ich duchu, żródłach, związku, i o rzeczach zawartych w pierwczym statucie dla Litwy, 1529 roku wydanym* (Krakow, 1861), I, pp. 16, 29.

[91] Ibid., I, pp. vii-viii, 4-6, 19, 25, 28-29; II, p. 292; Czacki, *Czy prawo rzymskie było zasadą praw litewskich i polskich? I czy z połnocnemi narodami mielismy wiele wspolnych praw i zwyczaiow? Rosprawa czytana w Krzemieńcu na otwarciu roku szkolnego 1808 w Gimnazyum Wołyńskiem* (Vilno, 1809), pp. 77, 94-95, 97, 99-116, 121-121.

[92] Czacki, note 91 above (1809), p. 99.

[93] Czacki, note 90 above, I, pp. vii, 7, 11, 16, 18, 19, 22, 29, 43-45, 49, 51-54, 56; II, pp. 292-293.

[94] Czacki, note 91 above (1809), pp. 121-122, 77, 85, 94-95.

into social existence).[95] These same ideas were developed by Rakowiecki: borrowed elements might be the primary foundation of culture and law of a people".[96] Czacki in 1800 wrote about the origin of general positive elements in law because of law being imposed on conquered peoples.[97] Rakowiecki expressed the same ideas between 1820 and 1822,[98] Maciejowski in his history of Slavic legislation,[99] among others.

Kołłątaj wrote about the worldwide human sociality and foresaw the possibility of universal legal uniformity: "so that all States simultaneously administered internally by uniform and the same principles of political law". The Napoleonic Empire he considered to be continental European and nonetheless foresaw the possibility that "that new entity in policies", a "great republic of enlightened peoples" encompasses the entire world if the level of civilization of all peoples "ripens". Such an empire/republic of the new type assumes the unification of small States into federations and the separate existence of large States. Despite Kołłątaj's emphasis on the deferential preservation of the freedom of peoples, there was no answer relating to the fully-fledged preservation of the legal orders of all or only large peoples. He pointed out that previously oppressed peoples should have been liberated. In his view, the uniformity of the law of national States might in full measure ensure the rights and freedoms of every person and become a pledge of the equality of peoples and international peace. It would create the foundation for the joint development of law by all peoples and the mutual taking of ideas and norms: "they are for us, we will work for them for the same and common good". The grounds for uniformization are that the "needs and duties of

95 Ibid., pp. 95, 122.

96 I. B. Rakowiecki, *Prawda ruska; czyli, Prawa wielkiego xięcia Jaroslawa Wladymirowicza, tudziez traktaty Olgi y Igora ww. xx. kiiowskich z cesarzami greckimi, y Mścislawa Dawidowicza x. Smoleńskiego z Rygą zawarte, których texta, obok z polskiém tłomaczeniem poprzedza Rys historyczny zwyczaiów, obyczaiów religiy, praw y języka dawnych słowiańskich y słowiańsko-ruskich narodow* (Warsaw, 1820), II, pp. 246, 254, 315.

97 Czacki, note 90 above, I, pp. 5-6, 8, 11, 45, 51-54, 97.

98 Rakowiecki, *O stanie cywilnym dawnych slowian. Rzech czytana na publiczném posiedzeniu Towarzystwa Królewskiego Warszawskiego Przyiacoł Nauk dnia 3 Maia 1820 roku* (Warsaw, 1820), p. 2; Rakowiecki, note 96 above, I, pp. 81-82, 128, 135; II, pp. 187-188, 254.

99 Maciejowski, *Historya prawodawstw słowiańskich* (Warsaw, 1832-1835), I, pp. 3, 5-6, 54, 67-69.

peoples are virtually the same, and therefore justice should be one for all", and differences emanate only from the "greater or lesser damaging of primeval customs". The French codes should be the basis of uniformization, especially the 1804 Code Civil, which Kołłątaj called the "universal book of enlightened peoples", the "universal foundation of future legislation".[100]

The Polish Jacobites, members of the Society of republicans, the ideological inspiration of which was Kołłątaj, proclaimed the principles and norms of French codes to be perfected and universally applicable, a symbol of universal civilized development. In a Memorial by Józef Zajączek (1752 - 1826) to Napoleon, the introduction of French legislation on Polish territories without changes was suggested.[101]

Bandtkie believed that peoples act as individuals in world society. He wrote about the identicalness and obviousness of the "rules of mankind and rationality" of all peoples, and the differences he linked with personal interests and human passions.[102] Bandtkie pointed to the uniform gradual process of human development ("progress and rotation") and uniform stages of development (enlightenment) of peoples.[103] The most ancient was the patriarchal state, for which the dominance of customs and non-professional elected courts were characteristic. Subsequently, with the emergence of the State, other sources of law emerge, and the courts become professional.[104] Niemcewicz also wrote about human civilization and its stages and social time.[105]

Roman law in Bandtkie's vision acquired special importance, the character of "leading", "eternal and immutable rules", the "Oracle of the world", a "universal model", "light".[106] However,

100 Kołłątaj, *Uwagi nad teraźniejszem położeniem tej części Ziemi Polskiej, którą od Pokoju Tylżyckiego zaczęto zwać Księstwem Warszawskiem* (Lipsk, 1808), pp. 94, 97-105, 108-110, 114, 182, 184, 205; M. V. Syrko, note 6 above, p. 88.

101 Grynwaser, note 1 above, I, pp. 23, 57; Gałędek, note 18 above, p. 11; Gałędek, Klimaszweska, and Pomianowski, note 1 above, pp. 240-241.

102 Bandtkie, note 73 above (1812), p. 259; Bandtkie, "Co stanowi prawnika", *Pamiętnik Warszawski*, VI (1816), p. 312.

103 Bandtkie, note 73 above (1814), pp. 5, 36.

104 Ibid., pp. 5-6; Bandtkie, note 102 above (1816), pp. 311-312.

105 [J. U. Niemcewicz], *Przestroga dla społziomków na rok 1809* (Wrocław, 1808), pp. 16-18.

106 Bandtkie, note 73 above (1812), pp. 219, 258; Bandtkie, note 73 above (1814), p. 29.

the views of Sobociński and Szymaniec concerning the natural law character of Roman law, in the eyes of Bandtkie[107] were not sufficiently substantiated. He considered the French codes the closest contemporary legislation to the grounds of Roman law, emphasizing their suitability also for other peoples.[108] But the conclusion of Galędek and Klimaszewska that Bandtkie believed the Code Napoleon to be a "universal work which is suitable for transplantation on to Polish territory without adaptation to specific Polish conditions, excluding secular marriages" is too categorical and not sufficiently confirmed.[109]

Prince F. Szaniawski noted the existence of "laws of the entire world" side by side with national law, but had in view the laws of the physical world establishing limitations and acting as an orientator (especially the notion of natural law or universal justice) for positive law.[110] Nonetheless, Szaniawski suggested the existence of an innate human legal consciousness, thanks to which the "fundamental rights of communities" are identical.[111] He also used the idea of civilization ("changes, advantages, and improvement of people which was caused by their combining into a community") as identical stages in the development of peoples in the world and simultaneously a certain worldwide social time, conformity to which he, just as virtually all authors of the works here analyzed, demanded of law.[112] In his work the problem of uniformity and diversity in law was separated out as an autonomous point. He asserted that *a priori* to reckon an ideal law for the entire world was complex, and to embody it was impossible because the circumstances of the life of peoples were different, social order historically created law, and not *vice versa*. Therefore, in the sphere of law individual societies should improve themselves and they will thereby improve mankind as a whole.[113]

[107] W. Sobociński, "Jan Wincenty Bandtkie obrońca Kodeksu Napoleona", *Rocznik Lubelski*, III (1960), pp. 160-161; P. Szymaniec, note 54 above, pp. 104-105.

[108] Litauer, note 15 above, p. 62.

[109] Galędek and Klimaszewska, note 62 above, p. 295.

[110] F. K. Szaniawski, *Wiadomości początkowe w nauce prawa* (Warsaw, 1817), pp. 2-3, 6-7,16-17, 19-21.

[111] Szaniawski, *Statyka prawa, czyli nauka porównywań w prawie* (Warsaw, 1819), pp. 70-71.

[112] Szaniawski, note 110 above, p. 34; Szaniawski, note 111 above, pp. 71-72.

[113] Szaniawski, note 111 above, pp. 58, 74-75.

In 1827 Hube named Roman law as the "sole model of legislative improvement", but it also had an "individual character inherent thereto".[114] Later he cast doubt on the harmoniousness, consistency, and "mathematical precision" of Roman law, pointing out its conformity only to certain social relations.[115] He called the French codes the perfect model in 1829, for they "bore the imprint of new general legal concepts" but emphasized that this was a relative and provisional model. Everything was subject to changes, and the state of the development of legal thought as well; therefore, these codes should be subjected to critical analysis. In addition, to overcome individual national distinctive features in law was impossible:

> There is no law, at least in the contemporary state of development, which might be called universal and which might be applied to each country. I do not dispute that all legislation might be orientated towards a single general level of perfection, and gradually the grounds of legislation at present so diverse would be simplified. But the moment has not yet come ... Perhaps in fact the time will come when a people is deprived of its own laws, when it accepts another's ideas, but soon this acceptance will show itself to be not particular. The social life of a people will remain, notwithstanding the reception, practically the same as before.[116]

Hube suggested that the material element of law; that is, "the very essence, base of concrete norms" might have not only an individual (national) but also a universal character.[117] He also wrote about the "spirit of our time" in law, the worldwide development of civilization (the maturing of man).[118] The concept of the Universal in law is present in Hube's work – as universal eras of legal development. But they are in no way objectified as something whole, but are immanent in the Particular, arise from the organic vision of the nation: the family structure as childhood and youth

[114] R. Hube, "O stanie nauki prawa w naszych czasach (1827)", in Hube, *Opera*, ed. K. Dunin (Warsaw, 1905), I, pp. 8, 12.

[115] Hube, "Niektore uwagi nad historya nauki prawa (1830)", in note 114 above, I, pp. 42-43.

[116] Hube, note 48 above, pp. 301-303, 307-309, 329, 332-335.

[117] Ibid., p. 313.

[118] Hube, note 116 above, pp. 35, 37.

of a people, the civil structure as its adult life as an autonomous person.[119] Hoffman also believed that the "most healthy grounds" of law were embodied in Roman law, and he also used the idea of a social time (spirit of the time, civilization).[120]

Zaborowski decisively rejected and ridiculed the idea of "universal laws extracted from reason, common for all times and generations", an "imagined uniformity" of an a priori philosophy. He excluded in general the possibility of the existence of a universal positive law, having regard to different political circumstances, needs, and legal ideas of peoples. Zaborowski acknowledged the influence on law of natural climatic conditions of the development of society, but opposed the idea of determinism of the physical world with regard to the moral, for the last in principle is not determined, does not give itself too "cold calculation", "physical equalization". At the same time, he used the ideas of civilization and innate ideas of people in understanding the universal factors of the development of law. He separated political and technical elements in law, noting that "technical" norms of law which are formed by science are rather similar throughout the world. Moreover, using the example of the reception of Roman law, Zaborowski demonstrated the possibility of the existence of relative and non-eternal but all the same lengthy factors of the unification of law of different peoples.[121]

Maciejowski in works produced between 1829 and 1830 used the idea of the universal evolution of the enlightenment of peoples which proceeds unequally and provides for the possibility of leadership and lagging behind: "We are the latest in European enlightenment and will not arrive rapidly at the point of improvement to which the peoples neighboring us have already become. Such is the path of human affairs that all peoples must embrace in order to achieve the moral level necessary for them". He also pointed to the existence of human rights common to all

[119] Hube, «История древнего наследственного права у славян» [History of Ancient Inheritance Law Among the Slavs], in Сборник исторических и статистических сведений о России и народах ей единоверных и единоплеменных [Collection of Historical and Statistical Information on Russia and Peoples of the Same Faith and Tribe] (1845), I, pp. 100, 104.

[120] K. B. Hoffman, "O stanie nauki prawa w naszym kraju", Themis Polska, I (1828), pp. 20, 27.

[121] [Zaborowski], note 56 above, pp. 213-214, 222, 225, 229-230, 238, 240; [Zaborowski], note 56 above, p. 366; Pomianowski, note 39 above, p. 138.

peoples. Roman law he proclaimed to be the most perfected of any created, or chosen, historical source of all developed legislation suitable on the whole for use by all peoples. He criticized from the positions of Roman law the French Code Civil as less perfected but nonetheless "one of the most perfected which so far human reason and labor could achieve". Finally, Maciejowski concluded that it is absolutely impossible to create a perfect law because of the imperfection of man himself.[122] Maciejowski also wrote about the possibility of the historical transfer of the social experience of a people from other peoples which preceded it.[123]

In Maciejowski's history of Slavic legislation, Roman law acts to a certain extent as universal – but only as a doctrinal and not a normative reality, a model for study, and also rather formally mentioned "civilizationness" and "spirit and needs of the time".[124] In general, he drew attention, as did Rakowiecki, to the doctrinal links of national legal orders, underlying which was the authority and prestige of foreign law (legal experience).[125] Moreover, Maciejowski pointed out that the development of one legal order may gave impetus to changes in another without borrowing concrete norms.[126]

Heylman denied the idea of metaphysical reason and a single reasonable law for all peoples, asserting that every law is reasonable. The world and God exist irrespective of their contemplation by man. An abstract human reason has the right to existence, but the attempts thereof to create law have been forced to adjust to human realities and are determined by the social order: "Legislation, either real or ideal, is nothing other and can be nothing other than relations between human reason, the external world, and the Creator of all things, having regard to the social order between people". Law is created by the relation between reason and the external world, and the moral grounds of law are created by the relation between reason and the "spirit of the Creator". Therefore, Heylman asserted, in the world diversity

122 Maciejowski, note 79 above, pp. 416-419; Maciejowski, "Uwagi nad artukułem 960 K.C.", *Themis Polska*, VII (1830), pp. 230, 232, 236, 248-249.

123 Maciejowski, note 79 above, pp. 414, 416-417, 419.

124 Maciejowski, note 99 above, I, pp. v, vii, ix, 2, 38, 67-69.

125 Ibid., I, pp. 3, 5-6, 54, 67-69; Rakowiecki, note 98 above, p. 2; Rakowiecki, note 96 above, I, pp. 81-82, 128, 135; II, pp. 187-188, 254.

126 Maciejowski, note 99 above, I, p. 6.

is uniform, and the former is invincible. However, Heylman used the ideas of world civilization, identical stages of the development of peoples, social time, and praised Roman law as a "universal source of particular legislation and the most perfected school of jurists". He also allowed for the possibility of the objectification of the Universal in law as worldwide custom which is formed on an identical level of enlightenment or "carried over from a people to a people" and may be reflected in legislation, but the "legislation of the whole human species" remains immutable as a generalized concept.[127]

Bieńkowski proclaimed that civil law (in the sense of all private law), unlike political, criminal, and police law is "embedded in the nature of things and man" and "is the same everywhere, without distinction". In addition to natural law, he named Roman law as the "universal source" of contemporary civil law, as well as universal principles of law drawn from the same Roman law, human reason and experience, and morality innate in every person, immutable, and uniform for the "entire human species".[128]

Bieńkowski saw the "majesty" of the Code Napoleon in the embodiment of these universal principles.[129] As Gałędek noted, Bieńkowski thereby suggested the possibility of future global unification of civil law on the basis of principles suggested back in Roman law.[130] In comparison with the leading model ("truths already known") of its day; that is, universal development (in a concrete instance – French civil code), national law might be evaluated by degree of proximity to the model – as more or less perfected, progressive or obsolete.[131]

In 1818 Daniłowicz, evidently relying on the ideas of Gaetano Filangieri (1753-1788), asserted that one should "search not for the absolute, but for the relative good" in any law.[132] He noted that the

[127] Heylman, note 52 above, pp. 6-11, 18-19, 24, 26, 48-51; Heylman, note 53 above, pp. 134, 137.

[128] Grynwaser, note 1 above, p. 86; Pomianowski, "Postulat narodowego charakteru prawa w pracach kodyfikacyjnych doby Królestwa Kongresowego", *Czasopismo Prawno-Historyczne*, LXXI, no. 1 (2019), p. 122. Also see Szymaniec, note 54 above, pp. 109-110; Pomianowski, note 79 above, pp. 405-406.

[129] Gałędek, note 18 above, pp. 23-26; Gałędek and Klimaszewska, note 62 above, p. 288.

[130] Gałędek, note 18 above, p. 24.

[131] Ibid., p. 25.

[132] Daniłowicz, note 68 above, p. 66.

development of society determines the need for changes in law on the basis of its own or borrowed ideas; he also suggested the possibility of the private law of various peoples being identical, for it was generated by identical needs of people.[133] Rakowiecki mentioned the universal spirit of the era in the development of law, although he did not emphasize this, and suggested the possibility of similarity between the law of peoples which did not disturb their individuality – if such elements arose within each people itself in the process of its development; but the universal history of law he acknowledged not to be an objective process, but merely a domain of research.[134]

Ideas relating to the Universal in Law are encountered in documents of State agencies. This is so especially in the publication of the 1809 Department of Justice; the Code Napoleon was called an "immortal work which revealed all imperfections of past legislators".[135]

Predictions of the future are found in works by Warsaw legal scholars. Staszic wrote about the sole linear stadial development of all peoples from barbarianism to civilization, which was an embodiment of natural law and the realization of all-human reason. When peoples achieve a high level of civilization, he suggested the possibility of their "accretion", including universally, on the basis of hegemony, which also suggested the forming of elements of a single legal order and simultaneously the uniformization of national law. To be sure, Staszic considered such a unification to be an ideal – unlike "accretions" of smaller scale.[136] Hoene-Wroskii suggested the possibility of creating a world federation of States which would become the realization of a "universal societiness" capable of cognizing the absolute truth. But States would not be destroyed in so doing.[137] Jastrżębowski affirmed the possibility

133 Ibid., pp. 33, 43, 65, 71.

134 Rakowiecki, note 96 above, I, pp. 129, 134-135, 244, 246, 252; II, p. 255.

135 Litauer, note 6 ab, p. 363.

136 T. Matlęgiewicz, "W kręgu myśli słowianofilskiej Stanisława Staszica", *Wschodni rocznik humanistyczny 2010-2011*, VII (2011), pp. 169-170; A. Wierzbicki, *Europa w polskiej myśli historycznej i politycznej XIX i XX wieku* (2009), pp. 48-49, 52, 70.

137 Wierzbicki, note 136 above, p. 53.

of a coming together of peoples even before the disappearance of differences between them, including in the legal domain.[138]

We turn to authors of non-legal works. Brodziński substantiated the universal character of social development and simultaneously the inevitability of the distinctiveness of peoples through the concept of a social world as a system where all peoples are linked physically, as in the example of planets rotating around the Sun, and each performs a certain function necessary for all. The spiritual life and values of each people are indispensable because the existence of the Universal is determined by the existence and interaction or correlations (contradiction, balance) of all the Particulars, "as each member of a people should invest in its good, so each people is active and in greater part aspired to the general good of the human species".[139] A view of mankind in the form of a solar system with an inalienable function therein of each people also is encountered in the work by Zygmunt Krasiński (1812-1859).[140]

The contemplation by Warsaw scholars of the Universal in law during the period here considered was rich in various ideas, some of which were not subsequently explored and evidently were referred to in a certain well-known discourse but not necessarily purely a legal discourse. Taken together, they deserve careful reconstruction.

Virtually all scholars denied the possibility of the objectification of the Universal in law in the form of a single world legal order. Some scholars pointed to the existence of a world societiness which might have assumed the creation of a single law, especially universal customs. But the view finally dominated of the impossibility of creating a perfected law acceptable to all, the more so the embodiment thereof, having regard at least to human imperfections. Moreover, despite the differences between each society, it was pointed out that even manifested in some unknown way, such a universal law will remain a dead letter, will not be realized.

The idea of the unification of law through the dominance and expansion of the legal order of one people to all the rest was considered by scholars both historically and under contemporary

[138] Ibid., pp. 55-57.

[139] K. Brodziński, *O narodowości Polaków* (1917), pp. 15-17, 25-29.

[140] Wierzbicki, note 136 above, p. 71.

conditions to be real. Examples were cited, especially the Roman Empire with Roman law, the Napoleonic Empire with the French codes. But it was noted that such unification, albeit enduring, was not eternal and universal, and did not remove the distinctiveness of the dominant and subordinate legal orders. There was no single and stable convention of positions with regard to the universal, regional, or national character of Roman or French law. The vision of Roman law as the doctrinal foundation of national legal orders and a factor in the preservation of their doctrinal unity and forming of universal principles of law was widely shared. Some scholars suggested the quality of national law be assessed by the degree of closeness to Roman law or Napoleonic law as selected examples.

The possibility of the uniformization of law on natural grounds was rejected by virtually all scholars: yes, the laws of the physical world are uniform, but the geographical and natural conditions are diverse. Moreover, the social world, unlike the physical, is a world of freedom, and not of determinacy.

The possibility of achieving universal uniformization supposedly underlay the widespread theory of a civilization (enlightenment) development identical for all peoples which presupposed the coming together of the law of peoples which were at at one stage of evolution, in one social time. The idea was even advanced of the possible creation under such conditions of a universal supranational political union ("accretion of peoples") with elements of universal law. But the disappearance of States and national legal orders was not suggested in so doing, merely the coordination and mutual exchange of legal innovations. The theory of the stages of civilization in the understanding of that time assumed a universal scale for assessing the development of national law and a presumption of its similarity under certain conditions, but not a world legal order. The degree of such similarity was not clarified by scholars.

Some scholars considered to be a factor of uniformization the identical nature of human needs and, respectively, the identical essence of law, or even the generality of innate legal consciousness of all humans. Yet another way of achieving uniformity suggested was the transfer by a people of its social experience by way of legacy to new peoples as "primary customs". But the majority of scholars rejected these factors – because of the differences in the conditions of the functioning of law and its creation by societies for own special needs and proceeding from own notions about these needs.

Ultimately, all scholars acknowledged the insuperability of the national form of law, which excluded the possibility of the objectification of a world legal order. The social world might be viewed as a single system, but its individual elements – national legal orders – were essential: the Universal was not situated above the Particular; it did not exist outside them and their links. The immanence of the Universal in the Particular was pointed to as uniformity of diversity, and the creation of this Universal in the process of development and interaction of individual national legal orders without the loss of distinctiveness by them.

Under these conditions, Warsaw legal scholars at the time developed the idea of forming an immanent Universal in law as a result of the dialogue of legal orders. The basis thereof was the theory derived from the works of German colleagues of the political and technical elements in law, of which the first was distinctive in greater degree, and the second – universal. A technical element might be formed in the process of self-development of national law, especially under the influence of the similarity of socio-economic development of the States and the cultural communication thereof. Individual scholars emphasized that a correlation might occur between national legal orders, mutual impetuses, and also there might be a mutual rejection. On the other hand, a technical element might be filled with universal content as a result of mutual borrowings, especially voluntary borrowings. But both the political and technical elements remained immanent in national law and might be singled out only intellectually.

§4.3. Conceptualization of Interaction of National Legal Orders

During the second half of the eighteenth and first third of the nineteenth centuries a general theory of the interaction of legal systems was formed in European legal thought. The grounds of conceptions in this sphere were compatible, and the most fundamental of them coincide: an understanding of contemporary legal orders as open, recognition of the inevitability of their interaction to greater or lesser advantage; recognition of the existence of similar problems in different legal orders and respectively an assumption of the existence of more perfected models for resolving them which might be borrowed; assumption of the possibility of carrying over elements of law from one legal order to another without loss of content; the idea of voluntary and limited reception emanating from cognized needs of the recipient society and the compatibility of legal orders; the requirement of adapting the form of borrowed elements and the correlation of their content in order to ensure conformity to the conditions of the recipient society; presumption of forming the immanent Universal in law as a result of historical, concrete, and constant interaction of legal orders. Moreover, an agreed complex of stable base concepts was worked out in this sphere.[141]

Polish jurists primarily determined the presence in national law of elements of Roman law, but the works of Czacki were a rare exception.[142] In 1800 Czacki asserted that in the Middle Ages, except for the Romanic countries, Roman law had a limited influence and only in individual regions of Germany, and the Scandinavian ("northern") and Slavic peoples remained free of its influence.[143] Czacki later actualized the problem of legal borrowings from Germanic peoples.[144] The synchronic interaction of legal orders he called a communion.[145] He pointed out that the result of borrowing might be a mixed legal order of a people.[146] He condemned the direct borrowing of legislation, but considered voluntary mutual influence in the forms of borrowing customs and doctrine to be a normal process, noting the carrying over of law together with the migration of populations.[147] Czacki also indicated the normality of borrowing foreign legislative models to regulate new types of legal relations.[148]

In the view of Kołłątaj, the reception of law on the whole was not humiliating, but created the possibility for the joint development of law. But the export of law ("to give law to others") also might be an important element and attribute of dominance.[149] Niemcewicz in

141 Kresin, note 89 above, II, p. 340.

142 Czacki, note 90 above, I, pp. vii-viii, 4-6, 19, 25, 28-29; Czacki, note 91 above, pp. 77, 94-95, 97, 99-116, 120-121.

143 Czacki, note 90 above, I, pp. 18-19.

144 Ibid., I, pp. vii-viii, 4-6, 19, 25, 28-29; Czacki, note 91 above, pp. 77, 94-95, 97, 99-116, 120-121.

145 Czacki, I, pp. 5-6, 8, 11, 45, 51-54, 97.

146 Ibid., I, p. 8.

147 Czacki, note 91 above, pp. 95, 122.

148 Czacki, note 90 above, I, pp. 5-6, 8, 11, 45, 51-54, 97.

149 Kołłątaj, note 100 above, pp. 14, 205.

1808 called French legislation and, especially, the Code Napoleon a "sacred thing which could be touched only with the greatest awareness", but he considered the adaptation of borrowed law to be necessary to the geographical, nature, and other peculiarities of the recipient country.[150]

Bandtkie devoted attention in his writings to the reception of elements of German, Roman, and canon law into Polish law, coexisting and correlating with autochthonic and received law, and proclaimed the study of the reception to be one of the tasks of historical legal research. He noted the fundamental positive influence of Roman law on the development of legal orders of all western European peoples.[151]

Just as Kołłątaj, Bandtkie noted that the reception of law is not humiliating, and also does not signify subordination or dominance of a certain people: "it is easier and more assured to move towards a certain goal through the path of the experience of another than to find it by one's own experience". In his view, historically the links between peoples, especially neighbors, at the early stages of development were closer and borrowing was much easier. But, at the same time he asserted that the more a people advanced "in enlightenment, the more willingly foreign views were borrowed".[152]

Historically, in the vision of Bandtkie reception primarily happened gradually and voluntarily, and the grounds were the cognized superiority of a legal model for regulating particular social relations, reasons of "influence and example" in an "insatiable aspiration for perfection". The law of a victor people might be received by the vanquished, or *vice versa*. But he acknowledged instances of the historical competition of legal orders and the aspiration to defend national law against the reception of foreign elements.[153] Moreover, in Bandtkie's view, the law of a country might be changed or carried over historically, just as language, in

[150] [Niemcewicz], note 14 above, pp. 16-18.

[151] Bandtkie, note 72 above, pp. 2-4, 32, 44-45, 53-54, 173-176, 197-199, 208, 211; Bandtkie, note 73 above (1812), p. 258; Bandtkie, note 73 above (1814), pp. 29-30.

[152] Bandtkie, note 102 above (1816), p. 312.

[153] Bandtkie, note 72 above, pp. v, vi, 2-3, 22, 44, 48, 174; Bandtkie, note 73 above (1814), p. 29; Bandtkie, note 102 above (1816), p. 312.

connection with a change of ethnic composition of a population, because of migration, for example.[154]

Of importance was the requirement of Bandtkie relating to the openness of national law to dialogue with others, for the need for legal regulation required new legal decisions irrespective of their origin. In Bandtkie's works, especially from 1815, the preservation of the historical distinctiveness of national law was no long a goal in itself. On the contrary, he substantiated rather modernization through a quest for the best law among those in Europe, but also taking into account certain not precisely drawn national grounds of law:

> We cannot assume that we will try, that through mediocre norms we will move on to better ones, we will pay for our legislation with experience because that experience is necessarily connected with harm to the country and placed us in a backward position in comparison with other peoples ... In the nineteenth century one cannot think about experience, having so many models and so many expensive experiences, both our own and foreign: one has only to consult history and the past.

He appealed to reject indecisiveness and use contemporary achievements in the name of law reforms useful for society.[155]

Bandtkie conferred a different status on elements of received law or foreign legal ideas. It might be operative in unchanged form, a source of national lawmaking, "have authority", be subsidiary, or referred to in a court proceeding or doctrine.[156] In his view, the prerequisite for the effective reception of law was the readiness of the national legal order and doctrine to accept it, and also the conformity of the borrowed elements to the grounds of national law. The carrying over of law by means of communion or

[154] Bandtkie, note 72 above, pp. 60, 66, 93, 204-205; Bandtkie, "O karze śmierci na kradzież stanowionéy rzecz podług kraiowych uwazana", in Bandtkie, *Zbiór rospraw o przedmiotach prawa polskiego* (Warsaw, 1812), pp. 285-286.

[155] Bandtkie, note 72 above, pp. iii, 53, 55, 60, 72, 174; Bandtkie, note 73 above (above), pp. 215-216, 218; Bandtkie, note 154 above, pp. 263-264, 280, 285-288; Bandtkie, note 73 above, pp. 5, 7; Bandtkie, note 45 above, pp. 170, 173-174; Bandtkie, note 102 above, pp. 311-312; Litauer, note 15 above, pp. 52, 62-66; Bandtkie, note 73 above (1825), pp. 39-40, 42.

[156] Bandtkie, note 72 above, pp. 53-54, 173-175, 198; Bandtkie, note 155 above, p. 42.

imposition might be successful only if it corresponded to the level of development of the people, to the needs which had formed, to the character and spirit. He pointed to the necessity to adapt borrowings.[157]

The grounds of law of various peoples might be more or less similar or even incompatible, which excluded the interaction thereof. If the grounds of autochthonic and received law are incompatible, the result is not a synthesis, but a mixture of law, and the prospects are that one will squeeze out the other.[158] If they are compatible, a synthesis will not necessarily occur, and one law may become basic and the other, subsidiary.[159] In this case the reception of law does not prevent the people to thereafter develop itself by its own path and is merely a supplemental factor of development.[160] But "foreign experience and the possibility of the use thereof combine ... peoples with peoples and bring the human species to a higher unity".[161] Bandtkie severely condemned the idea of the purification of law of foreign elements with a view to a return to the old, supposedly autochthonic models, for law must correspond to its own time: returned to the past, it becomes not in conformity with the development of social relations.[162]

In discussions with various legal scholars, Lelewel clarified certain issues of the reception of law using the example of Roman law. He wrote that one of the forms of interaction in law which, however, cannot be considered to be reception, is the unofficial authority of foreign law and also has a certain correlation with it in lawmaking, but without direct borrowing.[163] On the whole, he suggested this list of types of impact of one national law on another: binding force (operation), whole reception, auxiliary or referential law, "binding by some means", grounds, model of

[157] Bandtkie, note 72 above, p. 198; Bandtkie, note 73 above (1814), p. 29.

[158] Litauer, *Memoriał J. W. Bandtkiego o prawie hipotecznym z roku 1818* (Warsaw, 1915), pp. 62-63.

[159] Ibid., p. 66.

[160] Bandtkie, note 73 above (1814), p. 29; Sobociński, note 107 above, p. 162.

[161] Bandtkie, note 102 above, p. 312.

[162] Bandtkie, note 45 above, pp. 173-174; Bandtkie, note 102 above, p. 312; Litauer, note 158 above, pp. 52-53, 62, 64-66.

[163] Lelewel, "Rozprawy Jana Wincentego Bandtke o przedmiotach prawa polskiego (1815)", in Lelewel, *Rozbiory dziel obejmujacych albo dzieje, albo rzechy polskie roznymi czasy przez Joachima Lelewela ogloszone* (Poznan, 1844), pp. 228, 230; Lelewel, note 78 above, pp. 244-245.

legislation, authority, imitation, reception of an apparent norm, fashion, influence, legal or non-legal reference.[164]

F. Szaniawski devoted a separate point to the problem of imitation in law. He pointed to the significant prejudices in legal science with respect to the reception of law and corresponding public pressure. But borrowing was an entirely normal operation for man, "the example of one attracts others", and information about innovations in law is disseminated just as it is with respect to other useful inventions. Szaniawski stressed that borrowing (and mixing) was and is one of the principal factors of legal development; it requires a deeply pragmatic approach – the best model is chosen irrespective of its autochthonic or foreign origin: "it is not so easy to create new things, to make good inventions. In all human laws there is little useful originality, most of all imitation". But borrowed law must be reworked, adapted, assimilated in accordance with the needs of the recipient. In Szaniawski's view, the aspiration to absolute distinctiveness is an empty temptation, and thoughtless borrowing may prove to be harmful. Therefore, a conscious selection of the elements of law directed towards resolving problems of a concrete society is important.[165]

Rakowiecki noted that languages, cultures, and legal orders of peoples may be either "natural" (primarily autochthonic in origin of their norms and institutions) or "mixed" / "conventional".[166] He further observed that for the most part borrowing occurs in spheres of legal regulation directly created by the State ("political and police laws"), whereas civil law to a large degree preserves the distinctive national character and link with the culture of the people. Among the reasons for borrowings in law, he names the communion of peoples and migration, which lead to the mixing of people.[167] Daniłowicz wrote that borrowing sometimes may occur not because of necessity, but because of prestige and the extensive dissemination of a foreign legal model.[168]

Hube acknowledged the possibility of the reception of law, but considered this to be harmful and ineffective. The legal life of a

164 Lelewel, note 76 above, pp. 253, 258.

165 Szaniawski, note 111 above, pp. 72-74.

166 Rakowiecki, note 96 above, II, pp. 246, 254, 315.

167 Ibid., I, pp. 81-82, 128, 133, 135; II, 187-188, 254; Rakowiecki, note 98 above, p. 2.

168 Daniłowicz, note 68 above, pp. 38, 46, 51, 52, 67.

people was concentrated foremost in judicial practice, and it would ignore received law or rework the essence thereof, "adapting it to the people's concepts".[169] Proceeding from the idea of the identical essence of private law, Bieńkowski said that a successful legal model in this domain might be used by all peoples, although its adaptation to national interests and character in matters not violating general principles was possible.[170]

In Zaborowski's vision of the reception of law a condemnation prevailed of imposing law as a factor of "political supremacy and moral pressure". But physical coercion in law does not generate stable moral consequences and generates non-acceptance or indifference of the people. Zaborowski believed that borrowing (coercive or voluntary) may perform the function of the modernization of law, but any national law has the potential of renewal on the basis of rethinking and improvement of autochthonic law. Borrowed law violates the systemic interlinkage of legislation, judicial practice and scientific doctrine, and threatens national distinctiveness. But it is doomed to be rejected, ignored (not applied) or comprehensively reworked by the court and doctrine – which aspire to restore the harmony of national law and will necessarily achieve this: "custom and long practice of courts may ultimately assimilate them and impart the hue of the country to them". The same processes occur in legal doctrine after the dissemination of foreign legal ideas. The fully-fledged development of national law is restored only after the completion of the assimilation of material borrowed elements.[171]

As already noted, Heylman believed the carrying over of elements of law between peoples to be normal. He substantiated the possibility and advisability of borrowing the best foreign legal solutions en route to improving society: "The peoples fulfill their destiny when they assiduously aspire to the stage of social improvement and, in this matter, without trusting their own efforts, look to foreign legislation". In his view, the people by this means joins "with the feelings and education of the entire human

[169] Hube, note 48 above, p. 309; Hube, note 115 above, I, p. 36, 43.

[170] Grynwaser, note 1 above, p. 86; Pomianowski, note 128 above, p. 122. Also see Szymaniec, note 54 above, pp. 109-110; Pomianowski, note 128 above, pp. 405-406.

[171] Zaborowski, note 56 above, VI, pp. 363-371.

species", for the achievements of peoples know no boundaries and should serve all.[172]

Maciejowski considered the self-development of each people to be normal, but not the dissemination of the achievements of one people to others, which he viewed negatively. Borrowed elements contradict the spirit of the people, and mass borrowing may lead to the partial or complete erasing of the distinctiveness of a people and the national legal order, to the "mixing", or "alienation".[173] Among the reasons for borrowings in law he pointed to the migration of the population and communion of peoples.[174] He wrote about the impossibility of direct reception of legal norms – they are ineffective in the new milieu because of the loss of linkage with the original social relations and fail to conform to the new (although he evaluated positively on the whole the reception on the Code Napoleon in Poland).[175]

Individual ideas relating to the reception of law were expressed during the constant codification debates in lawmaking and other State agencies. The Memorial of the Directorate of Justice to Napoleon in 1807 asserted that the effective borrowing of law was possible only between countries with similar socio-economic and political relations and spiritual grounds, and also assumed the adaptation of the borrowed: "the legislator should not generalize his own law, but adapt it to local customs".[176] The same idea of the need to adapt even the most perfected law to natural and geographical conditions and customs is present in the Memorial of the Minister of Justice, Łubieński, of 1809.[177] Łubieński noted in his address to the Sejm in 1809 that the Code Napoleon emanated from natural human rights and "contains within itself that embryo of duration that does not depend on what necessarily must be subject to local and provisional conditions, as far as the providence governing the fate of the people", but at the same time with the aim of achieving real implementation affirmed the inevitability of

172 Heylman, note 52 above, pp. 51-52.

173 Maciejowski, note 99 above, I, pp. v, vii, ix, 2, 6, 35, 38, 67-69.

174 Ibid., I, pp. 3, 5-6, 54, 67-69.

175 Ibid., I, pp. v, vii, ix, 2, 38, 67-69.

176 Konic, note 6 above, pp. 210-213; Kraushar, note 6 above, p. 331.

177 The Report is produced in Litauer, note 15 above, p. 78.

the adaptation of borrowed law by taking into account the natural and geographical factors and historical tradition.[178]

The Report of the State Council to the Sejm in 1818 noted the unacceptability of the forcible imposition of law which might reduce the distinctiveness of the recipient people and cause material legal conflicts and a negative influence on social relations. It was further noted that adapted borrowed law might be fully considered to be national.[179] The Introduction to the draft Book One of the 1823 Civil Code of the Kingdom of Poland said that received law might play a role of a modernization and integrative factor for the national legal order and therefore be more acceptable to the development of social relations than the law of autochthonic origin. But the borrowing always is subject to adaptation to the "political state, the different economy of the country the different system of administration and finances, and other local peculiarities".[180] The deputies of the Sejm, Koźmian and Tymowski, averred that received law which had been assimilated may be considered to be national law.[181] We also recall that the proposals of Emperor Alexander I set out in the official letter of the State Secretary of 25 August (5 September) 1817 made provision for the "modification" of received law "with a view to adaptation to the customs of the country, state of civilization, and local circumstances".[182]

Wyczechowski in his addresses and drafts considered the mixing of elements of various national and supranational legal orders (folk customs, Roman and canon law) to be a characteristic feature of the legal development of European countries. We noted above, in his view the distinctiveness of national law is an illusion at least because of the influence of Christianity which generated (through principles, spirit, customs) the uniformization of law among European peoples, and then on other continents. He noted that borrowings in law are and will be acceptable and fruitful, but received law must be adapted to the socio-economic conditions of the country. The reason for reception of law may be innovations borrowed in socio-economic relations and new ideas or religious principles requiring embodiment and regulation, but the last do

178 Mowa, note 15 above, pp. 360-361.

179 Zarzycka, note 22 above, pp. 190-192.

180 Grynwaser, note 1 above, pp. 132-133.

181 Ibid., p. 156; Kodrębski, note 26 above, p. 163.

182 Grynwaser, note 1 above, p. 164.

not exist in the national law. He further noted that the borrowed subject-matter of regulation and the received regulation itself become an inalienable property of the recipient people: "national laws are those which will be deemed as most corresponding to contemporary civilization and convenient for consolidating the happiness of inhabitants of the Kingdom of Poland irrespective of the source from which they were taken". His approach to the technique of the reception of law was rather pragmatic; he proposed to compare all existing models in searches for the best decisions, choose one leading and some additional models, assess the suitability of the chosen norms for the country, integrate the results into the national code, and "choose the best of all and create the most perfected laws". Not only the norms of laws must be considered, but also commentaries and other doctrinal literature. The work results of lawmaking organs should be considered by courts, scientific and educational institutions, and agencies of executive power and local self-government, and the results of the consideration should be taken into account.[183]

It should be added that Daniłowicz wrote in 1818 that every people knows only its own law, is bound to it, does not know another's law, and therefore is not capable of comparing them, the more so impartially: "too much patience with one's own law and hatred for the laws of others originates from a mixture of ignorance and prejudice". Moreover, there are always forces in society which receive certain benefit from the preservation of their own law, albeit it imperfect or backward. Finally, a change of law "consecrated by the centuries" always is a complex process, stability and duration of legislation is a value which "should be higher than human passions", "combine and learn without restoring to discussions". But all this should not be grounds for rejecting either innovations in general or the borrowing of law in particular.[184]

Daniłowicz insisted on the fruitfulness of borrowings and on the need to adapt them to the spirit of the law of the recipient people and to the physical and socio-political factors of its development.[185] In his view, borrowing did not humiliate the

[183] Zarycka, note 22 above, pp. 176, 179-181; Gałędek and Klimaszewska, note 62 above, pp. 283-284; Gałędek and Klimaszewska, note 19 above, pp. 80-81; Pomianowski, note 128 above, p. 119.

[184] Daniłowicz, note 68 above, pp. 30-31, 41-43, 52, 66.

[185] Ibid., pp. 67, 69-70.

people; it was a normal and pervasive means for the development of law; on the contrary, "a people will never have a perfected code which neglects the experience of other peoples and begins to replace in law [their] concepts with its own".[186] That foreign law deserves attention which is "attested by lengthy observation" emanating from countries close in their conditions and character of development to one's own. Daniłowicz acknowledged the possibility of the "superiority" of one law in comparison with another and the borrowing thereof.[187]

During the period here considered, Warsaw jurists elaborated the elements of a doctrine of the interaction ("communion") of national legal orders. The view dominated that voluntary legal borrowing did not humiliate the recipient and was a normal phenomenon in the contemporary world. A significant portion of legal scholars affirmed that legal ideas and decisions, just as innovations and inventions in other spheres of human activity, might be adopted and serve all peoples. The idea was widely shared of a higher and lower level of the development of law in various countries and, accordingly, of a "better law" – progressive or more perfected models which might be used for the modernization of a national legal order irrespective of their origin.

These types of interaction were singled out: transfer of law by legacy from one people to another or to other new peoples ("primary customs"); carrying over of law together with the migrations of peoples; adoption of legal norms in connection with the adoption of a religion; conscious borrowing of elements of law in order to resolve certain problems, especially the regulation of new socio-economic relations, modernization of the legal order, acceleration of the development of society thanks to the experience of others, coming together of legal orders, or because of the prestige of a certain foreign law. Reference also was made to coercive carrying over of law (for example, to a subjugated people), which was unconditionally condemned as an element of political dominance and violation of the development of the recipient people.

Virtually all the authors of the works here analyzed unanimously were of the view that in the process of borrowing the received law cannot remain unchanged (except for coercive carryover); it must be adapted to the conditions of the recipient people, namely, to

[186] Ibid., pp. 68-69.

[187] Ibid., pp. 68, 71, 148, 173.

the natural and geographical conditions, needs, economy, system of administration, and historical traditions. Some legal scholars believed that law sufficiently assimilated ("appropriated") became the "inalienable ownership" of the recipient people. Others asserted that in the process of reception a mixed legal order was formed temporarily (until complete assimilation) or forever. A synthesis might gradually arise between the autochthonic and borrowed elements provided that the donor and the recipient were at the same level of social development; the borrowing was an answer to the real needs of the recipient and it was compatible with the national grounds (spirit, character). If the grounds of the two legal orders were incompatible, the law of the recipient remained a mixture with the prospect of one element or the other being squeezed out or subordinate. Legal scholars suggested various visions of the spheres and branches of law suitable to a greater or lesser degree to undertake borrowing.

Some authors considered a mixture (or conventionality) of national orders to be an inevitable phenomenon, widespread and constant, and the idea of preserving complete or primarily distinctiveness of law to be an illusion. In their view, the return of law to its original roots was a harmful slogan which gave new life to anachronisms and was contrary to the development of the people. For other legal scholars, original legal orders were the norm, and they advanced the idea of the conscious purification or self-cleansing of law: the original elements were always more active, for the entire life of the people was linked to them and they therefore in any event gradually squeezed out (or were immediately rejected, ignored, transformed) borrowings with the assistance of judicial practice.

During the period here considered, a classification was developed of receptions (most fully in the works of Bandtkie and Lelewel) that might be reduced to the following categories: complete carrying over of a legal order; reception of law in unchanged form; reception of an individual norm; subsidiary operation of borrowed law; foreign law as a source, grounds, or model of national lawmaking; authority, fashionability, or general impact of foreign law; correlation of national law with foreign or legal imitation; referential (or renvoi) significance of foreign law. Wyczechowski elaborated a detailed technique for undertaking the reception of law, and F. Szaniawski separated out the problem of the interaction of national legal orders as the subject-matter of autonomous contemplation.

Some legal scholars during the period here considered advanced the idea of radical condemnation of the interaction of national legal orders. They put forward the idea of the self-development of national law capable of modernization without borrowings. In their view, reception threatened national distinctiveness and led to "alienation". The carrying over also threatened the functioning of a legal order: received law could not be effective. It lost its link with social relations in its own country and could not be in accord with such relations in the recipient country. But even the most radical opponents of borrowings in law acknowledged the reality of the processes of reception and the need for legal science to investigate them.

§4.4. Theory of the Special in Legal Development

The idea of the social Special in law as an element of a comparatist scientific picture of the world was elaborated for the first time during the period here considered. This idea became a logical emanation from the contradiction between the *a priori* proclamation of the universality of legal development and the study of concrete mechanisms of interaction of legal systems, as well as from the contradictory nature of determining the limits of ethno-cultural frontiers of peoples not coinciding with the borders of States and the study of non-equal links between different national legal orders.

A theory of families of legal systems was developed as a middle and, simultaneously, maximal possible objective unit between a national legal order and universal legal development, an internally-connected phenomenon whose existence is materialized in the form of special immanent elements within national law. This Special in law, according to the views of legal scholars then, may be defined as the sum of material elements and interactions formed historically and being common to a certain group of legal orders. The problem of the Special in law and the classification of legal orders was separated out as a sphere of scientific knowledge by a number of legal scholars.

The most developed approach to the definition and classification of the Special in law was the linguistic-cultural approach, the principles of which became: the presumption of the conformity of the linguistic-communicative, spiritual-cultural, and legal development, on the basis of which the theory of linguistic families was carried over to the science of law as a theory of legal families; consideration of the legal family as an entity of legal development which in its characteristics approximates a national legal order; the confirmation of the forming of a legal family as a result of the separation of a single people with its single law at a certain stage of historical development and the preservation of its principal characteristics and vector of development by the peoples and their legal orders derivative from it; the notion of the legal family as a relatively and culturally solitary space of constant internal legal interaction (mutual borrowing, convergence, coordination) which does not grow into an integral supranational legal order.

In addition to the linguistic-cultural approach, other criteria were used to substantiate the definition of the Special in law, but the respective ideas discovered their own inconsistency, as well as subsidiary nature with respect to the theory of legal families – each of them was supported by merely some legal scholars. They had not sufficiently developed and relatively uncontradicted theoretical grounds and were always advanced together with the division into legal families. They are united by a search for a unit of legal development broader than the legal family which, during the period here considered, was not successful and not accompanied by the consensus of legal scholars.[188]

Most widely shared among Warsaw legal scholars was the variant of the idea concerning the inclusiveness of the people and national law in a broader association – was the theory of a Slavic community, but other conceptualizations worthy of attention were also present. In the present analysis of the problem, more attention is given to non-legal works because the ideas of Warsaw legal scholars might be regarded here primarily as referential. As Juliusz Bardach (1914-2010) noted, the methodological foundations of linguistics carried over to the history of law of peoples speaking the Slavic languages. Moreover, the revealed linkage of European languages with Sanskrit led to searches for the Indo-European roots of the Slavs and their law.[189]

188 Kresin, note 89 above, II, p. 340-341.

189 J. Bardach, "Historia praw słowiańskich. Przedmiot i metody badawcze", *Kwartalnik Historyczny*, no. 2 (1963), p. 255.

One factor in developing the idea of an association of peoples of the Slavic language family and the possible existence of a Slavic legal order was the political dimension of the Slavic issue. The last was perceived somewhat sluggishly and more as an ideological slogan, but all the same did not disappear. As a contemporary observer noted, the projects for a Slavic federation in the East of Europe were regarded at the highest level of French foreign policy back in 1797 during the Directorate and then by Napoleon by analogy with the Rhine Union.[190]

Prince Czartoryski in 1802 in a Memorial to Emperor Alexander I substantiated the possible creation of a federation of Slavic nations under the direction of the Emperor, the leading role in the federation to be played by Poland.[191] In an Appeal of 1811, Czartoryski called upon Poles to unite with Russia, having regard to the unity of genus, kinship of the language, and personality of the tsar as the hope of Slavic peoples.[192] The Manifesto of Alexander I dated 9 May 1815 concerning the results of the Congress of Vienna and the accession of the Duchy of Warsaw also addressed the Slavic problem: "this revives the bonds of brotherhood of the tribes mutually connected by a unity of origin".[193]

As contemporary observers note, the idea of Slavic unity, just as Slavophile ideology, was born on Polish territory back during the Enlightenment under the material influence of the ideas of Herder.[194] Bardach wrote about the first stage of the development of

190 S. I. Shchegolev, «Польша в системе наполеоновской Европы. Создание Герцогства Варшавского» [Poland in the System of Napoleonic Europe. Creation of the Duchy of Warsaw], Вестник СПбГУ [Herald of St. Petersburg State University], Series 2. History, no. 1-2 (2004), p. 75.

191 W. Djakow, "'Polskie słowianofilstwo' i jego wpływ na slawistykę polską (koniec XVIII w. – 1939 r.)", *Analecta*, II, no. 1 (1993), p. 12.

192 T. Matlęgiewicz, note 136 above, p. 166.

193 Available online. Also see N. Iu. Gromakova, «Польське питання» на Віденському конгресі 1815 р. й утворення Королівства Польського» [The 'Polish Question' at the 1815 Congress of Vienna and the Creation of the Kingdom of Poland], Збірник наукових праць Харківського національного педагогічного університету ім. Г. С. Сковороди. Серія «Історія та географія» [Collection of Scientific Works of the Skovoroda Kharkiv National Pedagogical University. Series "History and Geography"], no. 53 (2016), p. 156; S. M. Fal'kovich, «Польский вопрос в решениях Венского конгресса 1815 г. и причины краха венских договоренностей» [The Polish Question in Decisions of the 1815 Congress of Vienna and Causes of the Collapse of the Vienna Arrangements], Славянский альманах [Slavic Almanac], no. 3-4 (2015), p. 25.

194 Matlęgiewicz, "Idee słowianofilskie w Warszawskim Towarzystwie Przyjaciół

Polish Slavophilism dating from the end of the eighteenth century before the November uprising.[195] At the first session of the Society of Friends of Science in Warsaw on 9 May 1801, its President, Jan Chrzciciel Albertrandi (1731-1808), noted the kindship of Polish and languages extending from the "Novaia Zemlia to the Venetian territory, from Ragusa to the Chinese frontiers".[196] One of the early Polish Slavist historians and author of a book on the primeval history of the peoples of Russia was Jan Potocki (1761-1815).[197] The published study of the language and literature of the South Slavs by Jan Kossakowski (1755-1808) was satiated with the idea of Slavic unity.[198] The existence on Polish territories of a Slavophile masonic movement was noted.[199]

The idea of Slavic unity in Polish scientific studies in the early nineteenth century did not necessarily have a pro-Russian connotation: Russia as a participant in the Partitions of the *Rzecz Pospolita* could have been regarded as the "mongrel of the Slavic community" which should remain outside the reborn Slavic community. Poland should have become the leader and integrator of the Slavs and their link with France and the European community. A Slavic federation should have defended Europe against the Russian threat. A specific "third path" was suggested by J. Szaniawski: a Slavic federation headed by Poland should become independent both from Russia and from France. After Napoleon's defeat, Slavic unity was again to a greater degree seen connected with the leadership of Russia and acquired an anti-German orientation.[200]

The Memorial of 1806 to Napoleon by the Polish émigré Count Tadeusz Mostowski (1766-1842), the future Minister of Internal Affairs of the Duchy of Warsaw and Kingdom of Poland, pointed to the existence of a Slavic race having a uniform character and

Nauk (1800-1830)", *Athenaeum*, XXXIII (2012), p. 97; Matlęgiewicz, note 136 above, p. 186.

195 Djakow, note 191 above, p. 11.

196 Matlęgiewicz, note 194 above, pp. 98-99.

197 M. Iłowiecki, *Okręty na oceanie czasu. Historia nauki Polskiej do 1945 roku* (2011), p. 133.

198 Matlęgiewicz, note 194 above, p. 99.

199 Djakow, note 191 above, p. 12.

200 Matlęgiewicz, note 194 above, pp. 102-104.

customs.[201] The idea of Slavic unity is present in a collection of (supposedly) folk songs prepared by Bishop Jan Paweł Woronicz (1757-1829), published between 1803 and 1806.[202] Samuel Bogumil Linde (1771-1847) worked on a dictionary of Slavic languages but did not complete it.[203] He wrote in the preface to his dictionary of the Polish language that the Slavs are a single gens that in the past had a single language.[204] Kołłątaj in 1808 wrote about a single Slavic language divided into dialects.[205] The brother of J. W. Bandtkie, Jerzy Samuel Bandtkie (1768-1835) devoted his studies to Slavic linguistics and history in the early nineteenth century and wrote about the Indo-Slavic gods.[206]

The appearance in 1818 of a study by Zorian Dołęga-Chodakowski (Adam Z. Czarnocki) on Slavdom before Christianity was a significant event in Polish intellectual life that had considerable resonance and facilitated the appearance of numerous ethnographic studies by other scholars. Its influence was compared with the poetry of Adam Mickiewicz (1798-1855).[207] Czarnocki affirmed the historical existence of a single Slavic people who emanated from India (nonetheless, the Slavs have a "northern soul"), had a single State with the capital at Kyiv and a single customary law and will-established law, and were ruled by great khagans. He noted that the Slavs were a primary and integral, mono-cultural gens, and not a collection of exiles or units of destroyed States. The Slavs had a single common spirit linked by a common pagan cult, and later the adoption of Christianity weakened this spirit and confessionally divided the Slavs, "being orientated towards a foreign view, we became ultimately ourselves alien". But the common spirit was not destroyed, and the Slavs retain common features of character: "innate Slavic simplicity, gaiety, courtesy and sincerity ... intrepidness, love, and a perfected hospitality". Czarnocki upheld the idea of the unification of Slavic

201 Grynwaser, note 1 above, p. 21.

202 Szymaniec, note 54 above, p. 106; Matlęgiewicz, note 194 above, p. 100.

203 S. Dubisz, "Samuel Bogumił Linde (1771-1847)", in *Portrety uczonych. Profesorowie Uniwersytetu Warszawskiego 1816-1915* (2016), p. 334.

204 Matlęgiewicz, note 194 above, p. 99.

205 Kołłątaj, note 100 above, p. 90.

206 *Wiek XIX. Sto lat mysli Polskiej. Zyciorysy, streszczienia, wyjatki* (1907), II, pp. 283, 287.

207 K. Wł. Wójcicki, *Warszawa, jej życie umysłowe i ruch literacki w ciągu lat trzydziestu (od 1800 – 1830 r.)* (Warsaw, 1880), pp. 126-127.

peoples under the scepter of the Russian Emperor.[208] Skorochód-Majewski also developed the idea of the Indian origin of the Slavs as one of the most ancient peoples of the world and ascribed a common character to the Slavs.[209]

The Society of Friends of Science decided in 1821, at the suggestion of Skorochód-Majewski, to open a special scientific section called Slavic Archive; the common Slavic past became the subject-matter of consideration in the historical works of Franciszek Czajkowski and Adam Prażmowski (1764-1836), connected with the said Society.[210]

In 1807 Wawrzyniec Surowiecki (1769-1827) drew up a "Draft Work on Sources, Customs, and Religion of the Ancient Slavs" in which he suggested they originated in India and asserted that he was collecting materials on various aspects of the social and material life of the Slavic peoples, including their law. The Slavs were named as one of the large people in this project.[211] In later works Surowiecki affirmed the integral mentality of the Slavs, different from other groups of peoples and from the rest of Europe as a whole, the unity of Slavic languages, and the existence of a long-standing Germanic-Slavic conflict.[212] Calling the Slavs a people in the singular and plural, he also designated them as a species of people divided into sub-groups ("generations").[213]

In the legal studies proper of Warsaw scholars of that time, as noted above, ideas concerning Slavic unity in law were set out in rather fragmentary form and were to a considerable degree referential to respective notions formulated by representatives of other sciences.

[208] Z. Chodakowski (A. Czarnocki), "O sławianszczyznie przed chrzescianstwem (1818)", in note 206 above, II, pp. 387-390; Matlęgiewicz, note 194 above, p. 107.

[209] W. Majewski Skorochód, "Rozkład i treść dzieła 'O początku licznych sławiańskich narodów' (1818)", in note 206 above, I, p. 450-451; M. Taperek, "'Polscy aryjczycy'. Pomiędzy naukowymi podstawami mitu a mitycznymi korzeniami nauki w dyskursie słowiańskim XIX wieku", *Przegląd humanistyczny*, no. 3 (2018), p. 157.

[210] Matlęgiewicz, note 194 above, p. 107.

[211] Wójcicki, note 207 above (1879), pp. 65, 67.

[212] Matlęgiewicz, note 194 above, pp. 102, 106.

[213] W. Surowiecki, "Śledzenie początku narodow słowiańskich (1824)", in W. Surowiecki, *Dzieła* (Krakow, 1861), pp. 379, 381, 384, 389, 392-394, 415.

Czacki singled out the Slavic, Gothic/Northern (Scandinavian), and Germanic "generations" of peoples.[214] Underlying a generation, Czacki suggested, might by an origin from one people and a single, so to speak, primary law. A common spirit and feeling of brotherhood were inherent in a generation.[215] He wrote about the kinship of the Slavs with the Gothic peoples, and also about constant contacts with the Germans, the mixing of these generations, and the significant borrowings from them and other peoples in language and law, including customary law. Slavic law and Northern law Czacki considered to be free of the influence of Roman law.[216]

Bandtkie singled out the legal communities of the Germanic (German, Teuton) and Slavic peoples, whose law differed materially. He also called these communities "large tribes", and the peoples within the limits thereof "splinters" (*szczep*). The historical relations between these communities were characterized as hostile. "Slavdom" in Bandtkie's works figured rather as a country then simply a territory of the settlement of a group of peoples. Bandtkie idealized medieval Slavic law, the quality of which over time deteriorated because of foreign influences.[217]

Rakowiecki noted he was inspired to investigate the spirit of Slavic law by Herder's monograph on ideas on the philosophy of the history of mankind where reference was made to the existence of a single "Slavic people".[218] He singled out various "generations" ("aggregates", "circles", "brotherhoods") of peoples (Slavs, Goths/Scandinavians, Germans/Germanic, Anglo-Saxons, eastern peoples) united by origin from a single people, single language (or genetic link with a single language) and common motherland, and also a feeling of closeness and bond.[219] Rakowiecki wrote about the special spirit and character of the Slavs preserved despite their

[214] Czacki, note 90 above, I, pp. vii, 5, 19; Czacki, note 91 above, pp. 77, 95.

[215] Czacki, note 90 above, I, p. 7.

[216] Czacki, note 90 above, I, pp. vii, 8, 11, 25, 45-46; Czacki, note 91 above, p. 1, 94, 95, 97, 99-116, 120-121.

[217] Bandtkie, note 73 above, pp. 265-268, 280; Bandtkie, note 154 above (1814), p. 7. Also see Szymaniec, note 54 above, p. 106.

[218] Rakowiecki, note 96 above, I, p. 246.

[219] Rakowiecki, note 98 above, pp. 2-3, 6; Rakowiecki, note 96 above, I, pp. i, ii, vii, 4, 81-82, 128, 135; II, pp. 245-246, 312-313, 316.

separation; they are free peoples and adherents of a republic form of government.[220]

Every generation has its own historical aim. For each generation an inextricable unity of religion, customs, language, and law is characteristic ("the entire State civil and political laws, religious concepts, and folk singing, stably embedded character, traditions, customs, and ancient languages of our ancestors"), as well as of social development.[221] Following Václav Hanka (1791-1861), Rakowiecki suggested the existence of, so to say, primary law – a single medieval Slavic code.[222]

These generations in his work are natural enemies, borrowings in law between them are assessed negatively, but the historical influence of Gothic (Scandinavian) law on a Slavic law already formed (Germanic/German influence is denied), and, *vice versa*, the influence of Slavic law on Gothic and Anglo-Saxon, is acknowledged.[223] Moreover, Rakowiecki said that the Greek and Latin languages (and in his vision, also cultures and law) emanate from the Slavic.[224]

The generations at a certain historical time are divided into branches – peoples or small groups of peoples (also generations) and just as languages are divided into dialects.[225] The reasons for this may be geographical dispersion generating material differences in needs (evidently in economy, way of life, political relations) and anthropological differences, subjugation by other peoples, mixing with other peoples, influence of other peoples; the language and culture of some peoples may display greater purity, and others, be mixed.[226] In particular, among the Slavic peoples there were formed Eastern Slavic (Slavic-Russian) and Western Slavic groups whose law also has a special spirit but corresponding to an all-Slavic spirit; their characters may differ.[227]

220 Rakowiecki, note 96 above, I, pp. i, ii, viii, 81-82, 130, 227, 242, 245, 253.

221 Ibid., I, pp. 227, 315; Rakowiecki, note 98 above, pp. 3, 15-16.

222 Rakowiecki, note 96 above, I, pp. 242-243.

223 Ibid., I, pp. 128, 133, 135, 228, 244, 252-253; Rakowiecki, note 98 above, p. 2.

224 Rakowiecki, note 96 above, II, pp. 153, 243, and others.

225 Ibid., I, pp. vii, 81-82; Rakowiecki, note 98 above, p. 15.

226 Rakowiecki, note 96 above, I, pp. 81-83; II, pp. 187-188, 254, 313, 315.

227 Ibid., I, pp. ix, 128-129, 139, 198, 243; II, pp. 188, 243; Rakowiecki, note 98 above, p. 15.

With the assistance of knowledge of the culture of a people and its genealogy, one may understand the culture of all the peoples of a respective generation.[228]

As Fedor Zigel (Sigel) (1845-1921), noted, Rakowiecki's work on the *Russkaia Pravda* "was the first attempt to compare the *Russkaia Pravda* with other Slavic monuments and the first work where the single spirit was mentioned which permeates the legislation of the Slavs".[229]

Hube mentioned the "western peoples" but concentrated on singling out supranational legal communities (splinters, tribes, generations, genuses) according to linguistic families (especially Germanic people and Slavs). He ascribed to each such community separate "spirits of laws", "character of institutions", legal concepts, and peculiarities of legal thought. Slavdom in Hube's works figures, depending on the context, as the name of a country or State; he asserts the historicity of the existence of a single medieval Slavic legislation and of a single Slavic language. A factor in preserving the unity of such a community is the "innate link of blood and family unity" of the peoples (or tribes, splinters), their feeling of being natural brothers, customary law, and "primeval conceptions". The dominance of an "*obshchina* conception" is characteristic for Slavs, the dominance of the family and the collective over the individual, joint family ownership which gradually were changed because of a general trend towards individualization with the development of civilization. The Germanic peoples are an older formation than the Slavs; they have a synthesis of autochthonic customary and Roman law – despite the material differences of the spirit thereof. And the Slavs have developed in a struggle against Germanic people's aggression and simultaneously experienced the influence of Germanic law and institutions. In 1827 Hube activated the question on the "history of the legislation of Slavic peoples" as a separate sphere of scientific studies. He proposed the legislation be studied by analogy, which emphasized the presumption of their unity.[230]

228 Rakowiecki, note 96 above, I, p. 84; II, pp. 243, 245.

229 F. Zigel, «Славянское право» [Slavic Law], in Энциклопедия Брокгауза и Эфрона [Encyclopedia Brokhaus and Efron] (available online).

230 Hube, note 48 above, pp. 335, 338; Hube, note 115 above, pp. 37, 42-43; Hube, note 80 above, pp. 70-72, 75-76; Hube, "O starożytnych zbiorach praw Czeskich", *Themis Polska*, V (1829), pp. 1-3; also see the work of his brother, J. Hube, "Wywód praw spadkowych słowiańskich (Wywód spadków podług dawnych praw

Hube devoted significant attention to the spirit of Slavic legislation in his dissertation on inheritance by operation of law in Roman, Germanic, and Slavic law, defended at Warsaw University in 1830. He noted that over the centuries the Germanic peoples had exerted a determinative influence on part of the Slavic peoples, and therefore "the true character of the Slavic ethnos we must seek in the most remote period when the Germanic peoples had not yet come close to us".[231]

It is of importance that the Law Faculty of Warsaw University in 1828 announced a competition on the topic of the law of inheritance by operation of law in Roman, Germanic, and Slavic law.[232] Heylman singled out three groups (large tribes) of European peoples: Roman, Germanic, and Slavic. Of these, the law of the Germanic group was characterized by a mixture of autochthonic customary and Roman law. In turn, during the period of the resettlement of peoples the Germanic peoples extended to the peoples of other groups a social order inherent to them.[233]

Maciejowski recalled certain European peculiarities in the development of peoples, but attention was concentrated on Slavic and Germanic legal communities which were the heirs of Roman law. In his view, the Slavic peoples were on the same level in civilized development, and this was lower than other European peoples. The Slavs were a "tribe (splinter) of peoples" which has a common spirit and, in particular, the spirit of law (concept of justice, and others), and the peoples within its limits are brothers. They must be liberated from numerous historical legal borrowings from other peoples and develop law primarily on autochthonic grounds.[234]

In his later history of Slavic legislation, Maciejowski presented a fundamental study of the law of the peoples which belong to the Slavic linguistic family, having confirmed the existence of the respective legal family. Maciejowski had the idea to undertake this work back in 1820 when he participated in the Legislative Commission formed by Emperor Alexander I to review and

słowiańskich)", *Themis Polska*, VIII (1830), pp. 425-426, 428, 430-431, 433, 436-437, 441, 444, 454, 467, 472-473, 475, 497-498.

231 Hube, note 119 above, p. 61.

232 J. Hube, note 230 above (1830), p. 425.

233 Heylman, note 52 above, pp. 2-4, 27, 42; Heylman, note 53 above, p. 115.

234 Maciejowski, note 79 above, pp. 416-423.

correct laws in force of the Kingdom of Poland. The work was to demonstrate the originality and virtues of Slavic law in comparison with Roman and Germanic, the continuity and integral nature of its development ("we write not about antiquities, but the history of Slavic laws"), and also to show the possible use of the grounds of Slavic law in contemporary lawmaking. This notion was considered and approved by the said Commission, but the writing required twelve years.[235]

Maciejowski noted that when conceiving of his study he relied on the works of Friedrich Majer (1772-1818) and, by analogy with how the last had investigated the spirit of Germanic law, reconstructed an "image of Slavic legislation".[236] Maciejowski asserted the unity and inter-linkage of the anthropological and ethnic development, territory with its natural and climatic conditions, language, culture, political development and law of the Slavs, their common spirit and character, including the "spirit of Slavic legislation".[237] On the whole, he singled out groups of related peoples ("families") who originated from one people and whose law mutually reinforced one another and the linguistic and legal interaction proceeded primarily within a group.[238]

Using the example of the Slavs, Maciejowski considered a "family" to be a "large whole", suggested the possibility of the unification thereof into a "single community" or at least the coordination of the political and legal development of the peoples of the group, and confirmed the special destiny of the legal family, which should be guessed.[239] He condemned borrowings in law from peoples of another family (in the case of the Slavs, from the Germanic peoples and from Roman law) – "alienation", for this violates the unity of the group and the spirit thereof; however, he acknowledged the possibility of foreign impetus in the development of the law of a group of peoples. Maciejowski affirmed the hostility

[235] Maciejowski, note 99 above, I, pp. iii, 52; "Обозрение русских газет и журналов за первую треть 1858 года" [Survey of Russian Newspapers and Journals for the First Third of 1858], Журнал министерства народного просвещения [Journal of the Ministry of Public Enlightenment], no. 49 (July 1858), pp. 23-24.

[236] Maciejowski, note 99 above, I, pp. vi, 2, 53.

[237] Ibid., I, pp. iii-iv, vii-viii, 4-6, 11, 51, 53-56.

[238] Ibid., I, pp. x, 3-4, 6, 35, 55.

[239] Ibid., I, pp. 1, 53-54.

of the groups of peoples between themselves.[240] Groups of peoples might be divided into smaller groups ("splinters") for various reasons, including because of foreign influence (this especially concerned the division of the Slavs into Western and Eastern), but they preserve their spirit and character, including in law.[241]

It is important that Maciejowski prepared his history of Slavic legislation during the November Uprising of 1830-31 and was an active participant therein. In the view of Bardach, it was at this time that Maciejowski, under the influence of Lelewel, rejected the "Romanist conception of the development of medieval Polish law", abandoned work on the Commentaries on Roman and Slavic law, and moved on to investigate Slavic law exclusively.[242]

Also of importance is that Maciejowski in this scholarly activities after the Uprising received special assistance, often not public, from the Imperial Governor of the Kingdom of Poland and Orthodox Bishop of Warsaw, who attached ideological significance to his works.[243] The Russian and French translations of the history of Slavic legislation and certain other of Maciejowski's works were published at the expense of the Imperial treasury.[244]

Finally, it is important that the history of Slavic legislation received an "international resonance that no other historical synthesis from the pen of a Polish author had received"; despite scholars understanding of the fundamental shortcomings in Maciejowski's work, his "programmatic suggestions became the grounds which have been modified but not been subjected – so far – to substantiated revision".[245]

As modern observers note, the idea of the unity of the Slavic world at the time was perceived critically by the majority of Polish scholars.[246] Familiarization with numerous primary sources and

[240] Ibid., I, pp. vii, 2-3, 6, 35, 54-55, 67-69.

[241] Ibid., I, pp. 5, 70.

[242] Bardach, "Wacław Aleksandr Maciejowski 1792-1883", in *Portrety uczonych. Profesorowie Uniwersytetu Warszawskiego 1816-1915* (2016), pp. 339-340.

[243] Ibid., p. 342.

[244] Bardach, note 189 above, p. 257.

[245] Ibid., p. 257; Bardach, note 242 above, p. 348.

[246] Bardach, note 242 above, p. 342; I. S. Troiak, «Польская историческая россика первой половины XIX в.» [Polish Historical Rossica of the First Half of the Nineteenth Century], Гуманитарные науки в Сибири [Humanities in Siberia], no. 3 (2011), p. 84.

doctrinal literature have created a different impression in us – the idea of legal communities which were created on the basis of linguistic kinship was the most widespread embodiment of the doctrine on the Special in law in that period.

* * *

The idea of European unity was another variant of the inclusiveness of the Polish people and national law within wider communities. As Wierzbicki noted with regard to the earlier period, the "European-ness comprised for citizens of the *Rzecz Pospolita* one of the values of principle".[247] At the outset of the nineteenth century, Czartoryski had thought up the proposal of a European League – an international association with a codified international law. Later he proposed the formation of the League of Nations of Europe with supranational legislative organs.[248]

Niemcewicz in 1808 considered the French codes as uniform and universal books of law "for the greater part of Europe".[249] Samuel Gottlob Laube (1781-1835) in that same year asserted that the same key legal concepts are being used in the greater part of Europe.[250] The economist Dominik Krysiński (1785-1853) wrote about a European civilization which was united thanks to the Code Napoleon.[251]

Kołłątaj believed in 1808 that nature divided the world into parts and a system of empires should correspond to this as a whole, the empires being "large families" of peoples, "separate societiness". The seizure of territories on other continents he severely condemned. The Napoleonic Western Empire of a new type should encompass in the nearest future continental Europe up to the boundaries of the Russian (Eastern) Empire along the Dnipro and Dvina, relying on the high level of civilization of the European peoples. France was the metropolitan of this Empire. The uniformization of law which Kołłątaj would allow for the entire world in historical perspective should have been contemporary to the Western Empire, which would consist of national States and

247 Wierzbicki, note 136 above, p. 34.

248 Ibid., pp. 43-44.

249 Niemcewicz, note 14 above, pp. 20-21.

250 S. G. Laube, *Krótka nauka z cywilnego Statutu Napoleona Wielkiego. Sposobem słownika publiczności podana* (1808), p. v.

251 Szymaniec, note 54 above, p. 120.

federations of small States. The constitutions given by Napoleon "rest on the same foundations; or so close to one another that in the end they ultimately will all have to be subject to identical governments and to identical laws". And the French codes should become the basis of the uniformization of law.[252]

Bandtkie pointed to the existence of a group of western (European) peoples united by religious tradition, Roman legal (normative or doctrinal) legacy, closeness of customs and institutions, and high level of civilization development.[253] Rakowiecki acknowledged the unity and stadiality of the development of European law.[254] Maciejowski, together with legal families, singled out a "large family of European peoples", they being the "most civilized peoples".[255]

We observe that Brodziński in 1831 presented the vision of the Slavic world, uneven in its development, where the Polish people was the historical leader. The Slavs in his work arose as a splinter and simultaneously a single people, as well as part of the large European unity. The Poles also are defenders of Europe against the Russians as a Slavic but still barbarian peoples.[256] Jastrzębowski, dreaming in 1831 about a universal association and rapprochement of peoples, suggested for the moment an all-European association be formed with a single constitution and duality of "European laws" (international law) and national law. European law was to have been created by a single all-European Congress. Within such an association the differences between peoples should gradually disappear, which evidently would lead to the acquisition by the association of a State character. The association was to be voluntary and did not assume the hegemony of any State.[257]

One may also affirm the existence throughout the period here considered of Euro-skeptics. Czacki, for example, denied the idea of the legal unity of European peoples of the Middle Ages, pointing out that their law was exclusively national; there was no place in it for the influence of Roman law. To be sure, he wrote also about

[252] Kołłątaj, note 100 above, pp. 98-105, 108-110, 135- 144, 151, 157, 160, 182, 184.

[253] Bandtkie, note 72 above, p. 55; Bandtkie, note 102 above (1816), pp. 320-321.

[254] Rakowiecki, note 96 above, I, pp. 129, 134.

[255] Maciejowski, note 99 above, I, pp. 7, ix.

[256] Brodziński, note 139 above, pp. 14, 16-20, 24-25, 28.

[257] Wierzbicki, note 136 above, pp. 55-61.

similarity in the law of European peoples which had developed historically.[258]

* * *

The attempts during the period here considered to construct a multi-tiered Special in law that would combine the ideas of Europe, legal families, and supranational political formations are the most interesting for the observer.

Although for Kołłątaj the political people is actually the equivalent of an independent State, it might be combined with others in a federation, and also in an empire as supranational, supra-State formations.[259] Within the limits of an empire of the new type, peoples do not lose their statehood and are not oppressed, the freedom of each people and the integrity of its territory must be respected, although a metropolitan exists (and specifically, France).[260] Staszic also did not exclude the unification of several nation-States into an empire, but he regarded the last as a personal unie with a monarch at the head.[261] F. Szaniawski did not deny the possible existence of heterogeneous "vast" States composed of several countries, but asserted that to preserve the unity of law in them, and also the simultaneous observance of the public and private good in all parts was virtually impossible because of the differences in national life.[262]

Staszic in his works considered the European tribe to be the broadest association of peoples, China being the second center of such an association. Three integration attempts had occurred within the framework of Europe (Greek, Roman, Romano-Germanic) connected with the domination of certain peoples, but their success was provisional. Nonetheless, Europe is united by certain common immutable trends of development and equilibrium (non-constant) between the components thereof. Its evolution is a self-regulating process. Staszic foresaw in the future a possibility of a fourth political unification of Europe into a federation with the dominance of Russia. He presented an extensive vision of groups of peoples corresponding to linguistic families. They were called generations

[258] Czacki, note 90 above, I, pp. 16, 29.

[259] Kołłątaj, note 100 above, pp. 98-103, 210.

[260] Ibid., pp. 104-105, 108-109, 151.

[261] Pomianowski, note 128 above, p. 116.

[262] Szaniawski, note 111 above, pp. 74-76.

or splinters, each emanating from one historical people, over the centuries transforming into an internally linked aggregate of close peoples, and in the future a new "splicing" of splinter-peoples might happen. The European tribe was divided into three chips – Roman (Gallo-Latin), Germanic (Teuton), and Slavic. In turn, these large generations were divided into smaller groups, which among the Slavs were three. The generations have inherent features of character and mentality. The Romans and the Germans were inclined to expansion, aggression, and the Slavs, to peacefulness and goodness. As a result, there was the consistent expansion of the Germanic peoples and their aspiration to assimilate the Slavs, the colonial policy of the Romans and the Germanic peoples. All three groups migrated to Europe from Asia. Large generations (splinters) of peoples were immutable and the principal actors of history, and not individual peoples. The peoples are "temporary creations of history", arise by natural means and irrespective of the will of the men because of links within the splinters and political and migration processes, and then disappear for the same reasons.

Their leadership within the splinter also is temporary, which is merely a manifestation of the general concealed potential of the last. In order to realize this potential, the peoples of the splinter must unite, forming a natural integral entity, and the issue of leadership in such an association is secondary. Staszic supported the idea of standardization in the writing of Slavic languages, which should have led to their coming together (restoration of unity), as well as a federation of Slavic peoples as paths to their political unity and just system based on natural law.

In earlier works Staszic considered such unity under the leadership of Poland without the participation of Russia and as the defense of Europe against Russia. Later the hopes for political unity he linked with Russia, which also was relegated to Europe, but pointed to the intellectual-cultural leadership in a formed union of Poles, for they and the Russians he considered as elder brothers along the other Slavic peoples. A Slavic Federation would have dominated in Europe and would have established a new just and peaceful international order therein.[263] Matlęgiewicz noted: "From all this somewhat ambiguous terminology an image is extracted of a hierarchical order of individual aggregates. From the

[263] Matlęgiewicz, note 194 above, pp. 100-103, 108-110; Matlęgiewicz, note 136 above, pp. 169-186; Wierzbicki, note 136 above, pp. 49-52.

people as the smallest entity through a splinter becoming a tribe – the broadest group with a trans-continental character".[264]

Hoene-Wroński in 1818, although he advanced the idea of a "universal community", actually believed in the creation of a European federation of free national States under the hegemony of Russia. Smaller associations of States must exist within such a federation, each formed in accordance with language kinship – Slavic, Romanist, Germanic.[265]

During the period here considered, Warsaw scholars actively elaborated the idea of supranational communities of a linguistic-cultural, political, and legal character. The most detailed became the conception of legal families based on carrying over to the science of law the approaches of linguistics, namely, the theory of linguistic families. A concrete expression of this conception became the presumption that linguistic kinship of the Slavic peoples also has a political and legal dimension. It is suggested that this presumption was formulated by Polish scholars at the end of the eighteenth century and developed during the period here considered. Such a presumption had not only scientific, but also a political-ideological dimension and was actively used to substantiate projects for associations of Slavs into a separate federation or within broader empires (French, Russian). The Slavic idea often was combined with Aryan, but the clear racial content it acquired after the period being analyzed here.

The available materials enable the theoretical content of the conception of legal families to be reconstructed. During the period here examined, the last were called in the sources: large tribes, gens of people, races, generations, aggregates, groups, brotherhoods, splinters, and families. The linguistic family was defined both as one people and as the aggregate of individual smaller groups (generations, splinters) and peoples, and such an equivocal attitude was described as the correlation of language and dialects.

It was proclaimed that historically the family of peoples emanated from one (and, in all likelihood, politically united) people also having a single religion and primeval law. The reasons for the division of the initial people and the formation of a family of peoples were geographical dispersion, which generated differences

[264] Matlęgiewicz, note 136 above, p. 169.

[265] Wierzbowski, note 136 above, pp. 53-54.

in the needs of people, the gradual emergence of anthropological differences between different parts of the people, the subjection of part of the nation to other peoples, the mixing of parts of the people with other peoples, and the influence of other peoples.

The family of peoples retained the same or close spirit, character, mentality, customs, legal concepts, trends of social development, and a joint notion of their special destiny. The family was regarded as the space of constant social, cultural, and legal interaction. Relations between different families and peoples were considered to be competitive and hostile. Borrowings between them were condemned, but all the same were recognized. Depending on the presence of borrowings, the law of the peoples and entire families may be regarded as pure or mixed.

Among legal families, legal scholars named Slavic, Scandinavian (Gothic, Northern), Germanic (Teutonic, German), Romanist (or Gallo-Latin), Anglo-Saxon, and Eastern. Within the Slavic family, Eastern and Western were singled out, as was a third (evidently, Southern) splinter (group).

The idea of European unity was another vector for constructing supranational legal communities. This was permitted on the basis of Roman law (preservation of its normative or doctrinal influence), religious tradition, identical or similar (and higher than in other parts of the world) level of civilization development, historical processes of the coming together of law, and dissemination of the new French codes. All this too was considered to be grounds for the political unity of the European peoples, with the possibility of creating a continental empire as a "separate community" and "large family" of peoples. European law was mentioned as a single phenomenon that might be formed by means of all-European legislative organs. But the prospects for the preservation of individual European national legal systems were not subjected to any doubt.

The Special in law, in the view of Warsaw legal scholars, might also be personified in the legal orders of new just empires or federations of peoples, smaller in territorial scope than a certain continent. Such formations might be formed on the basis of the hegemony of one State or equality of States, but without eliminating the last and the national legal orders.

Staszic proposed the most interesting conceptualization of the Special in law during the period here investigated. He believed that the peoples are temporary formations, are formed and disappear as a consequence of processes within a generation (or family of peoples). Peoples belong to certain groups which, in turn, are parts of a generation (chip). The generation historically emanates from one people; the processes of the rapprochement of peoples within it is characteristic; under certain conditions it may again "coalesce", become the sole natural political whole. But it will not transform into one people; it will merely generate new peoples. The generation (splinter), and not the people, is the principal actor of social development, including legal. In turn, the generations are components of large tribes. Staszic pointed in particular to the existence of a European tribe and yet another community connected with China. Uniform trends of development and equilibrium of the components thereof are characteristic of a large tribe. The tribe is capable of political and legal integration on the basis of the hegemony of one of the generations or one of the peoples.

Chapter 5
Conclusions

Dramatic changes connected with the loss of multi-national statehood, repeated partitions and wars, and dispersion of the people among several empires were events serving as the political context of the development of legal thought on Polish territories. The realities of occupation and the aspiration to restore the State aggravated the searches for a new national identity, especially in the sphere of law. The realities of partial loss of the force of the old law of the *Rzecz Pospolita,* the forcible repeated introduction of foreign law, and the revolutionary political and social changes provided therein stimulated the development of legal thought and simultaneously required constant activity by jurists to adapt and introduce new norms.

All this activity was embodied in the operation of the entirely new infrastructure of lawmaking organs, educational and scientific institutions (School of Law, Warsaw University, Society of Friends of Science), and professional publishing projects. The reception in the Duchy of Warsaw of the codes of Napoleonic France became to a significant degree, directly or indirectly, the impetus for their creation and transformation of legal science and practice in principle within the framework of their activity. The new institutions created effective channels for the forming and dissemination of ideas and discussion platforms in the context of contemplating old law of the *Rzecz Pospolita,* received French, Austrian, and Prussian law, and the formulation of a new legal world outlook of the Warsaw jurists.

Powerful external impacts through education, foreign scientific literature and translations thereof, and others formed the intellectual context for the development of legal thought. Warsaw legal scholars primarily identified themselves with two schools, German by origin, but trans-European in their expansion and significance – historical and historical-philosophical, which by their character were two inter-connected facets of the formation of early positivism in jurisprudence.

The deep link between Polish legal science during the period here considered and the science of other countries of Europe should be noted, especially the German states. The education of a significant portion of leading Polish legal scholars in German universities testifies to this, as does the dominance among the translations of foreign legal works of those by German authors; the same dominance is seen in Polish scientific legal publications of references to German works, together with an orientation solely to German schools of legal thought and the proclamation of the superiority of German science in comparison with other countries. But such an orientation was a general European phenomenon, and Polish science was entirely responsive to this trend. It is difficult to deny, for example, that German classical philosophy had influence throughout Europe or that Göttingen University was the best on the continent during the period here investigated.

But this does not testify to the unoriginality or secondary nature of Polish legal science. When analyzing this Polish-German link, it is important to proceed not from the presumption of the standardness of German models and their correct or insufficiently correct translation in other countries, but from the originality of the selective acceptance and transformation of general European ideas which in German legal science were clearly expressed, conceptualized, and popularized.

Certain Polish works of the period here considered testify with regard to a comparison with German to the simultaneous nature of the development of ideas important in principle, and others should not be considered as simple imitation; one may see in them original searches for answers to common questions. Our analysis of Polish scientific works of this period shows that recourse to ideas of the German schools of legal thought played an initiating role, and not a final point of reflections. Nor should one forget the material influence on Polish legal thought of leading French, Italian, English, and other scholars, as also reflected in the present study.

Originality should be cognized not in a comparison of the forms of expression, but in the fundamental agenda of legal thought then – the forming of a positivist and social paradigm in the "moral" sciences, and also derivative doctrines on the empirical and comparative cognition of law and a non-metaphysical scientific legal picture of the world. The conceptions of the Warsaw legal scholars during this period were not an eclectic mixture, but an original synthesized system of general European and original ideas.

The assertions of some contemporary specialists on the exclusively applied orientation and also the limited confines of the national problems of Polish legal thought in the first third of the nineteenth century and the unsatisfactory level of training Warsaw jurists of that time have no basis. The principal ground of legal science in the understanding of the majority of Warsaw legal scholars was its independence from *a priori* and metaphysical philosophizing, and the forming of an own philosophical-legal discourse (philosophy of positive law) on the basis of a generalization and contemplation of the results of empirical studies.

It was acknowledged that the science of law should be a system new in principle for the organization of legal knowledge – positivist and social. Recognizing the historical and contemporary pluralism of such organization of knowledge, Warsaw scholars identified themselves with Central European legal science, the core of which was the German states.

Warsaw scholars believed that historical, dogmatic, and philosophical approaches underlay jurisprudence. Accordingly, they analyzed three relatively separate spheres of scientific knowledge which in aggregate might be considered as a single legal science or system of inter-connected legal sciences.

Depending on the emphasis in the views of scholars on the fundamental or applied facet of legal science, this system was seen variously, and as the subject-matter of jurisprudence – universal or to a large extent, national. One may assert that to some degree this correlated with the predominance in the view of certain scholars of the grounds of the historical-philosophical or historical schools.

But independently of these orientations, Warsaw legal scholars considered comparison to be a means of building generalized knowledge on law and the formation of the concepts and conceptions thereof. Among the scientific purposes of comparison there were singled out: cognition of the essence of legal phenomena in their development, cause and effect links and interactions, the forming of a philosophy of positive law; cognition of the distinctive features of national law by means of determining the autochthonic and borrowed elements therein, and also the sources of the borrowing; reconstruction of the supranational or inter-nationality Special in legal development – legal families. Among the practical purposes were named: expert examination of legal decisions; improvement of national law by way of reception and adaptation of borrowed elements or purification of these elements; drafting of new law; harmonization of complex national orders; coming together of legal orders within one legal family.

Warsaw legal scholars saw comparison as subject-matter-functional (and not normativist), multi-source, contextual, and historical. Original methods and consistent methodological techniques of comparative legal research were proposed and approved.

During the period here investigated, the question of the place of comparative-legal knowledge within the legal sciences became the subject-matter of lengthy quests by Warsaw legal scholars. For some of the observers, this should have been found in the history of law, which was understood also as positive jurisprudence in general in its universal-historical dimension. This knowledge should have been a generalization of empirical data obtained by various legal sciences and serve as the basis for the highest abstracting thereof by the philosophy of positive law. A consequence of this approach became the conceptualization of the comparative (universal) history of law first as a separate sphere of research and, in 1829, as a scientific discipline.

In the vision of another group of legal scholars, comparative-legal knowledge at a high level of generalizations acted as a basic means of forming the philosophy of law, its stage, and simultaneously formed an individual kind of philosophy – the philosophy of diverse laws (finally conceptualized in 1830), or a science at the juncture of empirical, theoretical, and philosophical cognition – the "science of comparisons in law", formulated in 1819. National legal systems were part of the subject-matter of the last, as well as the dialectic of their interaction, and also the comparison of legal conceptions and concepts. The aim was the forming of a general doctrine on law and the determination or creation of the better law with the purpose of the improvement of the national legal order.

Warsaw legal scholars were aware that they were not the first to suggest the singling out of comparative jurisprudence and the comparative history of law, and they presented a survey of the history of this singling out. Prince Frantisek Szaniawski in 1819 submitted the most comprehensive and systematic and also sole book-length conceptualization of comparative jurisprudence in the world during the first third of the nineteenth century, and Heylman and R. Hube in 1830 became involved in the most heuristic discussion of its time on the disciplinary organization of comparative-legal knowledge.

The development and contemplation of comparative-legal knowledge and construing of comparative-legal sciences were merely formal manifestations of the new quality of reasoning of the Warsaw jurists, who aspired to master the world of law on new non-metaphysical, positivist, and social worldview grounds with the assistance of the comparative methodology. One may assert that previously a purely legal picture of the world did not exist, and the generalization of empirical legal knowledge was intertwined within a theological or speculative philosophical picture of natural law based on an uncritical transference of the methodology of the natural and technical sciences. Constructing the first integral scientific legal picture of the world, the major features of which were empiricity, sociality, and pluralism became an essential manifestation of new comparative-legal reasoning.

The concept of positive and social national law formulated by Warsaw jurists during the period here considered became a key element of this picture. The majority of them rejected an understanding of natural law as proper law, relegating it to the sphere of physical and biological nature as an external condition of the development of the social world, having proclaimed the essence of the last to be the diversity and freedom of will. Moreover, the Warsaw jurists precisely demarcated the moral as an internal and non-normative subjective imperative of human intentions and the law as purely external, objective regulator of human behavior which became an obligatory consequence of its recognition by society. Law began to be understood as an element of the historical self-formation of society, was generated by the last, and exerts a reverse influence on it. Accordingly, the law of a national society is changeable and territorially localized, and the territories of the extension of national legal orders comprises the legal picture of the world.

During the period here considered, Warsaw jurists developed socio-volitional and organic theories of national law. To a great extent, the socio-volitional theory was inherited from a political understanding of the people in the *Rzecz Pospolita*. A new understanding of the nation became more inclusive, encompassed broader strata of the population, but universal, as for example in France, it was not.

The socio-volitional theory of Warsaw jurists proclaimed the conscious creation of law by the people through the collective will as a realization of individual and collective freedom in order to provide for social needs and the realization of ideals. The presumptions of this theory were: equality of peoples as the bearers of the social will, their right to determine the form and content of their law, and also the requirement of statehood as the political self-determination of the people. The last requirement formalized national law into an autonomous totality and separate unit of universal legal development.

The organic theory of national law in the vision of Warsaw legal scholars relied on a cultural-linguistic understanding of the nation and provided for an immanent and continuous national lawmaking irrespective of the existence of an own State. The nation as a metaphysical organism is one, and a person within it – merely a particle whose interests and aspirations are removed in this integral unit. The development of the law of a nation is a constant function of the last, has an evolutionary character, and is manifest especially in customary law and judicial practice, and in other sources. But irrespective of the form of the embodiment and origin of law (even imposed) it always remains in its realization dependent on the people's legal consciousness.

An important element of the theory of national law developed as the doctrine by Warsaw legal scholars concerning its distinctiveness, represented by two basic approaches which may be roughly called culture-centric and constructivist. An understanding of distinctiveness as autochthonic and inalienable, embedded in the culture and reasoning of a people is characteristic of a culture-centric approach, proposing the possibility of an absolutely distinctive, "pure" national law without borrowings. Under this approach, any interaction of legal orders is unnecessary and even harmful, the borrowed law does not survive, always is identified and subject to transformation in principle or removal for the restoration of the character of development peculiar to national law.

The constructivist approach provided that distinctive elements of national law are not immanent, but are formed historically, and by origin may be autochthonic or borrowed. Distinctiveness in this vision is rational; it is determined by the distinctive features of the selection of legal models and their adaptation to local conditions. And as a result of modernization processes and borrowings between peoples, it narrows and in the future may even disappear. But in fact the two approaches in the works of Warsaw jurists were primarily synthesized as recognition of the inevitable existence in national law, in various correlations, of autochthonic and borrowed elements.

The understanding by Warsaw jurists of what is the supranational and inter-national in legal development is beyond the limits of national law was rather complex and multi-tiered. The respective ideas were formed most intensively in the course of discussions concerning the reception and fate of French, canon, and Roman law. With regard to French law, the Warsaw jurists proposed both the preservation and repeal, reworking, adaptation, and augmentation. But in connection with political changes in Polish society the perception thereof changed from an imposed imperial law to national which preserves the existence of the people from a new imperial threat. The need to undertake an own Polish codification of law generated no material objections, but the majority of jurists proposed to do this on the basis of French law. Moreover, with regard to French and Roman law, the Warsaw jurists often upheld their special role in universal legal development, as well as the European identity of Polish law. With regard to canon law, the discussion unfolded between proponents of the integrity of national law, which did not allow for the existence of a competing supranational legal order and mixing with norms of moral content, on one hand, and proponents of the superiority of morality over national law and the church over the State, on the other.

All these discussions were a platform for the theoretical contemplation of the possibility of inter-national or supranational elements of legal development. Warsaw jurists resolutely rejected the idea of the objectivization of a world legal order, having regard to the differences and dynamic of the development of societies. The possible unification or uniformization of law was presented by them only as regional and relative, which did not overcome either the form or distinctiveness of national law. Instead, a doctrine was elaborated on uniformity in diversity – immanence of the Universal in the Particular (national law), the forming of such Universal in the process of the development and interaction of individual national legal orders without the loss of distinctiveness by them. The conception of the dialogue of legal orders providing for the possible filling in of certain elements of law with autochthonic, or borrowed, or formed under foreign influence was an element of this doctrine.

Within the conception of dialogue of legal orders, Warsaw legal scholars developed elements of the theory of interaction of national legal orders. Conditions and forms of borrowing in law were substantiated, a classification thereof was proposed, as well as a technique for undertaking reception. The basic reason for borrowing was deemed to be the search for the better legal models in order to resolve problems of development identified by society. A doctrine was formed on the adaptation and acculturation of received law which provided either for the complete assimilation of the last or the forming of a mixed and internally contradictory legal order. Moreover, the position of proponents of relatively autochthonic development and possible partial purification of national legal systems from borrowings was conceptualized in detail. The problem of interaction of legal orders was singled out as an autonomous subject-matter of scientific consideration.

Searches for the Universal and separating out the problem of the interaction of legal orders led Warsaw legal scholars to identifying the Special in law as a concrete general, common for a certain group of legal orders and, at the same time, certain group of historical and contemporary interaction. The theory of the Slavic family developed on Polish territories, based on the closeness of languages and transferred into the cultural and political spheres, ultimately was perceived by jurists, who substantiated the existence of a respective legal family.

In addition to a pure Slavic problem, Warsaw scholars developed a theory of the legal family as a Special in law. The elements thereof were presumptions of: the origin of a family from one people with a single law which in the course of history had become a group of peoples; preservation by the peoples of a single family having uniform or close spiritual and social characteristics, including customary law, and also a feeling of mutual closeness; preservation within the family of constant cultural and legal interaction and limitation of communication with peoples outside the family. Warsaw scholars proposed a list of legal families which on the whole was close to comparative-legal classifications topical until recently.

Other variants in determining the Special in law were mutually-linked ideas of "large families" – European unity and empires of a new type. But these ideas remained unfinished, contradictory, filled with little legal content, referential to ideological constructs and products of other sciences, and also subsidiary to the theory of the legal family.

Staszic proposed the most integral theory of the Special in law. He absolutized the doctrine on the legal family, actually presented it as the Particular in law and basic unit of legal development, removing the personality of individual peoples. Staszic suggested special entities, higher than legal families, which were spaces of cultural and political interaction and integration – and which might correlate with a somewhat later concept of local civilizations.

The present study shows that the legal thought of scholars from the Duchy of Warsaw and Kingdom of Poland from 1807 to 1831 cannot be perceived as a secondary mixture of foreign lègal ideas and influences, which has been typical of the assessments of a number of contemporary Polish observers. Instead, it is autonomous, integral and a rather original ideological complex which should be cognized separately and in the context of European scientific development.

There are grounds to assert that one of the leading lines of development here was the rise of a new system of positivist and social legal sciences with the assistance of comparative-legal knowledge, contemplation thereof, and forming of a scientific legal picture of the world that was comparativistic in essence. In this context, Warsaw scholars proposed a number of discoveries and innovations of all-European significance. These were the first monograph in the world, by F. Szaniawski, on comparative jurisprudence and an expanded substantiation of the principles of the institutionalization of comparative-legal knowledge by Heylman and R. Hube, together with the integral technique for the reception of law proposed by Wyczechowski and Daniłowicz and the integral theory of the Special in law by Staszic. Many more important ideas from this period remain to be discovered and considered.

Annex
THOUGHTS ON NATIONAL LEGISLATION

Antoni Wyczechowski

Biographical Note. Born at Objezierze, Kingdom of Prussia, *Rzecz Pospolita,* (now the West Pomeranian Voivodeship, Poland), on 10 June 1780, Antoni Wyczechowski graduated from the Law Faculty of the University of Halle in 1799 and until 1801 worked as a referendar in a court at Berlin. From 1803 he was an assessor at the Warsaw Regency. A member of the House of Justice (1806), appellate court of the Warsaw Department (1807), counsellor of the Ministry of Justice (from 1808), referendar of the State Council (from 1811), and supreme judge (from 1815), he was a member of the Governmental Commission of Justice and of the State Council (from 1816).[1]

Text. The present work, here published for the first time but frequently cited by Polish jurists, was by its nature a Memorandum submitted by Antoni Wyczechowski to Prince Adam Czartoryski in response to the latter's appeal to Polish jurists to submit a vision of the prospects and mechanisms for replacing the Code Napoleon with another law in the Kingdom of Poland. The work probably dates from October to December 1815. The manuscript reposes in the Czartoryski Library in Krakow: Rrkps 5259 IV, Myśli względem prawodawstwa narodowego przez Antoniego Wyczechowskiego, k. 59. Professor Dr. hab. Michał Gałędek made it available to the author.

* * *

There is no people in all of Europe in which laws changed so often and within such brief intervals as in the country at present comprising the Kingdom of Poland.

Virtually every family feels the consequences of the shock of legal relations which occur again and again.

[1] Biography based on H. Grynwaser, "Kodeks Napoleona w Polsce. Demokraca Szlachecka. 1795-1831", in Grynwaser, *Pisma* (Wrocław, 1951), I.

The entire present and possibly future generations will still feel them. The sufferings of many is the suffering of all. So far no one can cognize and calculate their scale. They will gradually show themselves when everything returns to quiet and each will be occupied with eliciting and dealing with his property relations. At precisely that moment we will feel obstacles and confusion; we will encounter unexpected losses of personal ownership; the abyss in which we are lost is the result of frequent changes of the laws.

We have to cognize and separate each era of changes before passing on to an analysis of opinions relating to future legislation.

We will address consecutively: a) Polish laws; b) Prussian laws; c) Austrian or Galician laws; d) provisional laws; that is, of the Governmental Commission and Central Government; e) codes of the Duchy of Warsaw; f) conditions and modifications with which all the aforementioned laws together have force.

A. Polish Laws

No Christian people now has its own original laws and customs. Religion made one family from these peoples. Brought from foreign countries, it also introduced foreign laws and customs.

Hence Roman and partially canon law became sources of the laws of all Christian peoples. Neighbors took laws from neighbors and from other relations. And just as in Antiquity, the Romans took models from the Greeks, so in later times the laws of the Langobards and Saxons, and others traveled to neighboring countries.

Not always laws proper, but often the dominant spirit and customs were carried over to a country.

That which we now call Polish national law is merely modifications of Roman and canon laws; it was formed by mixing such laws with national laws and customs; by means of the influence of neighboring laws and customs.

In every country, and consequently also in Poland, we have such sources of law as: a) laws which the Polish people created for itself, which are called statutes and constitutions (*ius scriptum*); b) folk customs (*ius consuetudinarum*), which may be of various types; Aa) foreign laws introduced in Poland through custom, as: Roman, canon, Saxon, and Magdeburg laws, Prussian Correktura, and others;[2] (Bb) original folk customs formed over the centuries, judicial practice, stable notions, authority of authors writing about laws with whom they [the courts] consulted in Poland, especially with respect to municipal matters and bills of exchange.

We shall briefly consider the gradual formation of these sources of law.

The fewer [court] cases there were, the simpler they were, the less governments engaged in legislation. History teaches that kings themselves were judges, and therefore could not write laws for themselves.

The increase of population for which there follows a multiplicity of interests and enlightenment of the mind, and court cases multiply, making them more sophisticated and confusing. Monarchs can no longer be judges, and those judges subordinate to them cannot judge without norms. For the general public it is not the same if a plaintiff or defendant triumphs in the case. A case lost unjustly not only offends the party which lost, it disturbs the quiet of all citizens, making their rights and property unreliable.

The unreliability of ownership deters investments and improvements and paralyzes all internal movement. Thus, norms become necessary not only for a judge who must decide a dispute between parties, but also in order to secure the rights and ownership of all citizens.

With the growth of civilization there is naturally gravitation towards the foreign laws of those peoples from whom we take light, customs, and requirements which underlie ideas. Insofar as a judge, not finding in the law and customs of the country a single norm for a new case, and possibly one taken from foreign customs, even if, in his view, he himself could consider the case well but his opinion cannot have that authority and confidence as an expression of a praised foreign law, and therefore he prefers to rest his decision on the provisions of another's law.

But judges do not always refer in the same cases to the same sources, do not always interpret them identically, and ultimately there are cases connected with the concrete position of the country. Hence new laws arise and the adaptation of foreign laws

[2] The original name was: Ius Terrae Nobilitaits Prussiae Correctum. A multi-branch incorporation of legal norms from 1598 to 1599 in the Kingdom of Prussia, then part of the *Rzecz Pospolita*.

and customs. When reading the laws of that era, we rarely can understand them unless we study first the state of legal interests and concepts of that time. These laws do not contain clear and precise provisions to which we are accustomed now, but rather with brief allusions establish norms sufficiently understood only by contemporaries and which subsequent generations may master [only with the assistance of historical knowledge].

As civilization develops, the sources of law become more numerous and confusing. This occurs to such an extent that judges apply them with difficulty, students study them with even more difficulty, and citizens whom laws serve are not virtually in a state to understand them.

This is an era when partial collections and explanations of the sources of law appear. Some facilitate cognition and combination of fatherland laws. Such collections here are inventories of laws. Others explain foreign laws taken into the country and demonstrate their correlation. Yet others collect folk customs and judicial practice or write comments on various aspects of law. We have many writings of this kind, but fewer than foreign ones, for many works were lost and because our class of burghers is less numerous, there are fewer literate individuals.

The most widely spread sources of existing customs and judicial observations were those which each knew in practice whose traces are found in court cases and archives, and the traces of others rest on habit and memory passed down from generation to generation.

The era of separate collections finished with a general digest of all sources. Lithuania compiled for itself a Statute under the title Lithuanian Statute, which was amended three times.[3] At various times in the Crown[4] the need was acknowledged again and again for the consolidation of law; draft worthy collections were drawn up many times, but unhappy circumstances obstructed completion of a matter much needed by the people.

The joint history of our legislation with neighboring peoples began with this. We cannot conceal the last era when neighbors enjoyed a happy period for the development of their legislation,

[3] Reference is made to the three successive editions of the Statute of the Grand Duchy of Lithuania, Rus, and Zhemaity of 1529, 1566, and 1588.

[4] The traditional unofficial name of the Kingdom of Poland as part of the *Rzecz Pospolita*.

and the Polish people, on the contrary, was subject to a continuous series of misfortunes, with each year its downfall approached.

The invariability of rule opens the path to abuses. Human passions, unless suppressed, show themselves in various forms. Certain causes at any time and in any place have identical consequences, and consequently also in Poland. National legislation and law enforcement fell behind. Therefore, whosoever wanted to take as a model the state of Polish legislation and jurisprudence of recent times would imagine them in an unjust light.

In addition to a worthy collection of laws there exists an even higher degree of legislation. One may create laws or collect those already created into a single corpus by taking into account only natural justice and the interests of the parties. But one may make laws by taking into account policy and the general interests of the country. When artificial forces of government received a significance possibly even greater than natural forces, it was cognized that legislation is an essential driving force in this artificial machine which supports and improves its movement. The simple collection and ordering of laws from that moment was not sufficient, and the need was recognized for the systematization of law; that is, targeting all legal relations to the general political vision of the country.

It is difficult to explain this question precisely and briefly. The example from Prussian legislation may superbly replace an expanded interpretation. Such Prussian provisions: a) Ordnance on deposits; b) Ordnance on mortgage; c) Ordnance on instructions in connection with the law on mortgage credit, garden and park institutions, banks, marine companies, and various monetary-credit institutions which everywhere subordinated private interests to themselves; that is, directed the last to the general interest in combination with favorable grade relations elevate credit in the country so much that, according to calculations before the War with France, there was in Prussia twice as much credits than cash. Therefore, having regard to the fact that there was more than one hundred million thalers in the country in cash, internal turnover occurred so rapidly and intensive than if, in fact, there were three hundred million thalers cash in the country.

To triple the financial strength of the country is the work of a branch which would be impossible without the assistance of judicial laws.

Ultimately, when applying such laws, we encounter various principles which do not correspond to natural justice and would not find an enthusiastic executor in the person of a judge who in a legal dispute would take into account only one specific case, consider the interest between private and private, but not take into account the general influence on the country of the scale of such interests.

In order to explain these thoughts more precisely, we take an example by analogy: a groschen withdrawn from an account by a depositor means nothing in the understanding thereof, but the withdrawal of one groschen by each depositor may bring several millions of losses. Therein lies the difference between the individual and the general consideration of cases, and this in the example cited everyone apprehends. There is the same difference in the case of judicial laws, but here a higher scope and cognition of relations is needed in order to be convinced how the creation of principles whose fulfillment sometimes may undermine natural justice with respect to an individual interest between the parties but ultimately should be fulfilled so as not to weaken the general result is essential for law in order to achieve major results.

Only those who thanks to practical service are accustomed to preciseness, the unity and fullness of its realization, always having in view the intentions of the legislator relating to the entire country and being convinced that for society even natural justice sometimes must be the victim may be the executors of such law.

At the time when the Polish people was equal in legislation with their neighbors and even to some extent exceeded them, the use of all natural forces was not needed. At that time the means of artificial enhancing the might of the country were yet unknown. When the financial system began theoretically and practically to develop, when for political reasons legislation began to be seen as closely linked with policy in order to realize the principles of governing in all legal relations, the era ensued of the decline of the Polish people, and therefore national legislation in this sphere was in its infancy.

Combining all the foregoing into a single view, this is the result: a) Polish legislation reached that level when it was necessary to order all the sources of law and assemble them into a single whole; b) insofar as written laws and the works of authors are not sufficient sources for creating a perfected Digest and even the practice of Polish law itself thanks to which knowledge of its legal foundations was passed from generation to generation was interrupted by foreign governments, it is appropriate to call upon Polish jurists who remain to work on the creation of a perfected Digest of fatherland laws.

These people at the present moment are very important for Polish legislation; we must stand up for cognition for contemporary youth and for descendants a memory of their paternal laws which depend only on information from presently living jurists.

B. Prussian Laws

By reason of the Partition of Poland, a large part of the contemporary Kingdom of Poland went to the Prussian monarchy.

The will of the Prussian Government was that all countries of this monarchy, although they consisted of different peoples, be guided by one law. Only local relations and exclusive types of trades had individual reserved laws. Thus, Prussian laws were divided into general and provincial.

When the country was captured, it was declared which legal subject-matter should be regulated by old Polish laws, which were considered to be provincial, and which by general Prussian law.

Insofar as the majority of the foundations of Polish law rested on the memory of the living and the administration of justice was undertaken not by Polish, but by Prussian jurists whom it was difficult to materially enlighten with regard to norms absent in printed and manuscript form, the result was that even in cases where Polish or provincial laws should have significance, Prussian laws often predominated.

The genius of Friedrich the Great artificially transformed the poor and underpopulated Prussian country into a first-class State. The Prussian monarchy was distinctive not only for the military arts, but also for administrative and financial institutions and the improvement of legislation. All its institutions were brought over to Polish territory. Fulfilled by Prussian leaders and officials, they did not feel any obstacles or unsuitability. The Government had no intention to adapt to the customs or notions of the country and locality; on the contrary, it always aspired to generalization of the system.

The ordering of mortgage credits, the flow of cash from Prussia, and credit, and most of all peace and trade in grain led this part of Poland to a high growth of internal prosperity.

Legal relations changed, concepts changed, and education changed, which led to a change of morality.

We tasted the fruits of peace and good government, but we did not learn the art of government. The Prussian Government, aspiring that our compatriots learned another language in order to fully carry over the knowledge of Prussian laws and institutions, thereby deprived them of offices and only the rising youth were given the possibility of serving the country.

In 1806, when the governing was changed,[5] the influence of Prussian domination showed itself most distinctly on the inhabitants of the country from the standpoint of reason.

The former Polish officials who were engaged with the affairs of the country soon understood that their failure to act for more than ten years was a loss to them and to the country; they found another character of legal interests, other notions, and morality. For them the people within which they lived and to which they had devoted their labor had disappeared.

The new officials who came from the Prussian school knew Prussian institutions and laws, but they could not substantively know Polish laws. Consequently, they were, in the sense of the old order of things, like foreigners in their own country.

It was impossible to turn the order of things back, but it also was impossible to foresee how long Prussian institutions and laws might still be suitable for us, for we saw their favorable consequences in that period when: a) they were realized in connection with the Prussian monarchy; b) they were realized by Prussian officials accustomed to all branches of their administration and skilled in unanimous and precise execution; c) they were realized during peace, uninterrupted trade, flow of money – in general, at a time of domestic prosperity.

But we could not know what would have been their effect under a completely different set of affairs.

[5] Transfer of part of the territory of the former *Rzecz Pospolita* to the power of France and the allies thereof.

Finally, it is difficult to agree to take the law of a people from under whose power we have succeeded in withdrawing.

C. Austrian or Galician Laws

That which was said about Prussian laws also partly concerns Galician laws, which were the law for countries previously under Austrian domination and now comprise nearly half of the Kingdom of Poland. The main distinction lies in the following: A) that the Austrian Government did not have a certain law for all the countries of its monarchy and thus allowed each part thereof to be guided by individual laws; B) that Galician laws were better adapted to localities, relations, morality and concepts of the inhabitants of the country; C) that they lacked that artificiality which the Prussian Government should have used when utilizing legislation to realize their own political purposes; D) that compatriots were allowed to serve in court proceedings, and thanks to the introduction of the Latin language in judicial magistrates, communication was facilitated between Polish provinces and old countries of the monarchy.

D. Provisional Laws of the Governmental Commission and Central Government

The era which separated the Prussian and Austrian rule from the permanent government of the Duchy of Warsaw cannot be avoided without provisional laws, namely in the parts which previously belonged to the Prussian monarchy. All the Prussian magistrates ceased to exist because they were made up of foreigners, and their place was taken by advisors with other notions. The publication of such instructions which would facilitate administration by compatriots and strengthen the spirit of their ancestors was absolutely necessary.

Even beyond the provisional laws or instructions, the change of persons in and of itself who were to realize the rights provided but were filled with other norms and concepts, should constitute a change in legal relations.

E. Codes of the Duchy of Warsaw

The era of introducing the Civil Code[6] in the Duchy of Warsaw differed to a great extent from the era of introducing Prussian and Galician laws.

The reforms which emanated from the new spirit of philosophy and French Revolution were carried over to the Duchy of Warsaw by granting the Dresden Constitution to the Duchy,[7] which contained basic features of these reforms, and a Civil Code which introduced the same principles in detail in all legal relations. Organs for the registration of acts of civil status and civil marriages and divorces were introduced. Changes occurred in relations between owners of estates and peasants. Inheritance rights disappeared based on old feudalism. Inhabitants of the country who previously had individual rights were equated in legal relations with all other inhabitants. Virtually all these changes noticeably affected all internal relations more than Prussian and Galician laws that, although they differed in individual aspects from ancient Polish laws, were derived from a common system.

The law of the Civil Code is implemented only by compatriots, and consequently of all foreign laws knowledge thereof is most widely disseminated, whereas, on the contrary, each of the other foreign laws is known only to one part of the country and only to persons who fulfilled duties during the Prussian and Austrian rule.

Earlier we heard praise of the Code, but today too many reproaches. But praise and reproaches are connected with the name of the ruler, who is considered to be the creator of the Code, and more detailed study of the sources indicates that this is erroneous. The so-called Code Napoleon is not a new creation, but rather a collection of laws of the preceding period. The innovation of the Code basically lies in the system of generalization. Just as with the Prussian legislator, so in France they became aware of the need for the entire nation to be guided by one law. Provincial laws, statutes, and customs disappeared, and one Code identically indicates for all inhabitants.

[6] Polish authors called the 1804 Code Civil of France (or Code Napoleon) which entered into force in 1808 in the Duchy of Warsaw and then in the Kingdom of Poland the Civil Code or simply the Code.

[7] Constitution of the Duchy of Warsaw, signed by Napoleon I Bonaparte and by the Governmental Commission at Dresden on 22-23 July 1807.

As for the praise and reproaches connected with the content of the law, one should differentiate between the principal parts thereof. The part encompassing so-called rights to a thing (*ius rerum*) is based partially on the immutable principles of Roman law which in France were purer than anywhere else, without the jumble of national and foreign laws and customs had preserved its form and therefore could not contain much materially novel. The part encompassing the rights of a person (*ius posesorum*) is a consequence of new philosophical ideas and a result of the French Revolution. It still did not signify that the present order of things fully contradicted all the foundations of the Code on the rights of persons. Ultimately, the French dynasty changed, and the return to the principles which existed before the Revolution did not happen.

Germany is proud that it knows how to use the grounds of the French Revolution without having become a victim of the revolutionary events. In the north, the Prussian monarchy is carrying over to its legislation the grounds of this part of the Coderee on persons which it considered suitable for its own country.

All this in aggregate shows that the grounds which the French Revolution so openly and solemnly proclaimed, although not all concerned every country and the views of each government, could not simply be cast aside because they are the fruit of the revolution; on the contrary, they should be better known and understood.

The unsuitability of the Code was complained of in the Duchy for these reasons: a) no one law could be completely suitable for another country; b) the law of the Code providing for such a large-scale reform of personal rights would be unpleasing to many; c) the law of the Code is being complied with only by compatriots who in such a brief period could not sufficiently understand its spirit, and therefore defects of execution may be considered defects of the legislation itself; d) knowledge of the provisions of the Code is most widespread, and therefore greater attention is devoted to it than to any other foreign laws.

That said here about the Civil Code also concerns the Code of Procedure, Trade Code, and court organization, which should be regarded as additional parts of the Civil Code.

F. Conditions and Modifications Which Apply to All the Aforesaid Laws

All the aforesaid Polish, Prussian, Austrian, and Provisional Laws of the Governmental Commission and Central Government, and also the codes, are all now in force, because every case should be considered according to the law during whose operation the events occurred.

The application of various laws is extended so long as cases from the preceding eras of legislation will come to courts.

Even in cases from the moment of introduction of the Code into force the mixing of laws occurs because: a) the Code is the civil law of the country; b) Prussian criminal law is the criminal law for the parts [of the country] which previously were under Prussian domination; c) Austrian criminal law is the criminal law for the parts [of the country] which previously were under Austrian domination; d) the French organization of the courts operates throughout the entire country.

Not only that, all our legal relations remain confused; we have lost even more because of the jumble of notions and concepts. There is not that unity which is a distinctive feature, soul, and power of the People and which is acquired and nurtured by lengthy work thanks to public education.

Representatives of various schools should judge in every court; that is, Polish, Prussian, and Austrian.

There is hardly a person who knows all these laws identically well. All assessors should be taught foreign law; that is, even the Code they do not know in such a brief time, and only this foreign Code became supposedly national because all have equal knowledge of it.

It is not surprising that with such a selection of elements so distinct from one another the cases move slowly and with great complications. That which seems fully comprehensible to one is to another strange because this is not compatible with the grounds of his School. Great uncertainty than elsewhere is the result of virtually all disputes.

If cases which originated from Polish, Prussian, and Austrian times were judged by Polish, Prussian, and Austrian parties themselves, one may assume that with regard to certain norms they would agree, but the judgment in a case rendered by an assembly of representatives of different schools is difficult to predict.

The difference of the schools influences even cases emanating from the Code, for each loves to teach and interpret it according to his own grounds.

In surveying the eras of changes of laws, we have learned our contemporary situation.

Let there be unity of norms throughout the country, unity of forms, unity of notions and customs by which a Pole would know a Pole; such would be the general proposal. But who should create this unity for the present and future generations? What should we do in this matter, we who have no such unity in our notions?

Some say that the wish is common to return completely to the old Polish laws, but soon it turns out that there are no longer those interests, those relations, those notions, those customs for which these laws were suitable. The present cases are more sophisticated, linked with notions which we took from foreign laws and peoples. This borrowing already has become our ownership; it cannot be erased, for no one can change the past.

For such instances the old laws do not contain any norms because they did not know the latter.

Therefore, here additions and changes cannot be avoided, and they will necessarily breathe with another spirit because they must correspond to matters which arose from notions accepted from abroad. Who can find the old character of fatherland laws after such changes and additions?

There will be suggestions to the benefit of Prussian and Austrian law, at least some parts and grounds thereof. If the new national legislation is read attentively, we will see that they have great influence on our notions.

But what would become of this? In the event of the application of Prussian laws, should the former Austrian provinces study them, and in the event of the application of Austrian laws, was there a similar need for the former Prussian provinces? Then one may justly reproach: if we had to accept the foreign law, for what reason should one cast aside that which is better known to both parts [of the country] and which now operates better than each of the aforementioned.

So should we remain with the provisions of the Code? But we already have seen above that without a selection one cannot accept the grounds thereof concerning the rights of persons, and we have heard statements concerning the unsuitability thereof.

Thus, if none of the suggestions made can be accepted in full, it remains to select the best in them and thus create a perfected law. However attractive this thought is, its realization is one of the most complex measures in legislation. Each law should be regarded as an artificial machine composed of parts, each of which facilitates the movement of others, aspiring to the harmonious movement of the whole.

Just as it is difficult to create a completely new machine from the parts of other different machines, so too is it difficult to create one from many systems of law.

Ultimately, the difficulties of the realization should not obstruct the [adoption] of a decision, and it should proceed not from the difficulties of realization, but rather from the convenience of the grounds for the country.

Also above we separately considered each system of law because the very basis of [our] work and importance of the subject-matter prove that to demonstrate the spirit thereof in a brief essay could not be our intention. But all the laws enumerated above should be investigated in detail and the correlation shown with the present state of the country, and a work of such great significance and size cannot be undertaken by one person. Only when all the combined forces will achieve the goal contemplated will the issue of national legislation be sufficiently comprehended.

Therefore, at this moment not a single decision may be adopted, but rather the raw material should be brought to a degree of proper maturity so that in time a substantiated decision may be adopted.

Hence follows a division of legislative activity into: a) preparatory work; b) constitutive work.

In the gradual development of these types of work it would be advisable, in our view, to act as follows:

I. First, it is pertinent to create a form of political organ; that is, a constitutional statute, because without these fundamental indicia legislative preparations cannot have any determined purposes, direction, and constancy.

II. It is pertinent to agree with the principle that national laws are those which will be deemed to best correspond to contemporary civilization and are most suitable for strengthening the happiness of the inhabitants of the Kingdom of Poland irrespective of the source from which they emanate.

III. Inasmuch as all preparatory works should have one order and one basis, they should correspond to the order of the codes now in force, that is, the Civil Code, Code of Procedure, Trade Code, and Organization of the notariat, for the following reasons: a) Polish laws have not been collected into a single whole in systematic sequence; b) Prussian and Austrian laws are not known everywhere, and therefore preparatory works cannot use the order thereof.

On criminal codes we speak below.

IV. A Commission should be appointed to prepare and illuminate materials of future national legislation in civil matters, which will be divided into four sections: a) the first section for Polish laws; b) the second section for Prussian laws; c) the third section for Austrian-Galician laws; d) the fourth section for the laws or codes now in force.

V. The first section, for the purpose of preparing and illuminating materials of future legislation on Polish laws in civil matters will be obliged to:

1. collect according to the order of codes now in force all Polish laws contained in both statutes and constitutions and various renvoi laws, and also various grounds and principles, both described in printed works and unwritten, which have been adopted in judicial practice, always citing the sources in the annotations from which they were taken.
2. draw up a historical survey of sources of Polish law and literature on them.
3. undertake the comparison of the grounds of Polish law with the grounds of the codes now in force, taking into account the constitution now in force, the contemporary state of the education and form of legal relations, and also the distinctive feature of the

position of the country, show with regard to each question which of the grounds of Polish law and which of the grounds of the law of the codes, in its view, are most convenient for strengthening the happiness of the inhabitants of the Kingdom of Poland.

VI. The second section for the purpose of preparing and illuminating the materials of future legislation on Prussian laws in civil matters shall: a) draw up a historical survey of the sources of Prussian laws that were binding for Polish provinces and the literature on this law; b) review all questions according to the codes now in force, citing for each question the place of Prussian law in which it is encompassed, show and illuminate the similarity or differences of the grounds of both legislation, and from this comparison draw a conclusion concerning the principles which, in its view, are most suitable for strengthening the happiness of the inhabitants of the Kingdom of Poland.

VII. VII. The third section with a view to preparing and illuminating the materials of future legislation on Austrian-Galician laws in civil matters will have the duties and prescriptions as the second section has.

VIII. VIII. The fourth section will engage in a survey and study of works of authors which illuminate the sources of laws of the codes and the literature on these laws. They may be considered as commentaries showing the spirit of the law in a broader light. Subsequently, the work which combines all this subject-matter together or works which encompass this subject-matter separately will be by the efforts of the section translated into the native language.

IX. IX. All four sections must complete their work within nine months maximum and submit it to the Court of High Instance of the Kingdom of Poland.

X. X. The Court of High Instance, having considered the work of each section, shall order to publish them, and transfer the originals for eternal memory to the chief archive of the country, which previously was called the Royal Metric.

XI. XI. With a view to the further study of legislative questions, the Court of High Instance will recommend to send the works of the four said sections to: a) scientific institutions: the Society of the Friends of Science in

Warsaw, the Academy in Krakow, the Academic Law Faculty in Warsaw; b) appellate courts; c) magistrates in the voivodeships, namely: 1) the ziemski and grodzki courts; 2) voivodeship councils and commissions. These magistratures in voivodeships will comprise a single general commission for discussion of the legislative questions.

XII. XII. The High Court shall call upon the magistratures of the country and scientific institutes no later than within three months to express their opinion with regard to the precision of the collection of laws, the sources and literature thereof, and also the conformity of the principles and grounds for future national legislation submitted by the sections.

Commentaries of the magistratures and institutes, and also ordered by the Court and preserved in the chief archive for eternal memory will be published for public familiarization.

XIII.XIII. After three months the High Court shall send all works of the sections and the commentaries of magistratures of the country and scientific institutes to the State Council.

XIV.In order to combine the grounds and comments into a single whole, consider them, and submit to the monarch the fundamental features of national law, and also the plan, that is, the structure of the books of law, a commission will be created from members of the State Council, Senate, and Sejm Chamber.[8]

XV. When the monarch confirms the grounds and plans according to which the future books of national law should be drafted, a competition shall be opened for the awarding of prizes to those who according to these grounds and plan submit the most substantiated draft of all law or part thereof. These drafts will be considered in the commission mentioned in point XIV, and it shall submit [the projects] adopted and collected into one to the monarch, who shall decree a decision with regard thereto in accordance with the grounds of the constitution.

8 The Senate and Sejm Chamber were the upper and lower chambers of the Sejm of the Kingdom of Poland.

XVI. The High Court, and also the commission for the preparation of laws and the sections thereof, and also the magistratures of the country, shall adopt for themselves an internal procedure for consideration of the legislative questions. The Government shall allot a certain sum to cover these needs, which shall be placed at the disposition of the High Court *salvo calculo.*

XVII. The organization of the commission for preparing the draft from the materials prepared, mentioned in point XIV, will be appointed at a time when these materials already will be assembled, from which only its work and orientations could be evaluated.

XVIII. Detailed rules for the actions mentioned in point XV also may be written only subsequently.

XIX. The Commission for preparing draft laws in the criminal sphere will be created at that time when the monarch confirms the grounds of civil legislation, to which criminal legislation should conform.

Sources

Antonetti, G. "La Faculté de droit de Paris à l'époque où Boissonade y faisait ses études", *Revue internationale de droit comparé,* XLIII, no. 2 (1991).

Askenazy S. "Zagrożenie Kodeksu Napoleona przy utworzeniu Królestwa Polskiego", *Gazeta Sądowa Warszawska,* no. 22 (28 May 1908).

Bandtkie, J. W. "Co stanowi prawnika", *Pamiętnik Warszawski,* VI (1816).

___. *Uwagi o potrzebie nauki prawa w naszym kraju w szczegolności, a o użytku onejże w ogolnością* (Warszawa: Nakladem Zawadzkiego i Komp., 1814).

___. "Myśli o zmianie prawodawstwa krajowego", *Rocznik Lubelski,* III (1960).

___. "O karze śmierci na kradzież stanowionéy rzecz podług praw kraiowych uwazana", Bandtkie J. W. *Zbiór rospraw o przedmiotach prawa polskiego* (Warszawa, Wilno: Nakladem i Drukiem Józefa Zawadzkiego, 1812).

___. "O poważaniu dawnieyszém w Polszcze prawników uczonych", *Posiedzenie publiczne Królewskiego-Warszawskiego Uniwersytetu, na uczczenie pamiątki uczonych mężow, a mianowicie polakow, odbyte dnia 15 lipca 1825 roku* (Warszawa, 1825).

___. "O uprawnieniu dzieci przez zaszly̧ zwiazek malzenski czynionem", Bandtkie J. W. *Zbiór rospraw o przedmiotach prawa polskiego* (Warszawa, Wilno: Nakladem i Drukiem Józefa Zawadzkiego, 1812).

___. "Wywod historyczny praw mieyskich w Polsce dawney obowiązuiących", Bandtie J. W. *Zbiór rospraw o przedmiotach prawa polskiego* (Warszawa, Wilno: Nakladem i Drukiem Józefa Zawadzkiego, 1812).

Bardach, J. "Historia praw słowiańskich. Przedmiot i metody badawcze", *Kwartalnik Historyczny,* no. 2 (1963).

___. "Wacław Aleksander Maciejowski 1792–1883", *Portrety uczonych. Profesorowie Uniwersytetu Warszawskiego 1816–1915* (Warszawa: Wydawnictwa Uniwersytetu Warszawskiego, 2016).

[Bieńkowski A.], *Upominek pogrobowy Ś. P. Kazimierza Pliszki Podlasianina Rzecz o sukcesji, czyli uwagi nad prawem przyrodzonym do spadku* (Warszawa, 1827).

Bentkowski, F. *Historia literatury polskiey, wystawiona w spisie dziel drukiem ogloszonych* (Warszawa, Wilno: Nakladem Zawadzkiego i Komp., 1814). 2 vols.

Bondaruk, V. O. (Бондарук В.О.). Розвиток юридичної науки і освіти в Замойській академії (1594-1784 рр.): Дис. ... канд. юр. наук (Київ, 2016). 241 p.

Brodziński, K. "O narodowości Polaków", *Z przedmową i objaśnieniami W. Rejndla* (Warszawa: M. Arcta, 1917).

Butler, W. E., Kresin, O. V. (eds.). *The Interaction of Legal Systems: Post-Soviet Approaches* (London: Wildy, Simmonds & Hill, Publishers, 2015).

___, Kresin, O. V., Shemshuchenko, Iu. S. (eds.). *Foundations of Comparative Law: Methods and Typologies* (London: Wildy, Simmonds & Hill Publishing, 2011).

Chodakowski, Z. (Czarnocki, A.) O slawianszczyznie przed chrzescianstwem (1818) // *Wiek XIX. Sto lat mysli Polskiej. Zyciorysy, streszczienia, wyjatki* (Warszawa: Naklad Gebethera I Wolffa; Krakow: G. Gebether i spolka, 1907). 2 vols.

Czacki, T. *Czy prawo rzymskie było zasadą praw litewskich i polskich? I czy z połnocnemi narodami mielismy wiele wspolnych praw i zwyczaiow? Rosprawa czytana w Krzemieńcu na otwarciu roku szkolnego 1808 w Gimnazyum Wołyńskiem* (Wilno: u J. Zawadzkiego, 1809).

___. "Mowa przy otwarciu Gimnazyum Wołyńskiego w Krzemieńcu d. 13 października 1805 r.", *Wiek XIX. Sto lat mysli Polskiej. Zyciorysy, streszczienia, wyjatki* (Warszawa: Naklad Gebethera i Wolffa; Krakow: G. Gebether i spolka, 1906).

___. *O litewskich i polskich prawach o ich duchu, źrzódłach, związku i o rzeczach zawartych w pierwszym Statucie dla Litwy 1529 r. wydanem.* T. I (Warszawa: w Drukarni J.C.G. Ragoczego, 1800).

___. *O litewskich i polskich prawach o ich duchu, źródłach, związku, i o rzeczach zawartych w pierwszym statucie dla Litwy, 1529 roku wydanym*. T. II (Krakow: Drukarnia "Czasu", 1861).

Daniłowicz, I. *Kodex Napoleona w porównaniu z prawami polskiemi i litewskiemi* (Warszawa: Księgarnia Jana Fiszera, 1905).

Djakow, W. "Polskie słowianofilstwo" i jego wpływ na slawistykę polską (koniec XVIII w. – 1939 r.)", *Analecta*, no. 2/1 (1993).

Dresner, T. *Similium juris poloni cum jure romano, centuria una. Auctore Thoma Dresnero Leopolitano* (Paris: ex offic. typogr. C. Morelli, 1602).

Dubisz, S. "Samuel Bogumił Linde 1771–1847", *Portrety uczonych. Profesorowie Uniwersytetu Warszawskiego 1816–1915* (Warszawa: Wydawnictwa Uniwersytetu Warszawskiego, 2016).

Dunin, K. "Jubileusz Kodeksu Napoleona", *Gazeta Sądowa Warszawska*, no. 22 (28 May 1908).

Egorov, A. V. (Егоров А. В.). Теоретико-методологические основания сравнительного правоведения: Монография. (Витебск: ВГУ им. П.М. Машерова, 2014). 207 p.

Fal'kovich, S. M. (Фалькович С.М.). «Польский вопрос в решениях Венского конгресса 1815 г. и причины краха венских договоренностей», Славянский альманах, no. 3-4 (2015).

Feuerbach, P. "O prawodawstwie", *Pamiętnik Warszawski*, II (1822).

[___]. "Wyciąg z dzieła Feuerbacha, pod tytułem: Ueber die Gerichtsverfassung und das gerichtliche Verfahren Frankreichs, in besonderer Beziehung auf die Oeffentlichkeit und Mündlichkeit der Gerechtigkeitspflege. (Giessen 1825)", *Themis Polska*, IV (1828); VIII (1830).

[Filangieri, K.] *Nauka prawodawstwa przez Kawalera Kaietana Filangieri napisana po włosku, tłómaczona przez W.R. Karczewskiego* (Warszawa: u Diufura, 1791-1793). 8 vols.

Gałędek, M. "Does War Deepen Distrust Toward the State? Reorientation of the Polish Political Thought under the Influence of Napoleonic Wars", *Del siglo XIX al XXI. Tendencias y debates: XIV Congreso de la Asociación de Historia Contemporánea, Universidad de Alicante 20-22 de septiembre de 2018* / Coord. M. M. Seco; eds. R. F. Sirvent, R. A. G. Lloret (Alicante: Biblioteca Virtual Miguel de Cervantes, 2019).

___. "The Problem of Non-Adaptability of National Legal Heritage. Discussion on the Reform of Civil Law in Poland in the Course of Work of Reform Committee in 1814", *Romanian Journal of Comparative Law*, VIII, no. 1 (2017).

___., Klimaszewska, A. "A Controversial Transplant? Debate over the Adaptation of the Napoleonic Code on the Polish Territories in the Early 19th Century", *Journal of Civil Law Studies*, XI, no. 2 (2018).

___., Klimaszewska, A. "Stosunek polskich elit do prawa francuskiego po upadku Napoleona – zarys problem", *Studia z Dziejów Państwa i Prawa Polskiego*, XXI (2018).

___., Klimaszewska A. "The Work of the Civil Reform Committee on the New Regulation of Catholic Marriages in 1814", *Krakowskie Studia z Historii Państwa i Prawa* (Zeszyt specjalny; 2018).

___., Klimaszewska A., Pomianowski P. Z. "Prace Komitetu Cywilnego Reformy nad przygotowaniem narodowej kodyfikacji prawa cywilnego i procedury cywilnej w przededniu utworzenia Królestwa Polskiego (1814–1815) – edycja źródłowa. Część I", *Krakowskie Studia z Historii Państwa i Prawa*, XII, no. 2 (2019).

___., Klimaszewska A., Pomianowski P. Z. "Prace Komitetu Cywilnego Reformy nad przygotowaniem narodowej kodyfikacji prawa cywilnego i procedury cywilnej w przededniu utworzenia Królestwa Polskiego (1814–1815) – edycja źródłowa. Część II", *Krakowskie Studia z Historii Państwa i Prawa*, XII, no. 3 (2019).

Godek S. "Już Napoleon w swoim Kodeksie rozwody upoważnia". Kilka uwag w związku z książką Piotra Zbigniewa Pomianowskiego, Rozwód w XIX wieku na centralnych ziemiach polskich. Praktyka stosowania Kodeksu Napoleona w latach 1808–1852", *Czasopismo prawno-historyczne*, LXXI, no. 1 (2019).

Gromakova, N. Iu. (Громакова Н.Ю.). «Польське питання» на Віденському конгресі 1815 р. й утворення Королівства Польського», Збірник наукових праць Харківського національного педагогічного університету ім. Г.С. Сковороди. Серія «Історія та географія», вип. 53 (2016).

Grynwaser, H. "Demokracja Szlachecka. 1795 – 1831", Grynwaser, H. *Pisma* (Wroclaw: Wydawnictwo Zakladu Narodowego im. Ossolinslich, 1951).

___. "Kodeks Napoleona w Polsce", Grynwaser, H. *Pisma* (Wroclaw: Wydawnictwo Zakladu Narodowego im. Ossolinslich, 1951).

Heylman A. "Myśli o nauce prawa i prawodawstwie w kraiu naszym", *Themis Polska,* VII (1830).

___. "Wywod zasad ogolnych nauki prawa i prawodawstwa", *Themis Polska,* VII (1830).

Hoffman, K. B. "O stanie nauki prawa w naszym kraju", *Themis Polska,* I (1828).

Hube, J. "Wywód praw spadkowych słowiańskich (Wywód spadków podług dawnych praw słowiańskich)", *Themis Polska,* VIII (1830).

Hube, R. "Krotki rys historyi literatury prawa", Hube, R. *Opera* (Varsaviae: Typis Michaelis Arct, 1905).

___. "Niektore uwagi nad historya nauki prawa", Hube, R. *Opera* (Varsaviae: Typis Michaelis Arct, 1905).

___. "O stanie nauki prawa w naszych czasach", Hube, R. *Opera* (Varsaviae: Typis Michaelis Arct, 1905).

___. "O starożytnych zbiorach praw Czeskich", *Themis Polska,* V (1829).

___. "Uwagi nad systematem Kodexu cywilnego francuskiego", *Themis Polska,* V (Warszawa, 1829).

___. «История древнего наследственного права у славян», Сборник исторических и статистических сведений о России и народах ей единоверных и единоплеменных (Москва: Типография Августа Семена, 1845).

Iłowiecki, M. *Okręty na oceanie czasu. Historia nauki Polskiej do 1945 roku* (Warszawa: Mada, 2011).

Jakubowski, J. "Pierwszy wykład prawa na Uniwersytecie Warszawskim", *Palestra,* no. 3/2-3 (1959).

Kant, I. *Projekt wieczystego pokoju; rozwaga filozoficzna przez E. Kanta z języka francuskiego z nowymi autora dodatkami* / przeł. z j. francuskiego S. Bielski (Königsberg (Królewiec), 1796; Warszawa, 1797).

___. *Wyobrażenie do historii powszechnej we względzie kosmopolitycznym przez Kanta* / przeł. J. Bychowiec (Königsberg (Królewiec): Druk. G.L. Heeringa i G.C. Haberlanda, 1799).

Karamzin, N. M. (Карамзин Н. М.). Мнение русского гражданина (available online).

Klimaszewska A., Gałędek M. "The Implementation of French Codes on the Polish Territories as Instruments of Modernization – Identifying Problems with Selected Examples", Albarian, A., Moréteau, O. (eds.), *Le droit comparé et... / Comparative Law and...: Actes de la conference annuelle de Juris Diversitas* (Aix-Marseille: Presses universitaires d'Aix-Marseille, 2015).

Kodrębski, J. "Prawo rzymskie a Kodeks Napoleona w Polsce XIX wieku", *Acta Universitatis Lodziensis. Folia Iuridica,* XXXVIII (1988).

Kołłątaj, H. *Uwagi nad teraźniejszem położeniem tej części Ziemi Polskiej, którą od Pokoju Tylżyckiego zaczęto zwać Księstwem Warszawskiem* (Lipsk, 1808).

Konic, H. "Nowy przyczynek do dziejów kodeksu Napoleona w Polsce", *Gazeta Sądowa Warszawska,* no. 13 (18 marca 1903).

___. "Nowy przyczynek do dziejów kodeksu Napoleona w Polsce", *Gazeta Sądowa Warszawska,* no. 14 (22 marca 1903).

Kraushar, A. "Przedmowa wydawcy", Daniłowicz, I. *Kodex Napoleona w porównaniu z prawami polskiemi i litewskiemi* (Warszawa: Księgarnia Jana Fiszera, 1905).

___. "W setną rocnicę Kodeksu Napoleona", *Gazeta Sądowa Warszawska,* no. 22 (28 May 1908).

Kresin, O. V. *Comparative Legal Studies: 1750 to 1835. Approaches to Conceptualization: In 2 vols.,* ed. and transl. W. E. Butler (London: Wildy, Simmonds & Hill, 2019). 2 vols.

___. "Criteria in Subject of Genesis of Comparative Jurisprudence", *Law of Ukraine,* no. 9-10 (2011).

___. "Genesis of Comparative Jurisprudence in German Universities", *Journal of Comparative Law,* VIII (2013).

___. "Social Law Doctrine and the Genesis of Procedural Comparative Jurisprudence", *The Journal of Comparative Law*, X (2015).

___. "The German Philosophy of National Law in the Late Eighteenth and Early Nineteenth Centuries and the Transformation of Legal Science", *The Journal of Comparative Law*, XIV (2019).

___. "The Periodization of Comparative Law: In Search of an Acceptable Model", *The Journal of Comparative Law*, V (2010), pp. 10-27.

___. (ed.). Видатні компаративісти: Творчий шлях, ідеї, праці (Київ: Інститут держави і права ім. В.М. Корецького НАН України; Видавництво „Логос", 2007).

___. (comp.). Порівняльне правознавство у системі юридичних наук: проблеми методології: Монографія / Кер. авт. кол. О.В. Кресін; за ред. Ю.С. Шемшученка (Київ: Інститут держави і права ім. В.М. Корецького НАН України, 2006).

___. (ed.). Порівняльне правознавство: Антологія української компаративістики XIX – XX століть / За ред. О.В. Кресіна; Упорядники: О.В. Кресін (кер. кол.), К.О. Черниченко, О.В. Ткаченко (Київ: Інститут держави і права ім. В.М. Корецького НАН України; Видавництво «Логос», 2008).

___. Порівняльне правознавство у XIX – XX століттях: проблеми становлення: Монографія. (Київ: Логос, 2011).

___. Становлення теоретичних засад порівняльно-правових досліджень у другій половині XVIII – першій третині XIX століття: компаративна концептуалізація: монографія (Київ: Інститут держави і права ім. В.М. Корецького НАН України; Видавництво «Логос», 2017).

___. Становление теоретических оснований сравнительно-правовых исследований во второй половине XVIII – первой трети XIX века: компаративная концептуализация: монография / Институт государства и права им. В.М. Корецкого НАН Украины (Одесса: «Фенікс», 2018).

Laube, S. G. *Krótka nauka z cywilnego Statutu Napoleona Wielkiego. Sposobem słownika publiczności podana* (Wrocław, 1808).

Lelewel, J. "Prawo rzymskie w Polszcze w sprawach kriminalnych, z powodu rozpraw J. N. Janowskiego", Lelewel, J. *Rozbiory dziel obejmujacych albo dzieje, albo rzechy polskie roznymi czasy przez Joachima Lelewela ogloszone* (Poznan: Nakladem ksiegarni Jana Konstantego Zupanskiego, 1844).

___. "Przypiski do dwu rozpraw Al. Mickiewicza i Franc. Morze", Lelewel, J. *Rozbiory dziel obejmujacych albo dzieje, albo rzechy polskie roznymi czasy przez Joachima Lelewela ogloszone* (Poznan: Nakladem ksiegarni Jana Konstantego Zupanskiego, 1844).

___. "Rozprawy Jana Wincentego Bandtke o przedmiotach prawa polskiego", Lelewel, J. *Rozbiory dziel obejmujacych albo dzieje, albo rzechy polskie roznymi czasy przez Joachima Lelewela ogloszone* (Poznan: Nakladem ksiegarni Jana Konstantego Zupanskiego, 1844).

Lerminier, P. "Uwagi nad stanem prawodawstwa francuzkiego", *Themis Polska,* VII (1830).

Litauer, J. J. *Memoriał J. W. Bandtkiego o prawie hipotecznym z roku 1818* (Warszawa, 1915).

___. "Przeciwnicy Kodeksu", *Gazeta Sądowa Warszawska,* no. 22 (28 May 1908).

Liubeznikov, O. A. (Любезников О. А.). «Попытки проведения Н.Н. Новосильцовым общеимперской национальной политики в Западных губерниях России и Царстве Польском в 1810–1820-е годы», Труды Исторического факультета Санкт-Петербургского университета, no. 11 (2012).

Maciejowski, W. A. *Historya prawodawstw słowiańskich* (Warszawa, Lipsk: W Księgarniach Brzeziny i Hinrichsa, 1832-1835). 5 vols.

___. "Ogłoszenie prenumeraty", *Themis Polska,* V (1829).

___. "Uwagi nad artykułem 960 K.C.", *Themis Polska,* VIII (1830).

Majewski Skorochód, W. "Rozkład i treść dzieła "O początku licznych sławiańskich narodów" (1818)", *Wiek XIX. Sto lat mysli Polskiej. Zyciorysy, streszczienia, wyjatki* (Warszawa: Naklad Gebethera i Wolffa; Krakow: G. Gebether i spolka, 1906).

«Манифест Александра I об окончании Венского конгресса от 9 мая 1815 г.» [фотокопія], Сайт «Отечественная война 1812 года». Проект Российской государственной библиотеки (online).

Manuale fundamentorum juris civilis ac Poloni quatuor disputationibus juridico-historico politicis comprehensum: ad quatuor libros institutionum imperatoris Justiniani publico examine ventilatum in illustri schola Auriaca (Bredae: ex offic. Joan. a Wasberge, 1647).

Matlęgiewicz, T. "W kręgu myśli słowianofilskiej Stanisława Staszica", *Wschodni rocznik humanistyczny*, VII (2010-2011).

___. "Idee słowianofilskie w Warszawskim Towarzystwie Przyjaciół Nauk (1800-1830)", *Athenaeum*, XXXIII (2012).

Mecke, Ch. E. "Dyskurs o zasadniczej myśli prawniczej w „Themis Polskiej" (1828–1830) na tle programu historycznej szkoły prawa w Niemczech", *Forum prawnicze* (2018).

Montesquieu, Ch. de. *Duch czyli treść praw albo o stosowności którą powinny mieć prawa z ustawą rządu każdego, obyczaiami, położeniem kraiu, religią etc. Z przydatkiem dociekania praw Rzymskich względem sukcessyi, praw francuzkich i praw lennych* (z francuzkiego P. Monteskiego) przetłómaczony (Lipsk, Drezno, 1777). 2 vols.

"Mowa J. W. Małachowskiego, Prezesa Senatu przy otwarciu Seymu miana w Senacie dnia 10 Marca 1809", *Gazeta Korrespondenta Warszawskiego i Zagranicznego*, no. 21 (1809) (Dodatek).

"Mowa J. W. Ministra Sprawiedliwości miana w Izbie Poselskiey 15 Marca 1809 roku", *Gazeta Korrespondenta Warszawskiego i Zagranicznego*, no. 25 (1809).

Mycielski, M. "Uniwersytet Królewski, 1816–1831", *Dzieje Uniwersytetu Warszawskiego. 1816–1915* (Warszawa: Wydawnictwa Uniwersytetu Warszawskiego, 2016).

[Niemcewicz, J. U.]. *Przestroga dla spółziomków na rok 1809* (Wrocław, 1808).

«Обозрение русских газет и журналов за первую треть 1858 года», Журнал министерства народного просвещения (July 1858), Ч. 49.

Ochimowski, F. "Dawne prawo polskie prywatne a Kodeks Napoleona", *Gazeta Sądowa Warszawska*, no. 22 (28 May 1908).

Oniszczuk, A. "Doświadczenia Księstwa Warszawskiego w zakresie edukacji prawniczej", *Krytyka Prawa*, VIII, no. 3 (2016).

Paszkowska, M. "Romuald Hube 1803–1890", *Portrety uczonych. Profesorowie Uniwersytetu Warszawskiego 1816–1915* (Warszawa: Wydawnictwa Uniwersytetu Warszawskiego, 2016).

Польша и Россия в первой трети XIX века. Из истории автономного Королевства Польского. 1815–1830. М.: Индрик, 2010.

Pomianowski, P. Z. "Główne nurty ideologiczno-metodologiczne w środowisku warszawskich prawników przed wybuchem powstania listopadowego", *Zeszyty Prawnicze UKSW*, XI, no. 4 (2011).

___. *Początki polskiego czasopiśmiennictwa prawniczego. Seria pierwsza „Themis Polskiej"* (Warszawa: Campidoglio, 2015).

___. "Postulat narodowego charakteru prawa w pracach kodyfikacyjnych doby Królestwa Kongresowego", *Czasopismo Prawno-Historyczne*, LXXI (2019).

___. "The National Codification of Civil Law in Poland at the Beginning of the 19th Century. Sources and Inspirations", *History of Law and Other Humanities: Views of the Legal World Across the Time*, ed. V. Amorosi and V.M. Minale (Madrid, 2019).

Posner, S. "Dziś a przed stu laty. Nasz stosunek historyczny do kodeksu", *Gazeta Sądowa Warszawska*, no. 22 (28 May 1908).

Rakowiecki, I. B. *O stanie cywilnym dawnych slowian. Rzech czytana na publiczném posiedzeniu Towarzystwa Królewskiego Warszawskiego Przyiacoł Nauk dnia 3 Maia 1820 roku* (Warszawa, 1820).

___. *Prawda Ruska; czyli prawda wielkiego xiecia Jarosława Władymirowicza tudzież Traktaty Olga i Igora ww. xx. kiiowskich z cesarzami greckimi y Mćisława Dawidowicza x. smoleńskiego z Ryga zawarte, których texta, obok z polskiém tłomaczeniem poprzedza Rys historyczny zwyczaiów, obyczaiów, religiy, praw y jezyka dawnych słowiańskich y słowiańsko-ruskich narodow* (Warszawa: Drukarnia XX Piiarów, 1820-1822). 2 vols.

"Raport ministra sprawiedliwości Feliksa Łubieńskiego w sprawie zmiany niektórych artykułów rodeksu Napoleona, dotyczących hypoteki", Litauer, J. J. *Memoriał J.W. Bandtkiego o prawie hipotecznym z roku 1818* (Warszawa, 1915).

Rosner, A. "Dzieje Wydziału Prawa i Administracji Uniwersytetu Warszawskiego w latach 1808–1831", *Zarys dziejów Wydziału prawa i administracji Uniwersytetu Warszawskiego*, ed. G. Bałtruszajtys (2d ed.; Warszawa: Wolters Kluwer, 2016).

___. "Jan Wincenty Bandtkie 1783–1846", *Portrety uczonych. Profesorowie Uniwersytetu Warszawskiego 1816–1915* (Warszawa: Wydawnictwa Uniwersytetu Warszawskiego, 2016).

___. "„Nauka prawa [...] stała się nieuchronnie potrzebną nie tylko przez swą użyteczność, lecz obowiązki, jakie nas łączą w obywatelskim stanie". O tradycji i nowoczesności w nauczaniu prawa w Księstwie Warszawskim i Królestwie Polskim (1807–1830)", *Krakowskie Studia z Historii Państwa i Prawa,* VIII (2015).

___. "Tradycja i nowoczesnośc w nauczaniu prawa. Doświadczenie Rzeczypospolitej szlacheckiej i Szkola Prawa w KsięstwieWarszawskim", *Nauka i nauczanie prawa. Tradycja i przyszłość,* ed. H. Izdebski (Warszawa: Liber, 2009).

Rundstein, S. "Kodeks Napoleona w Niemczech", *Gazeta Sądowa Warszawska,* no. 22 (28 May 1908).

Sedillez, M. L. E. *Considérations sur l'organisation des écoles de droit, suivies d'un tableau de l'enseignement du droit, présentées au Tribunat par M.L.E. Sedillez: Séance du 21 ventôse an XI.* (Paris: Imprimerie Nationale, XII, 1803).

Shchegolev, S. I. (Щеголев С.И.). «Польша в системе наполеоновской Европы. Создание Герцогства Варшавского», Вестник СПбГУ. Серия 2. История, no. 1-2 (2004).

Sobociński, W. "Jan Wincenty Bandtkie obrońcą Kodeksu Napoleona", *Rocznik Lubelski,* III (1960).

___. "Prawo francuskie w Niemczech a w Polsce: nowe opracowania niemieckie recepcji i refleksje porównawcze", *Annales Universitatis Mariae Curie-Skłodowska. Sectio F: Humaniora,* XXXVII (1982).

Sojka-Zielinska, K. "Nauczanie historii prawa w czasach przemian ustrojowych", *Humanizacja zawodow prawniczych a nauczanie akademickie,* ed. A. Turskiej (Warszawa: Liber, 2002).

___. *Wielkie kodyfikacje cywilne. Historia I współczesność* (Warszawa: Liber, 2009).

Sokolov, A. R. (Соколов А. Р.). «Русские в Варшаве в 1813 – 1815 годах: от Герцогства Варшавского к Царству Польскому», Новый исторический вестник, no. 2 (2018), p. 125-126.

Surowiecki, W. "Śledzenie początku narodow słowiańskich", Surowiecki, W. *Dzieła* (Krakow: Drukarnia "Czasu", 1861).

Syrko, M. V. (Сирко М.В.). Цивільний кодекс Франції 1804 року та його вплив на цивільне законодавство країн Європи (на прикладі Польщі та Румунії): Дис. …канд. юр. наук (Львів, 2015).

Szaniawski, F. K. *O usposobieniach potrzebnych do uczenia się prawa. Rzech czytana przy otwarciu Szkoły prawa w Warszawie dnia 14 Października 1808 roku* (Warszawa, 1808).

___. *Statyka prawa, czyli nauka porównywań w prawie przez X. Szaniawskiego D.O.P. i Professora w Królewsko-Warszawskim Uniwersytecie* (Warszawa: w Drukarni J.C.K. Mości Rządowéy, 1819).

___. *Wiadomości początkowe w nauce prawa* (Warszawa; Drukarnia J.C.K. Mości Rządowa, 1817).

Szaniawski, J. K. *Korespondencja w materiach obraz kraju i narodu polskiego rozjaśniających* (Warszawa: w Druk. Gazety Warszawskiey, 1807).

[___]. "O przyczynach wielu uprzedzeń i sarkań przeciwko prawnictwu", *Pamiętnik Warszawskim*, I (1815).

Szymaniec, P. "Nauka prawa jako działalność pro bono. Uwagi na temat polskiej nauki prawa w latach 1807–1831", *Pro publico bono – idee i działalność*, ed. M. Marszał, J. Przygodzki (Wrocław, 2016).

Szyndler, B. "Towarzystwo Warszawskie Przyjaciól Nauk w dobie Ksiestwa Warszawskiego (szkic do monografii)", *Teka Komisji Historycznej Oddziału Lubelskiego PAN*, I (2007).

Taperek, M. "„Polscy aryjczycy". Pomiędzy naukowymi podstawami mitu a mitycznymi korzeniami nauki w dyskursie słowiańskim XIX wieku", *Przegląd humanistyczny*, no. 3 (2018).

Troiak, I. S. (Трояк И.С.). «Польская историческая россика первой половины XIX в.», Гуманитарные науки в Сибири, no. 3 (2011).

Ustawa Rządowa. Prawo uchwalone dnia 3 Maia, Roku 1791 (Warszawa, 1791).

Wiek XIX. Sto lat mysli Polskiej. Zyciorysy, streszczienia, wyjatki (Warszawa: Naklad Gebethera i Wolffa; Krakow: G. Gebether i spolka, 1907).

Wierzbicki, A. *Europa w polskiej myśli historycznej i politycznej XIX i XX wieku* (Warszawa: Trio, 2009).

___. "Joachim Lelewel 1786–1861", *Portrety uczonych. Profesorowie Uniwersytetu Warszawskiego 1816–1915* (Warszawa: Wydawnictwa Uniwersytetu Warszawskiego, 2016).

Witkowski, W. "Warszawa jako ośrodek polskiej nauki prawa w dobie zaborów", *Krakowskie Studia z Historii Państwa i Prawa,* VIII (2015).

Wójcicki, K. Wł. *Warszawa, jej życie umysłowe i ruch literacki w ciągu lat trzydziestu (od 1800— 1830 r.)* (Warszawa, 1880).

___. "Warszawa, jej życie umysłowe i ruch literacki w ciągu lat trzydziestu (od 1800— 1830 r.)", *Biblioteka Warszawska. Pismo, poswiecone naukom, sztukom i przemysłowi,* I, no. 1 (1879), Serya V.

[Zaborowski, S.]. "Jurysprudencya sądu kassacyinego Xięstwa Warszawskiego i związek instytucyi kassacyinéy z ogólném życiem prawném w kraju", *Themis Polska,* VI (1829).

___. "Rozbiór krytyczny dzieła pod tytułem: Upominek pogrobowy ś.p. Kazimierza Pliszki Podlesianina; rzecz o sukcessii…", *Themis Polska,* VI (1829).

Zarzycka, A. "Próby zmian prawa rzeczowego z Kodeksu Napoleona w Królestwie Polskim w latach 1815–1818", *Krakowskie Studia z Historii Państwa i Prawa,* II (2008), p. 192.

___. "Rola organów władzy Królestwa Polskiego w pracach legislacyjnych nad narodowym prawem rzeczowym w latach 1815-1830", *Studia z Dziejów Państwa i Prawa Polskiego,* VIII (2003).

Żelazny, M. (comp.). "Bibliografia polskich przekładów prac Immanuela Kanta (do roku 2004)", *Filo – Sofija,* no. 1(4) (2004).

Zigel, F. (Зигель Ф.). «Славянское право», Энциклопедия Брокгауза и Ефрона (available online).

Ziuzin, A. M. (Зюзин А. М.). «Адам Чарторыйский и формирование государственной политики по польскому вопросу (конец XVII – начало XIX веков)», Всероссийский журнал научных публикаций, no. 5 (2011).

Index of Names

www.ingramcontent.com/pod-product-compliance
Lightning Source LLC
LaVergne TN
LVHW091529200926
848483LV00002B/336
* 9 7 8 1 6 1 6 1 9 6 5 8 5 *